The Incarnation of Language

BLOOMSBURY LITERARY STUDIES SERIES

Also available in the series:

Forthcoming titles:

The Incarnation of Language

Joyce, Proust and a Philosophy of the Flesh

Michael O'Sullivan

B L O O M S B U R Y
LONDON • NEW DELHI • NEW YORK • SYDNEY

Bloomsbury Academic

An imprint of Bloomsbury Publishing Plc

50 Bedford Square	1385 Broadway
London	New York
WC1B 3DP	NY 10018
UK	USA

www.bloomsbury.com

Bloomsbury is a registered trade mark of Bloomsbury Publishing Plc

First published in 2008 by the Continuum International Publishing Group Ltd
Paperback edition first published 2014 by Bloomsbury Academic

© Michael O'Sullivan, 2008

Michael O'Sullivan has asserted his right under the Copyright, Designs and
Patents Act, 1988, to be identified as Author of this work.

British Library Cataloguing-in-Publication Data
A catalogue record for this book is available from the British Library.

ISBN: HB: 978-1-8470-6047-1
PB: 978-1-4725-1295-6

Library of Congress Cataloging-in-Publication Data
A catalog record for this book is available from the Library of Congress.

Typeset by YHT Ltd, London

Contents

Introduction

The Incarnation story is a compelling one. John's Gospel – 'And the Word became flesh and lived among us' (John 1.14) – describes a mysterious union of the divine and the human, the transcendental and the material, the prelinguistic and the linguistic. Following the Council of Chalcedon, in 451, incarnation was taken to refer to the 'union of the divine and human natures in the person of the Word, or, equivalently, the union of the human nature to the divine person' (Cross 2002: 29). However, a philosophical and literary notion of incarnation is also now in evidence. Michel Henry's philosophy explicitly employs the union that the 'Word' embodies in Scripture to describe his 'phenomenology of life'. He describes the 'Word' as the 'Word of Life' and the 'Logos of Life' (Henry 2003: 220), that it is not only a 'generation but a self-generation. It is life's self-generation as its self-revelation. It is this power to reveal itself in generating itself that is expressed in the notion of Word; it designates the phenomenological power of absolute Life' (ibid. 222). This book examines a rhetoric of incarnation in phenomenology that is enabling of a reconfiguration of the relationship between the writer and the work. It takes up, in a new phenomenological light, the 'human analogue' concocted on the basis of the Incarnation, that the Scholastics employed in their investigation of the human word (Gadamer 1995: 421). Joyce and Proust share an interest in the notion of incarnation as a means for understanding the work of the writer.

Incarnation approximates to embodiment in much phenomenology; however, when phenomenologists dwell on its specific nature for their philosophies, they very often invoke some notion of spiritual flesh. Hans-Georg Gadamer differentiates between incarnation and embodiment. For Gadamer, the notion of embodiment that is integral to Platonic and Pythagorean philosophy 'assumes that soul and body are completely different'; throughout all its embodiments 'the soul retains its own separate nature' and its separation from the body is regarded as a 'purification' (ibid. 418). On the other hand, Gadamer believes that the 'Christian idea of incarnation' is central to the development of the concept of language because it prevented 'the forgetfulness of language in Western thought from being complete' (418). Elliot R. Wolfson also argues that '[t]he phenomenological parameters of embodiment must be significantly expanded if we are to comprehend the enigma of incarnation' (Frymer-Kensky *et al.* 2000: 254). Readings in literature can illuminate those blindspots in phenomenology where an incarnation of sorts has proved to be a point of contention.

A rhetoric of incarnation has a long history in phenomenology. Michel Henry and Maurice Merleau-Ponty describe states of being that privilege how the body and the flesh mediate experience. For Henry, a 'phenomenology of the Incarnation' implies the complete disruption of the traditional phenomenological account of the body so that the body 'is thought not as an object of experience but as a principle of experience' (Henry 2000: 172). Such a conception of flesh implies an understanding of life as a constant process of self-revelation where 'that which experiences and that which is experienced is one' (173). Natalie Depraz (1995) also rejuvenates Husserlian phenomenology with notions of incarnation and self-alterity. Jacques Derrida[1] and Emmanuel Levinas[2] have employed the notion of incarnation in describing what they believe are defunct theories of intersubjectivity and signification. Other philosophers have extended the range of the notion to encompass the act of reading. Ada S. Jaarsma argues that Luce Irigaray has mobilized 'religious narratives in order to restore the possibility of healing through sacred stories' (Jaarsma 2003: 45). Irigaray, who I read in more detail in Chapter 4, employs the term incarnation to refer to a 'process of moving and becoming that invokes the radical participation of the reader' (ibid. 47). Finally, for those who clearly want the notion of incarnation to retain something of its religious mystery, the narrative of incarnation can offer something of the inter-confessional faith[3] that is so important to philosophers such as Paul Ricoeur.

The 'theological turn'[4] in phenomenology has meant that religious figures have also become more important for the examination of literary works. Aldo Gargani suggests that 'a recovery of the signs of the religious tradition that have not been thought through to the end' may signify a 'recovery of the signs and of the annunciations immanent within the history of a religious tradition', so that they become '*figures for an interpretative perspective on life*' (quoted in Derrida and Vattimo 1998: 114).[5] Hent de Vries examines a 'turn to religion' in philosophy through its mediation of violence (de Vries 2002: 17). When violence is defined, for de Vries, as entailing 'any cause, any justified or illegitimate force, that is exerted – physically or otherwise – by one thing (event or instance, group or person, and, perhaps, word and object) on another', then de Vries regards such violence as finding its 'prime model [...] in key elements of the tradition called the religious' (ibid. 1). De Vries argues that by 'renegotiating the limits and aporias of the ethical and the political in light of the religious and theological we can rearticulate the terms and oppositions in which the most pressing and practical present-day cultural debates are phrased' (de Vries 1999: xii). This is investigated in this book through the notion of incarnation.

Literary criticism has long acknowledged its debts to biblical exegesis. In the *Anatomy of Criticism* Northrop Frye suggests that the ethical critic's work must come ultimately to approximate to religious exegesis: 'When poet and critic pass from the archetypal to the anagogic phase, they enter a phase of which only religion, or something as infinite in its range as religion, can possibly form an external goal' (Frye 1973: 125). In the *Rhetoric of Religion* Kenneth Burke also investigates whether 'theological principles can be shown to have usable secular analogues that throw light upon the nature of language' (Burke 1970: 2). Kathleen Norris promotes a special kind of writing that she describes as 'incarnational literature'. She argues that, for her, this phrase does not refer to 'writing centred on the life of Christ or the theology of the church, but simply literature that "shows" in such a way that it comes to life for the reader – one of the first lessons is that you must give up the illusion of control' (Davis *et al.* 304). The application of this 'soft' conception of incarnation to literature has resulted in theories of reading very similar to those proposed by reader-response theories that have their roots in phenomenology.

In inspecting the overlap between the literary and philosophical use of religious figures, it is important to note that the concept of incarnation has very different meanings for different faiths. Alan F. Segal examines the earliest Jewish writings on 'how matter and spirit could interact' in Philo, a contemporary of Paul and Christ (ibid. 116). He argues that the concept of incarnation 'results from the interplay of Greek philosophy with Hebrew thought' (116–17) and he alerts us to the fact that the word incarnation does not appear in the Hebrew Bible, the New Testament or the Apocrypha. In comparing the writings of Philo and Plato on such philosophical problems as the interaction between matter and spirit, Segal comes to the conclusion that 'it seems unlikely that any notion of incarnation could have made it into Christianity directly from Platonism or Philonic Judaism' (133). For

Plato, the miraculous meaning of the incarnation is an 'impossibility' and, for Philo, any suggestion that divinity became flesh would have been a 'disparaging statement about God or at best a statement that needs to be understood allegorically' (133). The interest Joyce and Proust display in the notions of incarnation, transubstantiation and metempsychosis, and their employment of these concepts as figures for the work of the writer, is itself enabling of a new understanding of these 'mysteries'.

Elliot R. Wolfson believes the 'embodiment of God in Judaism is not merely a rhetorical matter' but something that refers to 'the imaginal body of God'; it is in 'the physical space circumscribed by words of prayer and study, [that] the imaginal body of God assumes incarnate form' (Frymer-Kensky *et al.* 2000: 253). In other words, it is in the minds of rabbinic scholars and the prayerful that the 'imaginal body' of God is incarnated:

> Just as early Christian exegetes saw in Christ, God made flesh, so the rabbis conceived of the Torah as the incarnation of the image of God. In the rabbinic imagination, moreover, the sage is a personification of the Torah. It follows, therefore, that insofar as the Torah is the embodiment of the divine image, the sage can be considered the incarnational representation of God. (ibid. 247)

Different philosophical perspectives on incarnation, 'incarnate significance' and 'incarnate existence' are examined in Chapter 1. These philosophical perspectives have, in turn, contributed to different styles of criticism. How is an artist's understanding of the process of artistic creation influenced by a religious upbringing that teaches an event as fantastic as an incarnation?

Joyce and Proust put religious figures to very different uses in their work. They share phenomenology's interest in the figure of incarnation due to the potential it grants theories of intersubjectivity that privilege flesh and the synthesis that accompanies any suggestion of unmediated passage between word and body. The examination of the theme of incarnation in phenomenology is also enabling of a reading of Joyce and Proust that reveals their motivations for regarding transubstantiation and incarnation as vital figures for the writer. The reader's interiorization of the narrated events of a life contributes to the writer's potential for reinscribing such an incarnation between body and word. While Joyce and Proust never admit to a religious belief in the story of the incarnation, their devotion to their work, and to the process whereby a writer gives himself up to the artistic word, can be read as allegories for this scriptural moment of genesis. Their works also voice many of the philosophical ideas that phenomenology and other philosophies have aligned with incarnation. Joyce and Proust share a devotional attention to the artistic process that draws them to the concepts of incarnation and transubstantiation as motifs for artistic endeavour. They share an interest in the recording of the moments of perception and apperception that does not solely reduce perception to contemplation, as Henri Bergson[6] has suggested certain writers of their generation do.

Their early work records subjects contemplating heightened states of self-awareness inspired by interactions with everyday objects. The enlightenment is then offered up to the reader as both 'creative force' and 'critical act'. In their later work this emphasis on the scrupulous recording of a character's moment of enlightenment before these everyday, ready to hand objects shifts as they devote more time to writing and redrafting and to the experience before the enlightenment of the word. The early memories of ballast clocks and madeleines that were fit subjects for representing the context of the moment of enlightenment grow dim and the memory of the peculiar enlightenment that reading and redrafting bring becomes the favoured subject for representing this heightened state of self-awareness. In other words, the cyclical move inwards towards charting an enlightenment that begins and ends with the word records greater depths of being. It is only the sensitivity towards the materiality of the body and the flesh that can ultimately assure the writer that the work is not now entirely solipsistic. The means for recording these ever greater depths of being – 'life's high carnage of semperidentity' (*FW* 582: 15) – can only be brought out for the reader through a philosophy that privileges the body's mediation of experience through a commitment to its 'incarnate significance'[7] and auto-affection.

Religious figures are central to Joyce's conception of writing. However, while the Thomistic roots of these figures have been carefully traced in Joyce studies, their affinities with phenomenology and the recent 'turn to theology' have been neglected. Critics recall how Joyce's alter ego, Stephen Dedalus, refers to the work of the writer in terms of transubstantiation, a religious mystery that, for many, commemorates and symbolizes Christ's incarnation. Stephen describes himself as 'a priest of the eternal imagination, transmuting the daily bread of experience into the radiant body of everliving life' (*P* 186). However, the language of phenomenology enables us to rephrase

Joyce's attention to the body and to the 'moral history' (Joyce 1975: 83) of his characters in terms of the theories of subjectivity and signification that broach these issues today. Joyce's oft-cited employment of the terms epiphany[8] and epiclesis also places these theological terms in a 'new configuration', moving them away 'from ritual' (Ellmann 1972: 169) so as 'to give people some kind of intellectual pleasure or spiritual enjoyment by converting the bread of everyday life into something that has a permanent artistic life of its own', as Joyce explained to his brother (S. Joyce 1958: 104). Hugh Kenner describes the effects of Joyce's literary and formal interest in transubstantiation in an incarnational language that recalls the biblical notion of the Word becoming flesh: 'All is words, we are being reminded, and all words are now' (Kenner 1978: 48). Kenner describes how the language of *Ulysses* embodies speech in a special way: 'So the word finds speech [...] Common expressions are transubstantiated: Joyce found no more eloquent metaphor for the artist than the priest, in whose hands "the bread and wine of common experience" alter nothing of their appearance but nevertheless are changed, to afford spiritual as well as bodily food' (Kenner 1973: 107).

Julia Kristeva has examined Proust's interest in the figure of the incarnation. She argues that such figures allow modernist writers 'the motivation without precedent for an artistic expansion' presenting them with 'the figure for the indissociable, interconfessional passion of the felt and the feeling, of the Word and the flesh. The intermediary between the two – a state of grace – becomes a possible space. It is this time-space of faith as imaginary experience and, inversely, the experience of the imaginary as an imperative reality' that attracts these writers to these religious figures (Kristeva 1984: 545). Proust also conceived of the work of the artist in terms of an incarnation. In a letter to Lucien Daudet, written in November 1913, Proust praises Daudet for his review of *Du côté de chez Swann*, commending him for having achieved a manner of writing 'where the supreme miracle, the transubstantiation of the irrational qualities of matter and life into human words, is accomplished' (Proust 1984b: 342–3). Kristeva argues that Proust adopts such a style.

In the last few years criticism has been strongly influenced by accounts of alterity and difference inherited from Levinasian phenomenology and deconstruction.[9] Jill Robbins (1999) reminds us that the connection between Levinas's philosophical writings and his theological writings cannot be overlooked. Criticism can sometimes neglect the roots of the figures that it borrows from philosophy. If criticism then argues for an 'ethics of reading' or an 'ethics of writing'[10] in terms of these inherited notions of alterity, then these philosophical roots must be investigated.[11] I examine various philosophies of language in this book in assessing the differences between those that privilege notions of incarnation and those that privilege language's mediation of alterity and difference. Natalie Depraz's extensive study of Husserl's texts collected in the *Husserliana* archive rejuvenates Husserl's account of alterity.[12] In employing incarnation as a philosophical motif, she argues that Husserl does not regard the other as a 'radical alterity' but as 'a unity of constituted sensations' (Depraz 1995: 22). She describes a conception of intersubjectivity influenced by the theme of incarnation grounded on the discovery in myself of an intersubjectivity, in the form of a co-existence of two selves, one empathizing, the other empathized (ibid. 203). The final chapters of this book argue that the language and lifeworlds put in play by Joyce and Proust emphasize this sense of engagement for the reader.

Chapter 1 traces the influence of the concept of incarnation in philosophies that elicit an unresolved tension towards what has been termed 'phenomenological religiosity'. The chapter begins with Gadamer's examination of incarnation, then moves through various phenomenological readings of the term, and ends with a brief look at Giorgio Agamben's and Alain Badiou's rejuvenation of the context of incarnation. In the influential philosophical exchange between Derrida and Husserl, what is representative, for Leonard Lawlor, of the 'basic problem of phenomenology' (the subtitle to his book on Derrida and Husserl), Derrida's depiction of language's relation to the body can be seen to employ a rhetoric of incarnation. In Derrida's first three books, where deconstruction has its genesis, any account of presence that perpetuates what Derrida believes is a philosophy of 'ideality' in arguing for 'a unity of thought and voice in logos' (Derrida 1973: 74) is challenged. The first chapter examines Derrida's reading of signification in Husserl in terms of what he describes as a 'linguistic incarnation'. What literary criticism describes as 'deconstructive criticism' frequently neglects the subtleties of Derrida's account of signification. In *Speech and Phenomena* any understanding of being that retains a notion of an 'intentional animation that transforms the body of the word into flesh' and that 'makes of the *Körper* a *Leib*, a *geistige Leiblichkeit* [from body to incarnate body]' (ibid. 16) is representative of a 'tormented' (6) phenomenology; too much is assigned to the 'voice' and the 'spiritual flesh' (16).

Michel Henry's material phenomenology offers an invaluable alternative to Derrida's readings in the phenomenology of language. *Le*

Monde's obituary to Henry describes him as 'one of the most important French philosophers of the second half of the twentieth century' (Droit 2002), and yet the majority of his work is still unavailable in English. Henry's work in the sixties prefigured what the advocates of the 'turn to theology' acknowledged in the nineties. *Incarnation: Une philosophie de la chair* gives a phenomenological account of language that is grounded on the concept of Incarnation. Henry conceives of the body as 'flesh' in a way that is only possible once '*le corps mondain*', 'the worldly body', is understood as '*flesh already revealed to itself as living flesh in the pathētik auto-revelation of life*' (Henry 2000: 195, Henry's emphasis). His incorporation of the notion of incarnation into contemporary philosophical debates argues that our understanding of the body must be phrased in terms of '*a body that is no longer the object of experience but its principle*' (ibid. 160, Henry's italics).

Chapter 2 begins with a comparison of Joyce's early aesthetic and phenomenology's early accounts of language and perception. Even though many of the recent advances in criticism have their roots in phenomenology, Joyce has generally either been regarded as a Thomist or a deconstructionist. In his early work Derrida's close readings of genesis and what he describes as 'linguistic incarnation' demonstrate the weaknesses of phenomenology. Joyce and Proust describe another route beyond these limitations.

Jacques Rancière's *The Flesh of Words* examines criticism's roots in exegesis in the light of a phenomenological account of the space of the writer–text–reader. In a section entitled 'Theologies of the Novel' Rancière parallels the history of the Christian narrative with that of the novel. He argues that Peter's denial of Christ sets in motion the completion of the 'story of salvation' and with this, 'the true "life story" that is the novel is founded' (Rancière 2004: 74). Peter's denial fulfils the prophecies of Ezekiel in the Old Testament and inaugurates the figural economy of prefiguration. For Rancière, the figure unique to this narrative becomes 'a body announcing another body' (ibid. 75). It is this communion of bodies through the intermediary of inscription that leads, Rancière argues, to 'two conflicting interpretations of what the novel owes to the Christian equivalence of the incarnation of the word and the fulfilment of the Scriptures' (78). The first is 'based on incarnation and on the plenitude this confers on the representable body of literary narration; the other draws on this relationship of Scripture with itself that alone proves to be completely figuration' (78). The first privileges the relation between representation and corporeity while the second focuses on the intertext.

Rancière's 'history of the theological-poetic transfer' examines the transformation of 'sacred' writing into poetic writing, a moment in the history of writing that is subtly voiced by Joyce and Proust. The movement between the figurative and figural functions of the text is responsible for this transfer. For Rancière, the 'figurative' refers to the reality of the work's 'material production' and the 'figural' refers to the 'reality of its relationship with the body-to-come of its truth'. When the 'figural function glides beneath the figurative function', the 'religious text' is transformed into a 'poetic text' (81). Rancière argues that the 'promise of body' of the figure has now been incorporated into the 'matter of imagination to identify it with a promise of meaning' (83). I argue in Chapters 2 and 3 that Joyce and Proust allow the reader to make good these promises by allowing body and meaning to coalesce in their work, a process that can be accounted for phenomenologically.

However, in Rancière's history of the novel, the interpretation of the body of Scripture as a fictional body is upset by another aspect of the text's relation to the body. In referring to Paul's admission, 'I complete in my flesh what the suffering of Christ is' (Colossians 1.24), Rancière argues that the 'truth of the suffering body of incarnation requires that there must always be a new body to sacrifice itself in order to attest to it' (Rancière 2004: 84). It is such a belief that has contributed to the notion of the lifework in the history of the novel. For Rancière, however, this belief gave rise to ascetic theology where the ascetic 'give[s] it [Scripture] body again so that the letter can once again take form' (ibid. 84); in other words, the ascetic repeats the suffering, giving his own body so that 'incarnation fulfils its promise' (85): 'One must annihilate oneself and also annihilate one's claim to be an interpreter of Scripture, to let its truth come in the form, even if absurd, of wounding one's body' (85). In Chapter 4, I argue that Joyce and Proust give their bodies over to the word for a very different realization of the incarnation of language. Their acceptance of impotentiality and of a desire that remains immanent to itself enables them to transform their sacrifices for the word into a form of 'nourishment' for the reader.

Chapter 4 examines aspects of desire in Joyce and Proust in the light of the material phenomenology outlined above. Joyce's unrelenting examination of paternity in the context of impotentiality and 'universal love', a sexual politic so far only achieving a relatively minor status in 'feminist' readings that stop at equating the 'impotent/castrated' with the 'woman(ish)/inadequate' (Reizbaum 2004: 92), unsettles the narrative of paternal authority implicit in incarnation. My reading extends Marilyn Reizbaum's reading of impotence in Joyce, and her comparison of Stephen as an 'impotent' 'most finished artist' (ibid. 90) with the 'impotent' Bloom, through an examination of the manner in which Bloom's interiorization of impotence and impotentiality affects his self-image and his understanding of other aspects of creativity. Impotence is examined in the light of Giorgio Agamben's theory of impotentiality (Agamben 1999: 181–4). Joyce's analysis of figures, his epiphanic detailing of moments of perception that lead to artistic inspiration, and his desire for the word are also representative of an interrogation of desire as what can remain 'immanent to itself'. The desperate interrogation of physical union that impotence affords the cuckold and the artist leads to an interrogation of all forms of human interaction, ultimately splintering the association that exists between desire and human interaction. Joyce and Proust transferred their desire onto something that would always respond to their yearnings and that would also be as complicated and wilfully obscure as the most elusive lover: the word made flesh.

Chapter 1

Phenomenology and incarnation

Gadamer's history of the Christian idea of incarnation

Early accounts of Incarnation in philosophy have noted the difficulty of finding an adequate expression to detail what this mystery represents. For Kierkegaard, the Incarnation, Christianity's grounding belief, is responsible for introducing representation to the world and moving us beyond Greek thought. He argues that the Incarnation requires a belief in an 'incarnated individual' who 'sucks in the energy from all the others' (Kierkegaard 1992: 75) and that the Greek consciousness 'lacks the strength to concentrate the whole in a single individual'. For Kierkegaard, this has 'consequences for what follows'. Such a construction of individuality is important for the 'categories which the world-consciousness uses in different epochs' and it is even enabling of the 'spirit of the sensual erotic' (ibid. 75). In *Truth and Method* Hans-Georg Gadamer also regards the Christian mystery of the Incarnation as being influential for the 'development of the concept of language'. He perceives an important split in thinking in this development. While he acknowledges that language is 'fundamentally' taken to 'be something wholly detached from the being of what is under consideration; it is taken to be an instrument of subjectivity' (Gadamer 1995: 416/7), he argues that such a view of language ultimately leads 'to the rational construction of an artificial language' and 'away from the nature of language'. He is eager to explain that experience is bound up with words and that 'experience of itself seeks and finds words that express it' (ibid. 417). Greek philosophy, for Gadamer, was unwilling to accept this close relationship between 'word and thing, speech and thought'. For the Greeks, 'thought had to protect itself against the intimate relationship between word and thing in which the speaker lives' (417).

However, it is the next stage in Gadamer's description of the development of language that is most revealing. He argues that it was ultimately not a Greek idea that ends up doing 'more justice to the being of language', but the 'Christian idea of incarnation' (418). This Christian idea of 'the redemptive event' (the incarnation) is so powerful, Gadamer argues, that it 'introduces the essence of history into Western thought, brings the phenomenon of language out of its immersion in the ideality of meaning, and offers it to philosophical reflection' (419). The strength of this incarnational strain of thought lies in the fact that through it it became essential to 'reconsider philosophically the mystery of language and its connection to thought. The greater miracle of language lies not in the fact that the Word becomes flesh and emerges in external being, but that that which emerges and externalizes itself in utterance is always already a word' (420). In other words, the move away from the idealism of Greek thought towards an appreciation of the connection between the word and thought necessitated a privileging of speech as an incarnation of word and thought: the word 'has its being in its revealing' (421). The concentration on 'its revealing' looks forward to the phenomenological concern with the 'manner of appearing' of the object. Gadamer then plots the evolution of incarnation through the 'human analogue' that was concocted by the Scholastics on the basis of the Incarnation to assist them with the investigation of the human word (421). This analogue, which is 'more than a metaphor,' details how 'the human relationship between thought and speech corresponds, despite its imperfections, to the divine relationship of the Trinity. The inner mental word is just as consubstantial with thought as is God the Son with God the Father' (421). With this notion of the analogue, the Scholastics could now examine the relationship between the 'inner mental word' and thought that pertains to the human word, without feeling that they were objectifying any part of the Divine Word. They felt safe in the knowledge that their whole interpretative model was an analogue for this divine mystery.

Gadamer argues that 'the mystery of this unity is reflected in the phenomenon of language' (419) because it is the miracle of language that is itself described by the incarnation and that is, in turn, as the analogy with the emergence of the human 'inner word', 'supposed to illuminate' the 'mystery of the Trinity' (424). However, since the Scholastics presumed that the 'whole of the divine mind is expressed in the divine Word', there are aspects of the incarnation that will always remain incomprehensible to the human mind. What Gadamer describes as the 'processual element' in this word must then signify something for which they have no analogy. It is the singling out of this 'processual element in the word' that, for Gadamer, leads linguistic investigation beyond 'the theologians' way of stating this difference' (424) between the divine Word and the human word.

For Gadamer, the attention of the Scholastics is now drawn towards the human imperfection of the inner word and to the 'inner unity of thinking and speaking to oneself' which, we must remember, still corresponds to 'the Trinitarian mystery of the incarnation' (426). This aspect of the word will remain a sticking point for many philosophies and it will take on new significance for phenomenology and deconstruction in relation to the distinction they draw up between speech and writing. The concentration on the 'inner word' moves the 'human analogue' ever further from theology and the Divine mystery the description of the human word was modelled on, even though this mystery lies at the root of the Scholastic investigation of the word. The Greek idealizing of thought at the expense of the word is left behind, but recent phenomenologies of language will, once again, assign notions of 'intentional animation' and 'idealism' to their accounts of how the subject engages in self-communication.

There are two further aspects of Gadamer's history of the development of the concept of language in accordance with the 'Trinitarian mystery of the incarnation' that are taken up by phenomenology and later theories of literature. Gadamer argues that the inwardness of the word, what constitutes the unity of thought and speech (which itself corresponds to the mystery of the incarnation), makes it difficult to spot the 'direct and unreflective character of the "word"' (426). There is a subtle distinction at play here. While thought is capable of directing 'itself reflectively toward itself' in becoming an 'object to itself', 'there is no reflection when the word is formed, for the word is not expressing the mind but the thing intended' (426). A union is formed between the 'subject matter that is thought (the species) and the word' so that they 'belong as closely together as possible'. In continuing with the incarnation theme, Gadamer writes that 'the word is that in which knowledge is consummated' (426). The interest here in the fact that the word expresses not the mind, but the 'thing intended', will become a major concern of phenomenology when it pursues a return to the 'things themselves' through a reduction that divests the object of all ontological assumptions such as the reflexivity described above. While this earlier philosophy of the word does not yet share phenomenology's extensive interest in the thing's 'manner of appearing', phenomenology will be seen to employ an incarnational rhetoric in its description of signification that recalls this early 'human analogue' of the Scholastics.

The second aspect of Gadamer's history of language in terms of the concept of incarnation that has been revisited by recent philosophy is his description of the 'meaning of the word' as an 'event'. The difference that exists between the unity of the divine Word and the multiplicity of human words does not exempt the divine Word from multiplicity. Gadamer explains that for the Scholastics

> the proclamation of salvation, the content of the Christian gospel, is itself an event that takes place in sacrament and preaching, and yet it expresses only what took place in Christ's redemptive act. Hence it is one word that is proclaimed ever anew in preaching. Its character as gospel, then, already points to the multiplicity of its proclamation. The meaning of the word cannot be detached from the event of proclamation. *Quite the contrary, being an event is a characteristic belonging to the meaning itself* [Gadamer's emphasis]. (Gadamer 1995: 427)

The capacity of the event to act as a 'singular multiplicity' and to incite a concern for 'meaning,' or for that subject, namely philosophy, whose privilege it is to detail the conditions of meaning, has been rejuvenated in the philosophy of Alain Badiou. Badiou's intention to redefine philosophy, less as a concern for 'real ontology' but as 'the general theory of the event' (Badiou 2006: 100), voices many aspects of the event – its structure and its preservation of multiplicity – that Gadamer has assigned to the work of the Scholastics:

> In all these cases, the latent matrix of the problem is the following: if by 'philosophy' we must understand both the jurisdiction of the One and the conditioned subtraction from this jurisdiction, how can philosophy grasp what happens; what happens *in thought?* Philosophy will always be divided between, on the one hand, the recognition of the event as a supernumerary advent of the One, and on the other, the thought of the being of the event as a simple extension of the multiple. Is truth what comes to being or what unfolds being? We remain divided. The whole point is to maintain, as far as possible, and under the most innovative conditions of thought, that, in any case, truth itself is nothing but a multiplicity. (Badiou 2006: 104)

Badiou does not want his theory of the event and its preservation of multiplicity to be regarded as 'an obscurantist theory of creation *ex nihilo*' (ibid. 100–1) and Gadamer also stresses that, for the Scholastics, the emergence of the word, its creation, does also not arise *ex nihilo*: 'The word does not emerge in a sphere of the mind that is still free of thought' (Gadamer 1995: 426). The idea that the word, and its later reincarnation as signification, preserves multiplicity, and the difference that is implicit in such multiplicity, will also become a major concern in Jacques Derrida's reading of Husserlian phenomenology.

Derrida's incarnational reading of Husserl

While it cannot be suggested that Derrida rejects outright the possibility of 'embodied "meaning" ', Jack Reynolds argues in his study of Derrida and Merleau-Ponty that Derrida's failure to pursue the 'question' of 'embodied "meaning" ' marks an 'important omission in his work' (Reynolds 2004: 54). There is a tendency in criticism to regard deconstructive criticism, and by implication Derrida, as engaging in a textualization of the body. Reynolds separates Derrida from such claims, reminding us that Derrida recognizes how 'the problem of writing as subordinated by speech and the problem of the body as subordinated by the mind are similar problems' (ibid. 48). However, I examine in this chapter how any hint of a relation between word and body, is, for Derrida, aligned with a problematic notion of 'linguistic incarnation'.

Derrida's struggle with Husserlian phenomenology is wide-ranging and protracted. We can now plot the evolution of this struggle due to the recent publication of his Master's thesis, *The Problem of Genesis in Husserl's Philosophy* (written in 1953 and 1954). Derrida devotes the first 15 years of his philosophical 'career' to his battle with Husserl, from *The Problem of Genesis*, through *Edmund Husserl's Origin of Geometry: An Introduction* (1962), up to *Speech and Phenomena: And Other Essays on Husserl's Theory of Signs* (1967). It is not until the essay 'Difference' is published in 1968, an essay included in *Speech and Phenomena*, that Derrida finally gives up the critique of Husserl to devise his own clearly demarcated philosophical programme. It goes without saying, then, that Husserl is integral to the evolution of Derrida's philosophy. However, the question remains: if Derrida had essentially formulated coherently and persuasively his differences with Husserl in 1953, why does he persist in outlining these differences? One is led to believe that, for Derrida, it is not so much Husserl who is at fault but the entire history of philosophy for its dissemination of a metaphysics that Derrida finds it most convenient to attack through Husserl.

The principal points of contrast between Derrida's early philosophy and Husserlian phenomenology become evident when we investigate what each philosophy regards as fundamental. Leonard Lawlor writes that, for Derrida, 'there is a non-foundation below' the 'founding validity of presence' (Lawlor 2002: 2); the emphasis is on the elements of delay, displacement and difference that imply that '[s]ubjective presence is always already passing away' (ibid. 5). James Richard Mensch supports this argument by implicating Derrida in a 'post-modern movement' that, in attacking foundationalism, 'nonetheless continue[s] its practice of getting to the basis of things and of using this basis to account for them' (Mensch 2003: 8). This results in a situation where, as Lawlor suggests, the other as 'a phenomenological necessity' is 'the center of Derrida's thought' (Lawlor 2002: 4). Derrida has himself referred to his own work's capacity for 'reintroducing the difference involved in "signs" at the core of what is "primordial"' (Derrida 1973: 45–6n). Husserl has a very different understanding of the foundation, or first philosophy, that is important for both his conception of objectivity and intersubjectivity. In the 'Fifth Meditation' of the *Cartesian Meditations* Husserl writes that when we abstract '*we retain a unitarily coherent stratum of the phenomenon world* [...] I obviously cannot have the "alien" or "other" as experience [...] without having this stratum in actual experience [Husserl's emphasis]' (Husserl 1970d: 96). The emphasis, then, for Husserl lies with a sense of belonging or unifying comprehension upon which the essential aspects of difference and otherness play their parts.

Derrida's criticisms of Husserlian phenomenology are far too numerous to detail here. However, many of the weaknesses Derrida perceives point to two related themes in Husserl's work: 'the problem of genesis' and what Derrida refers to, in commenting on Husserl's understanding of writing, as his notion of 'linguistic incarnation' (Derrida 1989: 76). Derrida reminds us that Husserl 'always says that the linguistic or graphic body is a flesh, a proper body (*Leib*), or a spiritual corporeality (*geistige Leiblichkeit*)' (ibid. 88). This is a description of Husserl's conception of the linguistic, or graphic, body in terms of a rhetoric of incarnation, a ploy Derrida returns to in the introduction to *Speech and Phenomena*. For Husserl, language is also the means by which 'Ideality comes to its Objectivity' (Husserl 1989: 76). But it is a quite distinct understanding of language that mediates this movement between Ideality and Objectivity, and Derrida goes to great lengths in describing the linguistic incarnation that sustains this movement.

In *The Origin of Geometry* Husserl is quite explicit in presenting his views on writing, a topic he says very little about in the *Logical Investigations*. Husserl argues here that '[t]he important function of written, documenting linguistic expression is that it makes communications possible without immediate or mediate personal address; it is, so to speak, communication become virtual' (Derrida 1989: 164). In giving a modified translation of this piece, Derrida argues that, for Husserl, '[t]he possibility of *writing* will assure the absolute traditionalization of the object, its absolute ideal Objectivity – i.e. the purity of its relation to a universal transcendental subjectivity' (ibid. 87). Derrida takes Husserl's conception of writing to imply that if the

> text does not announce its own pure dependence on a writer or reader in general (i.e., if it is not haunted by a virtual intentionality) and if there is no purely juridical possibility of it being intelligible for a transcendental subject in general, then there is no more in the vacuity of its soul than a chaotic literalness or the sensible opacity of a defunct designation, a designation deprived of its transcendental function. The silence of prehistoric arcana and buried civilizations, the entombment of lost intentions and guarded secrets, and the illegibility of the lapidary inscription disclose the transcendental sense of death as what unites these things to the absolute privilege of intentionality in the very instance of its essential juridical failure. (Derrida 1989: 88)

Derrida's writing becomes quite impassioned and lyrical at this point. The topic is close to his heart, as it will be his revolutionary philosophy of writing and signification that will ultimately show him the way forward, beyond Husserl's metaphysics. It is the 'transcendental function' of writing that Derrida believes is important for Husserl. But if writing is haunted by such a 'virtual intentionality' or 'transcendental function', there must be something that unites the 'text' or the 'lapidary inscription' with this intentionality so that the writing is more than a 'defunct designation'. Derrida describes this union in terms of an incarnation. He argues that, for Husserl, '[t]he possibility or necessity of being *incarnated* in a graphic sign is no longer simply extrinsic and factual in comparison with ideal Objectivity: it is the *sine qua non* condition of Objectivity's internal completion' [my emphasis] (Derrida 1989: 89).

Derrida sees a direct link, then, between Husserl's understanding of writing and 'ideal Objectivity' (ibid. 89): as long as ideal Objectivity '*can* not be engraved in the world – as long as ideal Objectivity is not in a position to be party to an incarnation [...] then ideal Objectivity is not fully constituted' (89). For Derrida, Husserl can only then posit the act of writing as 'the highest possibility of all '*constitution*' even though such a constitution is always measured against the 'transcendental depth of ideal Objectivity's historicity' (89). In other words, Derrida's commentary would appear to imply that Husserl privileges writing to such an extent that it incarnates, or makes material, 'ideal Objectivity'. Ideal Objectivity is only regarded as 'fully constituted' when it can be 'engraved in the world' or made 'party to an incarnation'. The resulting 'text' or writing will be more than a 'system of signals'. Writing's incarnation, a writing that cannot be a 'chaotic literalness' (88), will preserve and elicit 'ideal Objectivity' at the same time as 'ideal Objectivity' will call for its constitution in writing. But what is the nature of this incarnation writing must be party to? In a footnote to this section, Derrida describes the particular nature of the 'linguistic incarnation' that he regards as integral to Husserl's understanding of language and writing:

> The precise place of the properly termed realizing [*réalisante*] embodiment is ultimately therefore the union of the sensible form with sensible material, a union *traversed* by the linguistic intention which always intends, explicitly or not, the highest ideality. Linguistic incarnation and the constitution of written or scriptural material, suppose, then, a closer and closer 'interconnection' of ideality and reality through a series of less and less ideal mediations and in the synthetic unity of an intention. This intentional synthesis is an unceasing movement of going and returning that works to bind the ideality of sense and to free the reality of the sign. Each of the two operations is always haunted by the sense of the other: each operation is already announced in the other or still retained in it. Language frees the ideality of sense, then, in the very work of its 'binding' ('interconnecting' [*enchainement*]) [Derrida's emphasis]. (Derrida 1989: 89)

Derrida takes the description of this 'linguistic incarnation' a stage further. Not content to fault Husserl on his presumption that writing must 'suppose' the 'union of the sensible form with sensible material' in an 'intentional synthesis,' he goes on to compare both entities in this incarnation to different kinds of body:

But did we not just find out that writing, inasmuch as it was grounding (or contributing to the grounding of) truth's absolute Objectivity, was not *merely* a constituted sensible body (*Körper*), but was also a properly constituting body (*Leib*) – the intentional primordiality of a Here-and-Now of truth? If writing is *both* a factual event and the upsurging of sense, if it is both *Körper* and *Leib*, how would writing preserve its *Leiblichkeit* [living truth-sense] from corporeal disaster?' (Derrida 1989: 97)

This is about as far as Derrida takes his description of the specific conception of writing he finds problematic in Husserl. He will return to these accounts of different kinds of body in *Speech and Phenomena* in his investigation of Husserl's notions of indication and expression. The analogy Derrida draws here recalls the Scholastic 'human analogue' that Gadamer described early in his accounting for language and its association with the concept of incarnation. That Derrida must ultimately resort to such an analogy in detailing the weakness of Husserl's account of writing and language, describing writing as both a 'constituted sensible body' and a 'properly constituting body', would only then suggest his aversion to this incarnation analogue in general and the means with which it details the relationship between writing and the body. It will be some years before Derrida will come up with an alternative description of how writing leaves its trace on the body.

In *Speech and Phenomena* Derrida returns to a discussion of the difficulty with which language can deal with the kind of movement that is involved in a linguistic incarnation, where there is some synthesis of ideality and reality: 'In fact no language can cope with the operation by which the transcendental ego constitutes and opposes itself to its worldly self, its soul, reflecting itself in a *verweltlichende Selbstapperzeption*' (Derrida 1973: 12). Derrida reminds us that Husserl invests in the 'enigmatic concept of "parallelism"' (ibid. 12) to deal with these difficulties, but, for Derrida, it is a dangerous paralleling of 'phenomenological psychology and transcendental phenomenology' (12). It leads to further difficulties, for 'it renders more mysterious still' the concept of 'a *worldliness* capable of sustaining [...] *transcendentality*' (13). Derrida believes that Husserl's parallelism muddies the distinction between the disciplines he is paralleling and he urges us to 'maintain the precarious and fragile distance between the parallels' (13). He argues that any 'polemic for the possibility of world and sense' must take place in this '*difference*'. Derrida wants to preserve and privilege this site of difference between world and sense, a difference that cannot reside in the world, but only in language: 'language preserves the difference that preserves language' (14).

I now want to inspect more closely the genesis of this notion of difference in Derrida's account of language by looking at Derrida's reading of Husserl's 'theory of signs' in *Speech and Phenomena*. His commentary on Husserl's 'theory of signs' is compelling and it, once again, presumes a fundamental ontological duality in Husserl's thinking. Jean-Luc Marion and Michel Henry have questioned Derrida's reduction of Husserl's philosophy, however. Michel Henry's material phenomenology, also developed after a lengthy critique of Husserl, urges a 'return to life' (what is reminiscent of Husserl's 'Living Present') but it is something that must take place through the 'denunciation of phenomenology'. For Jean-Michel Le Lannou, Henry argues that 'it is not enough to recall the duality of the modes of givenness of the real, it is necessary, once again, to understand the possibilities and the modalities of the passage from one to the other' (Le Lannou 2002: 984). This would seem to urge a rethinking of the very 'linguistic incarnation' or movement between ideality and reality that Derrida wants to describe in terms of '*difference*' (Derrida 1973: 14). Henry argues that interpretations that have sought to investigate receptivity solely from the perspective of its receiving what is an 'exterior content' have been unwilling to accept the real conditions of the essence of the manifestation as representation. Henry's reading, therefore, urges an inspection of any separation or *déliaison* that Derrida might offer as a key to interpretation. Henry urges us to move beyond the 'vacuity of finitude' to which phenomenology has brought us. His project of *dé-finitisation*, speaking of the means of moving beyond phenomenology, does not have an English equivalent. It speaks for both our abstraction from a phenomenology of finitude, and a rigorous defining of our terms, processes that must occur simultaneously. The project of *dé-finitisation* seeks to conjoin the separation involved in phenomenology's ontological duality with what such a separation must consistently remove itself from, what Henry terms *l'ekstatique* (Henry 1973: 984).

Jean-Luc Marion's *Reduction and Givenness* also questions Derrida's reading of Husserl's theory of signs. He employs similar language to Henry in reminding us of Husserl's claims that his 'whole life's work has been dominated by this task of elaborating' a 'correlational *a priori*' (quoted in Marion 1998: 31). Marion offers a different account of Husserlian objectivity to that employed by Derrida in *Speech and Phenomena*. Marion argues that

[T]he object consists only in certain acts, acts whose primacy stems from their ability to allow the given to appear as an intentional lived experience. Whoever refuses here the 'legitimate source' of any appearance, namely lived experiences, cannot be refuted since he excludes himself from the terrain of givenness, where alone an argument becomes possible. (Marion 1998: 9)

Derrida's account of objectivity and language would then seem to neglect the manner in which Husserl believes expressions must be 'lived through', thereby excluding his reading from what Marion believes is that 'legitimate source' of givenness.

In *Speech and Phenomena* Derrida argues that Husserl assigns a 'radical distinction' to expression and indication, Husserl's 'two concepts of the sign'. He argues that the distinction connotes phenomenology's fundamental ontological duality. In making this claim the ground is then prepared for his next work, *Of Grammatology*, in which he critiques the privileging of speech in Western thought. He moves to the appraisal of the body of writing, and away from an idealized notion of a transcendental meaning that posits the trace and the inscription, as secondary. It is an appraisal of the body of writing that Hent de Vries traces to Levinasian responsibility where an '*incarnation* of sorts [...] instantiates, diffuses and disseminates itself before and beyond the concrete' (de Vries 2002: 321). It is a liberating philosophical move that questions established approaches to signification. Derrida introduces the difference involved in signs at 'the core of what is primordial' (Derrida 1973: 46 footnote). In emphasizing the divergence between the notion of a transcendental signified and its signifier or between the 'solitary mental life' and its voice or intuitive idealisation of self, Derrida speaks with a 'middle voice'.

In the introduction to *Speech and Phenomena* Derrida gives the most explicit outline in his work of the problematic form of presence that he believes grounds Husserl's work and much of metaphysics. Presence, a notion strongly related, if not identical, to Husserl's 'Living Present', is the 'original self-giving evidence, the *present* or *presence* of sense to a full and primordial intuition' (Derrida 1973: 5). It would seem to describe a form of union between 'sense' and 'primordial intuition', thereby taking the place of the 'difference' that he urges us to respect between 'world' and 'sense' above. Derrida questions the phenomenological concept of the sign on the basis of what he describes as Husserl's wish to expose 'degenerated' metaphysics for its blindness to the 'authentic mode of ideality' (ibid. 6). Husserl sees ideality as 'what may be indefinitely *repeated* in the *identity* of its *presence*' (6), an ideality that is not 'an existent that has fallen from the sky; its origin will always be the possible repetition of a productive act' (6), an account of ideality Derrida cannot accept. In looking closely at the difficulties Derrida has with Husserl's indication and expression, we can understand more clearly why Derrida's model of language presents the linguistic incarnation as a sticking point.

Husserl's 'theory of signs' argues that 'every sign is a sign for something but not every sign has "meaning"' (Husserl 1970a: 269) and that there are 'two concepts connected with the word "sign"' (ibid. 269). He refers to these two concepts as expression and indication. Indication applies 'more widely' when 'one limits oneself to expressions employed in living discourse' (269). In communicative speech meaning is always distinct because communication requires the indicative relation. But there is more to meaning than indicative relations: 'meaning is also capable of occurring without such a connection'. Expressions present us with this larger account of meaning, for it is expressions that 'function meaningfully even in *isolated mental life, where they no longer serve to indicate anything*' (269). In indication 'all marks belong, as characteristic qualities suited to help us in recognizing the objects to which they attach' (270). They are '[s]igns to aid memory' such as the flag as a sign of a nation. For indications, 'certain objects or states of affairs *of whose reality someone has actual knowledge* indicate to him *the reality of certain others or states of affairs,* in the sense that *his belief in the reality of the one is experienced* (though not at all evidently) *as motivating a belief or surmise in the reality of the other*' [Husserl's emphasis] (270). This is described by Husserl as a relation of 'motivation' representative of a *descriptive unity* among our acts of judgement. The essence of indication lies in this unity. In indication, therefore, one object or state of affairs does 'not merely recall another, and so points to it, but also provides evidence for the latter' (274).

Expressions, on the other hand, are, for Husserl, *meaningful signs*; 'each instance or part of *speech,* as also each sign that is essentially of the same sort, shall count as an expression, whether or not such speech is actually uttered' (275). An expression, as a case of speech, is phenomenally one 'with the experiences made manifest in them in the consciousness of the man who manifests them' (275). Expressions include 'the sensible sign, the articulate sound-complex, [and] the written sign on paper' (276). However, the point of contention is that 'all expressions in *communicative* speech function as *indications*' (277). They serve the hearer as signs of the 'thoughts' of the speaker, i.e. of his sense-giving inner experiences. Indications, therefore, are only evident when another person has to be understood, when intersubjective communication has to rely on something other than the 'inner word' for communication. Husserl also writes that 'ordinary speech permits us to call an experience which is intimated an experience which is *expressed*' (277), thereby unsettling the distinction. The distinction is upset further when Husserl describes the indications that take place in communicative speech as expressions. The underlying idea here is that they are essentially expressions yet they *function* in an indicative way:

> So far we have considered expressions as used in communication, which last depends on the fact that they operate indicatively. But expressions also play a great part in uncommunicated, interior mental life. *This change in function plainly has nothing to do with whatever makes an expression an expression.* Expressions continue to have meanings as they had before and the same meanings as they had in dialogue. (Husserl 1970a: 278 [my emphasis])

If indications, then, are fundamentally expressions, and are merely 'functioning' indicatively, does this imply that their materiality, what is generally regarded as their distinctive feature, is contaminated by the 'presence' that Derrida assigns to expressions? It is a question that cannot be answered here, but it would seem to imply that Husserl, and not only Derrida, is doing his best to unsettle any rigorous distinction devised between indication and expression. Since communication relies on the attachment of the physical manifestation of the meaning to the expression in its pre-communicative state, indication would appear to be made up of the expression coupled with an 'outer sign', vocal manifestation or gesture that completes the effort to communicate. Importantly, the dialogue has not altered the meaning of the expression. It would have the same meaning for the subject uttering it, if the indicative components were omitted. Husserl will later claim that '[w]hat we are to use as an indication, must be perceived by us as existent. This holds also of expressions used in communication, but not for expressions used in soliloquy, where we are in general content with imagined rather than with actual words' (Husserl 1970a: 279). It appears, therefore, that expressions are also to be regarded as being employed in communication. This is a further example of the subtle relation existing between the two 'concepts' for Husserl.

Husserl does sharpen this distinction, however: 'It seems clear therefore that an expression's meaning, and whatever else pertains to it essentially, cannot coincide with its feats of intimation [...] Shall one say that in soliloquy one speaks to oneself, and employs words as signs, i.e., as indications, of one's own inner experiences? I cannot think such a view acceptable' (Husserl 1970a: 279). For Derrida, it is this privileging of the unmediated inner voice, of communication free from any trace of inscription and difference, of a linguistic incarnation whose infinite potentiality for repetition patches up all difference, that is problematic. The incarnation, or manifestation of meaning in self-communication, that Husserl and later phenomenologists account for with the words 'life', 'incarnate significance' and 'Living Present', does not preclude all conceptions of difference. While they do not equate difference solely with the infinite deferral and difference that Derrida assigns to the sign, the difference that Husserl would seem to neglect in his phenomenology is still important to later phenomenologies that follow Husserl in privileging 'life' and 'auto-affection'.

Giorgio Agamben has spoken of the dangers, for Derrida, of making 'presence and origin' 'purely insignificant':

> In our tradition, a metaphysical concept, which takes as its prime focus a moment of foundation and origin, coexists with a messianic concept, which focuses on a moment of fulfillment. What is essentially messianic and *historic* is the idea that fulfillment is possible by retrieving and revoking foundation, by coming to terms with it. When these two elements are split up, we are left with a situation like the one so clearly witnessed in Husserl's *Crisis of European Sciences*, that of a foundation which is part and parcel of an infinite task. If we drop the messianic theme and only focus on the moment of foundation and origin – or even the absence thereof (which amounts to the same thing) – we are left with empty, zero degree, signification and with history as its infinite deferment. (Agamben 2005: 103–4)

Agamben argues that deconstruction gives up completely 'the nostalgia for origins' and in doing so inaugurates a 'principle of infinite deferment', where the movement of *Aufhebung* 'neutralizes signifieds while maintaining and achieving signification' (Agamben 2005: 103). Agamben questions the workings of this system because, for him, '[a] signification that only signifies itself can never seize hold of itself, it can never catch up with a void in representation [...]. In this way, the trace is a suspended *Aufhebung* that will never come to know its own *plērōma*. Deconstruction is, then, a thwarted messianism, a suspension of the messianic' (ibid. 103). The ability of an interpretation to 'seize hold of itself' recalls the notion of auto-affection and the question of 'embodied "meaning"' that Derrida has already problematized through the 'linguistic incarnation'.

In returning to the indicative function, we recall that indication relies on the subject's '*belief in the reality of the one*' being '*experienced* (though not at all evidently) *as motivating a belief or surmise in the reality of the other*' (Husserl 1970a: 270). It would appear, then, that the '*descriptive unity*' at work in indication privileges a theme of unity over difference. Derrida's description of the sign does not dwell on what Husserl's understanding of belief might suggest here. Belief epitomizes the kind of self-communication that is in question throughout Derrida's commentary. Belief relies on a great deal of self-interrogation, introspection and self-communication. In persuading himself that he believes the subject may very well have to overstep what Derrida here assigns to indication, since, as Husserl suggests, indication relies on belief. The capacity to believe that something is communicated in solitary mental life does not leave an accessible mark or trace behind that can then be interrogated for evidence that something has been communicated.

Derrida argues that indications are not involved with 'truths of reason' or with the '*content* of the truths involved' [my emphasis] (Derrida 1973: 29) and he reminds us that he is employing 'classical terms' (ibid. 29) and therefore speaks of truth and of a 'content of truths'. But what understanding of truth is implied here? Derrida argues that the '*whole system of essential distinctions is a purely teleological structure*' (101) and that sense is defined in general in phenomenology 'on the basis of truth as objectivity' (99). Husserlian phenomenology is deconstructed, therefore, through its understanding of objectivity. Derrida assigns to phenomenological thought a relation to objectivity, however, that is never wholly relinquished even in his own writing. The critique of the metaphysics of 'presence' or of that 'philosophy as knowledge of the presence of the object' (102) rests on the understanding of presence, objectivity and a relation to objects that Derrida takes from Husserl. There are a number of phrases in Derrida's commentary that enable us to understand the particular kinds of presence and objectivity he locates in Husserl. What is the particular 'possibility of a relation with the object' (99) that is so distasteful to Derrida's understanding of sense, meaning and *Différance*? How can our relation to objectivity and materiality impel a critique of metaphysics that offers in their place 'primordial division and delay', 'substitutive supplementation' and 'primordial self-deficiency' (88)? Derrida faults an account of presence and objectivity, described as 'the presence of the object', because it allows for an idealization of solitary mental life. He perceives a problematic stratum of presence based in language that he regards as responsible for phenomenological idealism. Even though Derrida does suggest that Husserl's account of language and of meaning can, in some instances, be removed from what Husserl regards as 'its normal meaning' (qtd. in Derrida ibid. 96), from the necessity that it be fulfilled by some object, the distinction between 'meaning-intention' and ' "eventual" fulfilment by the intuition of the object' (97) is always, for Derrida, under the 'command' of the 'theme of full "presence" ' (97).

The crux of Derrida's disagreement with Husserl, and with phenomenology in general, is found in *Speech and Phenomena*, in his reading of a particular kind of grounding objectivity ascribed to the *phōnē* or voice. He regards phenomenology as having to affirm an essential tie between *logos* and *phōnē*, one represented by phenomenology's notion of a 'living vocal medium', what then affords consciousness its privileged status (ibid. 15). However, Derrida then argues that 'self-consciousness only appears in its relation to an object'. Voice, therefore, must also have an 'essential tie' with this sense of objectivity and with the constitution of ideal objects. The constitution of ideal objects belongs to 'the essence of consciousness' and therefore to history, a fact that, for Derrida, makes the respective elements of consciousness and language 'more and more difficult to discern' (15). This introduces what Derrida refers to as 'difference' into any Husserlian 'pre-expressive stratum of experience'. Derrida wishes to investigate this 'difference', this site where it becomes difficult to distinguish language from consciousness. He suggests that Husserl emphasizes his particular account of *phōnē* to 'cover up' the difficulty of investigating this site. The situation is, therefore, that Derrida has problems, firstly, with phenomenology's distinct separation of logos and *phōnē*, and, secondly, with the emphasizing of a particular notion of voice that is employed by Husserl to 'cover up' the site where logos and *phōnē* diverge. However, Derrida's commentary on *voice*, while eliciting a supposed weakness in Husserl's philosophy, may also demonstrate why his own commentary must look for a rhetorical response to its methodological 'difficulty'. Derrida's description of this phenomenological voice indicates that he has a disinclination to accept a particular kind of conceptual or onto-theological transformation, or understanding of objectivity. The sense of objectivity of the *phōnē* or voice that Derrida does not accept is one located in the voice phenomenologically taken, speech in its transcendental flesh, in the breath, the intentional animation that transforms the body of the word into flesh, makes of the *Körper* a *Leib*, a *geistige Leiblichkeit* [from body to incarnate body]. The phenomenological voice would be this spiritual flesh that continues to speak and be present to itself – *to hear itself* – in the absence of the world. (Derrida 1973: 16)

Leonard Lawlor helps us read this passage. He reminds us that for Husserl, in *The Origin of Geometry*, writing is simultaneously a 'constituted sensible body (*Körper*), but also a constituting body proper or flesh (*Leib*). However, Lawlor recounts that, for Derrida, 'Husserl is not going to immobilize his analysis within this "ambiguity"' (Lawlor 2002: 120). Derrida continues: 'Although, in the word, *Körper* and *Leib*, body and flesh, are in fact numerically one and the same being, their senses are definitely heterogeneous and nothing can come to the latter through the former [Lawlor's translation]' (qtd. in Lawlor, 120). In other words, Derrida seems to have transplanted, once again, his reading of two kinds of sign, namely indication and expression, onto his reading of these two kinds of body, namely *Körper* and *Leib*. In order to describe the work of language, Derrida seems to have invested in a rhetoric of incarnation, or in a 'human analogue' for an incarnation, that employs notions of constituted sensible body and constituting flesh.

In the above passage Derrida has returned to the language of the linguistic incarnation that we have seen him outline so clearly in his introduction to Husserl's *Origin of Geometry*, some years earlier. We get a clearer understanding here of the notion of presence or 'relation to objects' that Derrida regards as problematic. It is a presence or objectivity that requires an 'intentional animation' for its being, one that 'transforms the body of the word into flesh'. Michel Henry shares Derrida's interest in moving beyond Husserl's understanding of intentionality, but he replaces it with notions of 'auto-impressionality' and a rejuvenated notion of 'flesh'. Henry argues that every life understood according to 'the overturning of phenomenology' (Henry 2000: 241) must 'withdraw from the intentionality of thought'. For Henry, it is 'in the auto-impressionality of the flesh, that each life reveals an impressional form' (ibid. 241). In the phenomenology of the impression we 'are sent back to a phenomenology of the flesh, which draws its own possibility from life' (241). Derrida will take a different route. His difficulty with an account of objectivity based on an 'intentional animation' does not withdraw to a consideration of impressionality. It does not dwell on the nature of the transformation grounding this problematic phenomenological objectivity. This 'spiritual flesh', or notion of objectivity that is founded on the transformation of the 'body of the world into flesh', is, for Derrida, enabling of a metaphysics that is 'present to itself' and can exist comfortably 'in the absence of the world'.

Natalie Depraz has also described a state of incarnation in Husserl in order to better reveal his notion of intersubjectivity. It can also assist in the examination of Joyce's motivations for employing interior monologue and stream of consciousness narration to mediate intersubjectivity. For Depraz, incarnation refers to the 'passage from the corporeal sensible to the conscious lived sense' (Depraz 1995: 275). It is a notion of intersubjectivity that is accepting of alterity, but of an alterity found *within* through attentive self-communion. In *Transcendance and Incarnation*, Depraz describes the kind of incarnation Husserl puts in play between word and thing:

> However, contrary to the logico-linguistic version of expression that establishes an asymmetrical relation between expressing (the word) and expressed (the thing), that is ever reshaped in the presentation of the indicative relation between bodies and living things, where the meaning of 'the expression' is not linguistic but intentional, his [Husserl's] indicative inter-empathetic version privileges a symmetry where the expressed (the flesh) becomes equally the expressing. (Depraz 1995: 176)

Depraz's basic argument is that Husserl does not regard the other as a 'radical alterity' but as 'a unity of constituted sensations' (Depraz 1995: 22). Other phenomenological accounts of alterity presume, for Depraz, that the 'intentional constitution of otherness' is based on a 'process of exteriorisation' (ibid. 22). This neglects, Depraz argues, a basic element of the phenomenological constitution of otherness which obliges us to take into account 'its dimension of associative resemblance to me and then to root its real content in a genetic structure of self-alterity which is co-originally temporal and spatial, and therefore image-like' (22). The move to regard the experience of otherness and of language as analogous rejuvenates Husserlian phenomenology. She argues that the subject is obliged to 'exhibit the genetic deep-rootedness of the experience of otherness as self-alterity through its simultaneously reflexive and incarnated matter' (23). However, the fact that she relates this reinterpretation of otherness as self-alterity, with its inauguration of the movement of incarnation, to what is 'image-like', and ultimately to language, is most important. In discussing Husserl's notions of indication and expression, she gives a reading of indication that departs from Derrida's more celebrated reading of this concept.

Because Husserl's conception of language is rooted in corporeity, Depraz argues that his notion of indication, even though it is representative of a rupture with any relation with an 'ideal identity' (ibid. 175), such as in expression, confers on 'the expression a meaning endowed with alterity'. Far from substituting itself to this alterity, the sign is now 'no longer reduced to its mundane empiricity, but re-evaluated in its phenomenological dimension, which implies a process immanent to the construction of otherness' (17-6). For Depraz, the most basic Husserlian expression is 'that of the fleshy bearing (*Aussehen*) as the flesh of man' (*Husserliana XV*, quoted in Depraz 1995: 176). Depraz argues that Husserl's conception of otherness necessitates an understanding of empathy grounded on auto-affection. It is through the 'foreign body that my primordial flesh is able to express itself as human' and 'corporeal' (qtd. in Depraz 1995: 176). But in the reduction of communicative speech, Depraz argues that Husserl confers more than an intentional sense on the indicative expression in forging in *Ideen II* an analogy with a 'linguistic anchorage' (ibid. 177) between intra-expressions (expressions of psychic lived experience) and inter-expressions (expressions of language and of thought). The analogy implies that the other is to language what the psychic living sense is to thought. Depraz argues that at the base of this analogy is the substrate of language. Her novel approach opens up the possibility whereby the experience of the other is apprehended as analogous to the functioning of language. Depraz argues that

> if the analogic *logos* forms 'a point of departure for the comprehension of the psychic life of otherness' (*Ideen II*, § 56, h, 240–1), owing to the fact that bodily movements correspond to the indications of living experiences and form a 'system of signs,' a 'signifying system of "the expression" of psychic events' analogous to 'the system of language', then the analogic experience of otherness gains through its analogy with empathy and language a living, fleshy anchorage' (Depraz 1995: 177).

It is the flesh that 'forms the point of departure from which is thematised the relationship between term and meaning' (Depraz 1995: 177). Depraz reminds us of Husserl's privileging of the notion of

incarnation in his work: 'the totality of discourse is the unity of flesh
and spirit' (quoted in Depraz 1995: 177). She argues that the 'flesh is
therefore the entrance way for a strange analogy which converts the
body into spirit and the term into meaning, and which transposes the
extrinsic duality of the form ("term") and of the content ("meaning")
onto the classical comprehension of symbolic language'. Depraz,
therefore, realigns the difference that Derrida has posited between
indication and expression through this analogy with the body. In
rooting the definition of indication and the communicative encounter
it inaugurates in the body, she describes the 'corporeity within' that is
primordial for Husserl and, as we shall see later, for Joyce and Proust.

Michel Henry, incarnation and the ends of 'phenomenological religiosity'[1]

The majority of Michel Henry's work is unavailable to English readers
despite the fact that *Le Monde*'s obituary to Henry describes him as
'without doubt one of the most important French philosophers of the
second half of the twentieth century' (Droit 2002). In his introductory
preface to the posthumously published four-volume collection of
Henry's essays, *Phénomenénologie de la vie*, Jean-Luc Marion also writes
that Henry's work harbours within itself 'a possibility still scarcely
glimpsed' (Henry 2004a: 8). This section examines two of Henry's most
celebrated philosophical motifs – flesh and incarnation – in the light of
more popular strands of phenomenological thought that privilege
what Michael Purcell calls 'incarnate existence', and in relation to
Merleau-Ponty's celebration of the flesh through his accounts of
'incarnate significance' and the 'subject incarnate'.[2]

   While the flesh has long been privileged in phenomenology as a
means for navigating otherness and intersubjectivity, Henry's privileging of flesh and incarnation, in a material phenomenology infused
with religious imagery, describes a 'phenomenology of life' that challenges descriptions of flesh and corporeity grounded on a privileging
of alterity. Henry privileges specific accounts of manifestation, auto-
affection and incarnation. Michael Purcell's recent study of the work of
Levinas, *Levinas and Theology*, also examines Levinas's description of
'incarnate existence', arguing that this conception of existence is
essential for understanding how Levinas's work straddles the divide
between philosophy and theology: Levinas pulls 'phenomenological

thinking back to think on ordinary incarnate existence' (Purcell 2006: 82).

These very different phenomenological arguments appear to hinge, then, on interpretations of incarnation and 'incarnate existence' that are frequently traced back to distinct exegetical practices. However, Purcell claims Levinas believed he was not 'an especially Jewish thinker' (ibid. 58), and Michel Henry has claimed that his work on ' "Christianity"?' does not intend to 'ask whether Christianity is "true" or "false" ', but instead to discover 'what kind of truth it offers to people' (Henry 2003: 1). The examination of such notions as incarnation, transcendence and manifestation in these different philosophies throws up the question of how it is possible to differentiate between 'confessional' writings and philosophical writings. The tendency to mediate the principle themes of a philosophy of intersubjectivity through such notions as 'incarnate existence' and incarnation has led many to suggest that phenomenology has lost its way in following for too long the 'disastrous consequences of philosophy's "linguistic turn" ' (Badiou 2006: 17). Dominique Janicaud also argues that the 'theological swerve in phenomenology' means that 'phenomenology has been taken hostage by a theology that does not want to say its name' (Janicaud 2000: 43) while Alain Badiou's understanding of the event and the mathematical offers a clear alternative to such 'phenomenological religiosity'.[3]

Paul Ricoeur has summed up most clearly what must presumably limit philosophical investigations that rely too much on any purported 'phenomenological religiosity'. In tackling such concepts as intersubjectivity and appearance with a phenomenology of religion, one must consistently be wary, Ricoeur argues, of how one's investigations regard 'religions other than my own' (Ricoeur 2000: 132).[4] He regards a phenomenology of religion as a guide to broader philosophical research 'by which one is to understand a regulative ideal projected on the horizon of our investigations' (ibid. 132). His work in the phenomenology of religion seeks to enunciate a 'wish for an interconfessional, interreligious hospitality, comparable to the linguistic hospitality that presides over the work of translating one tongue into another' (132). However, can such an interconfessional approach, dependent on the linguistic hospitality of translation, get off the ground when the linguistic hospitality itself is threatened by philosophies that consistently trace the meaning of fundamental terms, such as incarnation, back to religious practices and beliefs that cannot simply be translated from 'one tongue into another'? Are we left at a phenomenological dead end, having exhausted the discourse's resources for contributing to debates on alterity and intersubjectivity?

A rhetoric of incarnation has a long history in phenomenology.[5] Henry and Maurice Merleau-Ponty have both sought to describe a state of being that privileges how the body and the flesh mediate experience. In his last interview, in January 2002, Henry reiterates the major theme of his final phenomenological work, *Incarnation*: 'Only life gives us access to life, it reveals itself according to a pathetic *immédiation* which is a concrete auto-impressionality, a "flesh" ' (Henry 2005: 154). Henry uses the term 'flesh' to describe an understanding of the body as 'our body that feels itself at the same time as it senses all that surrounds it' (Henry 2000: 8) and he incorporates the Christian notion of Incarnation into his philosophy for two reasons: first, in order to differentiate his understanding of 'flesh' and enfleshed, 'incarnate living' from other philosophies that describe humans in terms of 'inert bodies' or 'types of computer that understand nothing of that which they are made' (ibid. 8) and, secondly, so as to describe the founding 'hallucinatory proposition' (10) of Johannic Christianity ('And the Word was made flesh') and its resultant style of thought, as a philosophical style of thinking. His employment of the notion of incarnation explicitly situates his own material phenomenology at the end of a philosophical trajectory that begins with the confrontation between 'Greek thought' or 'ontological monism'[6] – what he describes in terms of the Logos and its fundamental inauguration of an opposition between 'the sensible and the intelligible' (11) – and the genesis of Christian thinking. He describes the enormity of the struggle involved in assimilating the notion of Incarnation into a system of thinking in terms of those early Christians 'who tried hard to understand what they did not yet even have the means to understand' (11).

Henry wishes to move beyond the 'circular character' of the philosophy of representation. While Henry spends less time than Levinas and Derrida documenting the philosophical aspects of the subject's encounter with alterity, a consideration that makes his work vulnerable to attacks from advocates of deconstruction, he does write that this 'circular' nature of the monistic argument can be overcome, not by fleeing the jurisdiction of interiority, but by clarifying its 'essence of manifestation', a process that necessitates our rethinking of 'receptivity'. One of Henry's most important philosophical moves is to rethink the 'essence of receptivity' (Henry 1973: 237) from a state of interiority that redefines received understandings of monism, receptivity and what he refers to as the 'exterior content'. For Henry, interpretations that have sought to investigate receptivity solely from the perspective of its receiving what is an 'exterior content' have been unwilling to accept the real conditions of the essence of manifestation as representation. Henry regards the central movement of receptivity as that of an 'essence whose property is that of itself receiving *itself*' (ibid. 237). He believes that the 'problematic of receptivity' must be 'capable of understanding itself in its own ontological meaning'. It is only 'once the reception whose content it must give basis to is interpreted, no longer as a being, but as the pure ontological element which permits it to appear' that the problematic of receptivity, and hence the essence of manifestation, can be clarified. Henry replaces conceptions of exteriority, interiority and otherness with a foundational 'pure ontological element' that does not yet know, or sense, individual beings, or differences.

The concepts of transcendence, immanence and horizon are integral parts of Henry's phenomenology. The manifestation of Being is, for Henry, '*the condition of all possible manifestation of any being in general*' [Henry's italics] (ibid. 137). In *The Essence of Manifestation* Henry describes his unique conception of manifestation:

[I]f the horizon manifests the essence, it is in an [...] altogether different meaning, namely in the sense in which 'to manifest' means 'to be the appearance of something', nevertheless, in such a way that that which manifests itself in this appearance is not the thing of which it is the appearance, but merely refers to this thing as to that which does not show itself in the effective phenomenological content of the appearance itself. In this sense 'to manifest' signifies 'to hide', as well, or more precisely, to indicate something as differing in itself from the appearance which indicates it. (Henry 1973: 240)

The Essence of Manifestation introduces his understanding of transcendence, immanence and horizon and the kind of exteriority they are responsible for in a phenomenology of ontological monism. Henry does not only wish to denounce the ambiguity lying at the heart of representation, he also seeks to explain that it is possible to conceive of exteriority in terms of non-difference. Henry is unwilling to accept a philosophical tradition that makes 'inaccessible' to itself '*the very idea of a reception which would not be essentially the reception of an exterior content and one foreign to the power which receives it*' [Henry's emphasis] (Henry 1973: 237). The event referred to in the phrase 'essence of manifestation' works to imaginatively reconfigure what is prior to consciousness, representation and exteriority, and all those concepts that have worked in recent times from a presumption of primordial difference. Henry elaborates a phenomenology that readily acknowledges the centrality of exteriority for ontological monism, yet an account of exteriority that does not necessarily privilege difference. The receptivity and horizon that are essential to the event that belongs to the essence of manifestation find their nature in what they already contain. Henry believes that if the pure ontological content that the essence represents to itself belongs to it in such a way that it is in no way foreign to it, '*the mode of this belonging* is what must be determined from the ontological point of view' [Henry's emphasis] (ibid. 238). He continues:

> *Exteriority designates precisely the ontological character of this belonging, namely, the mode according to which the reception by the essence of this pure content which it itself is, takes place.* To give a rigorous ontological meaning to the concept of an exterior content is to extend it to all represented reality in general, and primordially to the ontological reality of the essence insofar [...] as it projects itself under the form of a horizon into the pure milieu of exteriority. Precisely because it is constituted by this horizon, namely by a milieu of pure exteriority, the ontological content, which the essence represents to itself in the act whereby it objectifies itself in it, is an exterior content, *and this in a radical sense in conformity to which exteriority, which qualifies such a content, is not a property added-on, but rather determines this content itself in its own ontological reality* [Henry's emphasis]. (Henry 1973: 238)

Henry's phenomenology wishes to step beyond being as a foundation for the event that allows such a state to appear. He describes a specific state of receptivity that allows for the 'essence of manifestation to receive itself' (ibid. 236) once receptivity is:

> [C]apable of understanding itself in its own ontological meaning, once the reception whose content it must give basis to is interpreted, no longer as a being, but as the pure ontological element which permits it to appear, it is obviously the essence itself that constitutes the content which it receives. By what right can such a content be qualified as 'exterior' to the essence if it is actually nothing other than the essence? (Henry 1973: 237)

These extracts display Henry's interest in immanence, what I examine in more detail in Joyce and Proust in Chapters 2, 3 and 4. Once Henry has explained his radical conceptions of representation and exteriority

as necessary components of phenomenology, the rest of his phenomenological vocabulary falls more easily into place.

The distinction between immanence and transcendence is a primary
distinction for Henry. Henry recognizes that Husserl's distinction
between immanent contents and transcendental contents is 'non-
essential because the essence of these contents is exactly the same'
(Henry 1973: 230). Henry believes that what makes the reception of
both sets of contents possible is transcendence. For Henry transcendence is the 'act or orientation of consciousness' (ibid. 230) the
'foundation' (222) and the 'manifestation of the foundation itself'
(216). If we conceive of immanence in terms of the event that is the
'essence of manifestation', then we might, for simplicity's sake, align
transcendence with the manifestation, and immanence with the
essence. It can then be suggested, very loosely, that transcendence is
the more abstract side of this equation and essence the more concrete
or 'material' side. The abstract side to transcendence implies that it is
impossible for it '*to lay its own foundation and thus to constitute the essence
of the foundation*' [Henry's emphasis] (210). Transcendence is removed
from phenomenality and as such it loses its concrete sense when it
must move beyond thinking of the 'condition of phenomenality as the
becoming of exteriority which has been realized in phenomenality'
(214). In other words, transcendence becomes abstract when it no
longer speaks of 'becoming' and instead speaks of the end product or
the 'is'. Transcendence is, however, fundamental for the human
capacities of imagination and intuition.

What Henry refers to as 'the internal possibility of surpassing'
(Henry 1973: 258) coincides with transcendence. Humanity is different
to the world of objects because it has the capability of remaining 'in
itself'. From such a state it is then possible that it also comes to 'surpass
itself'. Even though Henry regards transcendence as losing its essential
abstract quality once it becomes phenomenalized, its unique capacity
to trigger such 'surpassing' arises from its combining of worldliness
with an extra-worldliness. The ever-present 'possibility of an arrival of
transcendence' (ibid. 263) creates a space for the work of the imagination. Transcendence also brings to light the essential opposition that
Henry's work is consistently seeking to unravel: the opposition between
objectivity and movement, an opposition that is also connoted by the
phrase 'the essence of manifestation' itself.

Henry believes that immanence, intuition and essence voice more
completely the phenomenal or concrete world of existence. Immanence '*is the original mode according to which is accomplished the revelation of*

transcendence itself and hence the original essence of revelation' [Henry's emphasis] (227). Immanence designates the 'mode according to which the reception of a content takes place' (229) and the '*essence of the original receptivity which assures the reception of transcendence itself is immanence*' [Henry's italics] (228). Henry later describes immanence as 'the Being-interior-to-itself' (258). This state of being will be taken up again in Chapter 4, when I examine desire in Proust and Joyce in relation to what Gilles Deleuze has described as its capacity to remain 'immanent to itself' (Agamben 1999: 236). However, Henry argues that if transcendence loses itself in becoming concrete, or in speaking of the constituted and the immanent, it is immanence that preserves the notion of an essential primordial space of receptivity. Henry seeks to unravel the 'presuppositions [that] have determined the problem of receptivity' in the philosophical tradition. He believes that this tradition has been chiefly concerned to present the 'problem of receptivity ... as that of the reception of an exterior content' (Henry 1973: 236). Henry argues that 'we should attribute the characteristic of inadequacy to the manifestation of the essence under the form of the horizon' (ibid. 240). The recognition of inadequacy and 'radical passivity' is important for the examination of impotentiality in Chapter 4. These states require a sensitivity to Henry's understanding of auto-affection.

Auto-affection describes the event referred to by '*the manifestation of the essence to itself* [Henry's emphasis] (Henry 1973: 234). Henry argues that the 'act of appearing' is prior to being. What is important for the 'act of appearing' is that it occurs as an 'appearing to itself of the appearing' (ibid. 234). It must involve 'the self-appearance to self of this act', what Henry describes as a '*retro-reference of the act of appearing to itself that ultimately determines this act in its essence*' [Henry's emphasis]. Auto-affection is as important for Henry's phenomenology as '*Différance*' is for the philosophy of Derrida. Henry believes that the essence has the priority it has because it alone is capable of '*affecting itself*' and of being able to manifest '*itself to itself*' [Henry's emphasis] (235). He believes that it is an 'ontological necessity' that there is a state, or an essence, that is capable of entering into a relationship with self through what he calls 'effective phenomenal becoming wherein it realizes itself'.

The notion of auto-affection is closely related to another concept, that of auto-impressionality, that becomes important when Henry relates the phenomenology of ontological monism to his philosophy of Christianity. Henry shares Joyce's predilection for borrowing theological terms and investing them with a new meaning within the confines of his work. In *Incarnation: une philosophie de la chair*, Henry describes auto-impressionality as the 'original affectivity', one that 'accomplishes for itself the auto-revelation of life' (Henry 2000: 90). This 'original affectivity is the phenomenological matter of the auto-revelation that constitutes the essence of life' (ibid. 90). All these concepts recall the 'retro-reference' that Henry regards as essential also to the 'act of appearing' that grounds his earlier philosophy. The auto-revelation makes of this phenomenological matter 'an impressional matter', 'that is never an inert matter' or 'the dead identity of any thing'. It is 'an impressional matter that senses itself and that never ceases to do so' and this 'living auto-impressionality is flesh' (90).

Henry's re-evaluation of the body as flesh is a philosophical project that evolves over a long period in his work. His second book, *Philosophie et phénoménologie du corps*, begins this investigation. The philosophy of Maine de Biran is important for Henry. For Henry, Biran wishes to 'strip' the Cartesian cogito of the 'immobility of the thought-substance', in order to make of it 'the very experience of an effort in its accomplishment, an effort in which begins and ends the very being of the self' (Henry 1965: 72). Biran stresses movement and resistance rather than force. For Henry, his understanding of the body, '*in uprooting not the idea but being itself and the reality of movement in the sphere of the transcendent being* [...] *defines the real body, and not the idea of the body, as a transcendental and subjective being*' [Henry's italics] (ibid. 79). Henry's own conception of the body as flesh forces us to address the unique kind of affectivity and sense-experience that flesh embodies. When Henry later comes to describe his philosophy of Christianity, the mystery of incarnation proves very congenial to his philosophy of flesh.

Henry's aim is to discover whether the 'simplest experience', that which inhabits the internal structure of immanence (Henry 1973: 462), the 'immediate experience of self', can be 'recognised and grasped': 'THAT WHICH IS FELT WITHOUT THE INTERMEDIARY OF ANY SENSE WHATSOEVER IS IN ITS ESSENCE AFFECTIVITY' [Henry's upper case] (ibid. 462). Such an account of affectivity, felt without the intermediary of 'any sense', is also integral to Proust's vision of the reader. The writer provides 'nourishment' across time for the reader, as his incarnate word becomes the reader's very own 'inner book of unknown signs'. The reader's apprehension of the sacrifice of life made for the word can unleash a profound reciprocity whereby the reader returns a 'nourishment' that sustains the writer more than the life the writer has foregone for the word. For Henry, such affectivity is the concrete 'essence of auto-affection', it is the 'phenomenologically effective "self-feeling by self" ', what ultimately proves that 'feeling does not differ from the essence' (463). Because affectivity is never that which is given to us through the intervention of a sense, Henry emphasises that '[a]ffectivity has nothing to do with sensibility' [Henry's italics] (463).

A philosophy of the flesh and incarnation is privileged in Henry's later work. *Incarnation: Une Philosophie de la Chair* marks the culmination of Henry's work in material phenomenology for which there is no English translation. Roger-Pol Droit writes that 'the question of knowing whether these final works, marked by a quasi-mystical apology of Christianity [...] are to be considered as a continuation of his previous work, or as installing, on the contrary, a rupture in his thought, equally remains open' (Droit 1987). *Incarnation* is divided into three sections: 'The Unsettling of Phenomenology', 'Phenomenology of the Flesh' and 'Phenomenology of the Incarnation: Salvation in a Christian sense'. The first section outlines Henry's position in relation to phenomenology in general and it enables us to understand what kind of philosophy the theme of incarnation inaugurates for him. Henry, like Levinas, recognizes the importance of placing 'phenomenology before ontology' (Henry 2000: 43). However, for Henry, phenomenology's 'great weakness is precisely its deep-rooted phenomenological indeterminacy, its tendency to focus on the appearance without explaining what it consists of, or how it appears' (ibid. 43).

Henry also critiques the attention phenomenology pays to Husserl's understanding of intentionality, what Levinas refers to as '[t]his conditioning of the mental in "one's own body" that makes up what is called sensibility, this "incarnation" of thought' (Levinas 1990c: 62). Henry writes that phenomenology traditionally argues that it is 'in intentionality that intuition has its phenomenological power, the power to institute itself in the condition of the phenomenon and with this to suddenly unleash phenomenality'. Henry believes that phenomenology's greatest strength leads to its greatest weakness: 'the most profound project of Husserlian phenomenology was to have thought life – the transcendental life of the ego that Husserl has a tendency to confuse with the absolute' (Henry 2005: 154). Henry, in arguing against this understanding of intentionality, believes that an 'important misconception must therefore be set aside. If intentionality belongs to the reality of the conscience, while the object to which it is related is situated outside of it, is it not then advisable to place the power that reveals, namely the revelation itself, "inside" the conscience? Otherwise is it not the case that the "interiority" of the conscience will be opposed to the exteriority of the object?' (Henry 2000: 51). Therefore, even though Levinas and Henry do stress, as Michael Purcell suggests, 'this incarnate life within the world which is the locus of salvation', because 'consciousness finds itself always and already *here in the world*' (Purcell 2006: 80), a closer inspection of their accounts of incarnation reveals very different philosophical perspectives.

The second section of *Incarnation*, 'Phenomenology of Flesh', revises some of the arguments that appear in Henry's earlier works, such as *Phénoménologie matérielle*. Henry reiterates the main points of his material phenomenology, employing a rhetoric of embodiment and incarnation in advancing his philosophy. He argues that

> [T]he unsettling of phenomenology is the movement of thought aimed at understanding that which precedes it: this self-givenness of absolute Life in which it comes to itself in itself. The unsettling of phenomenology thinks the precedence of Life over thought. The thinking of the precedence of life over thought may very well be the event of a kind of thinking [...] it is only possible because, in the order of reality and according to philosophical reflection itself, life is already revealed to itself. In the thinking of the precedence of life over thought, it is therefore life, in its effective phenomenological accomplishment – life always already accomplished in which this thinking is given to itself – which allows for itself, firstly, to be a kind of thought, a *cogitatio*, and secondly, to be, eventually, this particular yet essential thinking which proceeds from the unsettling of phenomenology and which shows itself capable of thinking the precedence of life over thought as a condition interior to itself. (Henry 2000: 136)

Henry argues that philosophies that conceive of the 'sensible body' in terms of an 'empirical body' have their roots in the writings of Galileo: 'The substitution of the sensible body for a material, extended object assimilable to the geometrical object constitutes a reduction' (Henry 2000: 143). Henry offers his philosophy of the flesh as an alternative to the philosophies of Condillac and Husserl who, he believes, have been influenced by this strand of scientific thought.

However, it is in the last section of *Incarnation*, 'Phenomenology of Incarnation: Salvation in a Christian sense', that Henry clarifies his move towards a philosophy of Christianity in advancing his phenomenology of Incarnation. Henry believes that 'the "theological turn" of contemporary phenomenology is not a "deviation" or distortion of phenomenology, but its fulfilment' (Henry 2005: 154). Henry explains why he employs a rhetoric of incarnation. He argues that even among 'those who are Christians there are those who follow Greek thought and who are not able to accept the Incarnation' (Henry 2004d: 235). What he does not accept in the dualism of classical Greek thought, however, is that it essentially defines man as 'an animal', as something of 'no great importance' that is yet provided with a '*logos*' (ibid. 235). Henry employs incarnation as a term that describes an essential element of Judaism and Christianity that is opposed to this conception of man: '[A]s regards the body (the incarnation), Greek thought is a dualist thought; there is the soul that opens itself up to the intelligible – the ηοῦς that is eternal – and then there is a perishable body. Such dualism is neither in Judaism nor in Christianity' (235). Henry argues that since the New Testament the flesh has been associated with both salvation (according to John, the Word 'brings men salvation') and damnation (auto-eroticism is regarded as idolatry in the Old Testament). Henry asks how 'flesh can be at the same time both the site of salvation and damnation? The phenomenology of flesh discovers its limits at this point and only a phenomenology of Incarnation is capable of enlightening us further' (2000: 238).

Sébastien Laoureux's reading of Henry examines some interesting points of intersection between material phenomenology and Derridean deconstruction. Even though Laoureux argues that Henry certainly '*"escapes" in a certain manner the Derridean reading of Husserl*' by not '*espousing the metaphysical presuppositions that Derrida finds in Husserl*', for Laoureux, this does not imply that Henry '*completely "escapes" a Derridean deconstruction*' [Laoureux's italics] (Laoureux 2005: 90). For Laoureux, material phenomenology, or Henryian phenomenology, is chiefly concerned with preserving a certain 'heterogeneity' between what is primary and what is secondary, or between an 'originary' phenomenological element and a 'derived' element, something Henry has inherited from Husserl's understanding of 'phenomenological originality' (ibid. 88). This heterogeneity manifests itself most clearly, for Laoureux, in Husserl's distinction between 'perception or originary representation' and 're-presentation or re-production' (88). However, Laoureux acknowledges that even though Henry strives to preserve a sense of this Husserlian heterogeneity, his understanding of 'self-presence' 'has nothing to do with Husserl's understanding of this term' (86). For Laoureux, Derrida and Henry do not accept Husserl's conception of a 'purely immanent apprehension' (80) and they recognize the 'impossibility for Husserlian phenomenology of accepting the problematic of the unconscious' (85). In other words, while both

Derrida and Henry do not accept Husserlian presence or intention-ality, and while they both acknowledge that the originary impression's interaction with what Henry refers to as the 'temporal flux' (Henry 2000: 75) introduces a foundational element of 'Différance' (ibid. 75) into phenomenology, what ultimately comes to divide them is the place they assign such 'Différance' in their larger philosophical schemas. Henry, for his part, would, according to Laoureux, suggest that '*the analysis proposed by Derrida will not always be coherent because it only conceives of one kind of phenomenality*' [Laoureux's italics] (Laoureux 2005: 83).

Henry refers to Derrida's notion of 'Différance' only once in *Incarnation* in discussing Husserl's understanding of the impression's rela-tion with temporality. Henry refers to 'Différance' (Henry 2000: 75) in passing as he privileges language promoting a sense of 'synthesis' (Henry 2000: 77) that serves to unify what is present and what is 'retentional'. He suggests that a strict adherence to 'Différance', what he equates with 'temperal flux' or the 'paradoxical incapacity of the consciousness of the here and now to give to the present that which is in itself never present but always in flux', is only in truth 'an attempt to camouflage the idea of continual synthesis according to which a retentional consciousness ties itself to this consciousness of the here and now' (ibid. 77). In other words, Henry chooses, in acknowledging the importance of 'Différance', to persevere with a phenomenological project that consistently unravels aspects of personhood that, for him, elicit illuminating degrees of immanence and incarnation.

The Levinasian 'time-lapse' and 'incarnate existence'

Before examining Emmanuel Levinas's understanding of 'incarnate existence' and his reading of incarnation in Merleau-Ponty, I want to look briefly at his notion of the time-lapse, because it is important for his understanding of narrative time. The 'time-lapse' is an aspect of Levinas's work that has been neglected by literary critics in favour of his understanding of alterity. In *Otherwise than Being* Levinas returns to a description of time that first appears in *Time and the Other*. In seeking to move beyond a formulation of the 'temporalization' of time, where everything 'is crystallized or sclerosized into substance', Levinas thinks it is necessary to admit a time-lapse, or an irrecoverable element of time, that is still integral to this movement of temporalization: 'in the recuperating temporalization, without time lost, without time to lose, and where the being of substance comes to pass – there must be signaled a lapse of time that does not return, a diachrony refractory to all synchronization, a transcending diachrony' (Levinas 2006: 9). Why must there be such a time-lapse that does not return and would it ever offer anything that could be returned? It is this element of time, represented by the 'transcending diachrony', what is caught irrevocably in the 'recuperating temporalization' (ibid. 9) that relates ethics to what is described in terms of narrative in Levinas. The notion of a transcending diachrony is important for investigating Levinas's comments on narrative because it is integral to Levinas's understanding of signification as that which absorbs subjectivity and inaugurates the privileging of the relationship with the other:

> Diachrony is the refusal of conjunction, the non-totalizable, and in this sense, infinite. But in the responsibility for the Other, for another freedom, the negativity of this anarchy, this refusal of the present, of appearing, of the immemorial, commands me and ordains me to the other, to the first one on the scene, and makes me approach him, makes me his neighbor. It thus diverges from nothingness as well as from being. It provokes this responsibility against my will, that is, by substituting me for the other as a hostage. All my inwardness is invested in the form of a despite-me, for-another. Despite-me, for-another, is signification par excellence. And it is the sense of the 'oneself,' that accusative that derives from no nominative; it is the very fact of finding oneself while losing oneself. (Levinas 2006: 11)

Having devised this conception of the transcendental diachrony of time, Levinas goes on to refer this element of the 'beyond-time' to a way of speaking that can, for him, be too easily likened to a 'narrative' 'way of speaking': 'But this is still perhaps a quite narrative, epic, way of speaking. Am I the interlocutor of an infinity lacking in straightforwardness, giving its commands indirectly in the very face to which it ordains me?' (Levinas 2006: 13). This 'narrative, epic, way of speaking' is consonant with an obedience and a responsibility that must obey the order to be responsible before this order 'is formulated', as though the order 'were formulated before every possible present, in a past that shows itself in the present of obedience without being recalled'. In other words, the reason for obeying this order to be responsible cannot be found, or must consistently be referred back to 'him who obeys in his very obedience' (ibid. 13).

For Levinas, a narrative 'way of speaking', therefore, presupposes an inescapable responsibility to the 'order' and to the other, a responsibility in which subjectivity is 'absorbed in signification' (13) and which amounts to 'the glory of transcendence'. Substitution fills the void when subjectivity has been absorbed in signification – '[s]ubstitution is signification' – but 'substitution as the very subjectivity of a subject'. This state of the subject replaces the 'ego' and any 'modality of being' because it comes from 'the impossibility of escaping responsibility, from the taking charge of the other' (14). This signification, as subjectivity, has nothing to do with 'transubstantiation' or with the shutting up of myself 'in another identity' (14). It cannot be concerned, therefore, with aspects of signification that are phrased in terms of embodying two disparate meanings at once, something I will examine later in this section in relation to what Michael Purcell describes as Levinas's privileging of 'incarnate existence' (Purcell 2006: 73).

Levinas returns to the time-lapse in Chapter 2 of *Otherwise than Being*, in a section entitled *'Despite Oneself'*. The saying, the 'anarchy of responsibility', the 'refusal to be assembled into a representation' (Levinas 2006: 51) 'has its own way to concern me' and it is through the *'lapse'*. However, the impossibility of representing the 'transcendental diachrony', or the fact that it does not have a 'representable present', also means that the resulting 'responsibility for another' may not 'devolve from a *free* commitment' (51). To assume this state of responsibility means to assume the state of 'the sacrifice of a hostage designated who has not chosen himself to be hostage' (15). The removal of this freedom inaugurates the Levinasian ethic where the 'temporality of time is an obedience' (52). What is investigated here, therefore, albeit briefly, is the implications for literary criticism of the merging, in Levinas's philosophy, of the time of books, plot and narrative with the time of the other, especially as it colours his distrust of the theme of incarnation. Levinas argues that 'to make signs to the point of making oneself a sign is not a babbling language' (143). For Levinas, signification, or this making of signs, inaugurates, once again, the state of 'for-the-other' where 'incessant signification' is only concerned with 'pure signification'. Derrida's essay on Levinas, 'Violence and Metaphysics', claims that Levinas denies the 'moment of the concept' (Derrida 2002a: 185). Even though language in its 'original possibility as *offer*' is non-violent, Derrida argues that there is no phrase which 'does not pass through the violence of the concept' (ibid. 185). Levinas is so concerned to describe the non-violent that, for Derrida, his descriptions of plot, narrative and even the language of books remains at the state of 'pure signification', a state that is inherited from the responsibility to the other because the central time-lapse does not differentiate between lived time and narrative time. One important corollary of this unwillingness to clearly differentiate narrative time and lived time, or to describe more than a philosophy of 'pure signification', is that, for Derrida, it demonstrates the need to 'find other grounds for the divorce between speech and thought' (190).

Jill Robbins examines Levinasian language in relation to the long-running debate on how to differentiate Levinas's philosophical work from his 'confessional' work. She argues that the distinction in Levinas between the 'philosophical and the nonphilosophical writing is not absolute' (Robbins 1999: xvi). In claiming, however, that Levinas sought to keep his ' "confessional" writings' separate from his philosophical texts, at least until 1975, 'as the difference between an exegetical adherence and a phenomenological inquiry aware of its own presuppositions' (ibid. xvi) she does not examine the manner in which something akin to an 'exegetical adherence' may have been embraced by the recent 'turn' to 'phenomenological religiosity'. She argues that Judaism, what informs Levinas's style of commentary, 'is so oriented toward the exterior and the outside, it seems to lack even the possibility of such interiority' (44), an interiority found, Robbins argues, in the 'Christian "drama" of personal salvation'. The fact that, for Robbins, the Christian imagination can be 'characterised by its movement from sensory to nonsensory', whereas Judaism refuses this movement through 'its perpetual recourse to the interhuman' (47) leads, Robbins argues, to Levinas's distrust of representation, figuration and anything that might serve to idolize or make an icon of the interhuman.

How do Levinas's writings and the criticism his work has inspired respond, then, to the work of writers that might be regarded as making an 'icon of the interhuman'? Joyce and Proust may very well be regarded as making an 'icon of the interhuman' that includes the reader. How do Levinas's writings on signification respond to the work of authors who privilege a conception of interiority that is grounded on a representation of the 'movement from sensory to nonsensory'? Robbins suggests that Levinas regards all rhetoric not as 'intersubjective persuasion' but as 'trope'. In other words, Levinas's 'confessional' practices might be regarded as influencing his understanding of trope, a consideration that must be kept in mind when we read Levinasian criticism.

Alterity, manifestation, transcendence and incarnation are central concepts for Levinas that have come to act as tropes within literary criticism. At the beginning of *Totality and Infinity* we learn that '[t]he metaphysical desire tends towards *something else entirely,* toward the *absolutely other'* (Levinas 1969: 33) and that '[f]or Desire this alterity, non-adequate to the idea, has a meaning. It is understood as the alterity of the Other and of the Most-High' (ibid. 34).[7] The two important features, therefore, of Levinasian alterity are that it is *'absolutely other'* and that the inescapable desire for it is equivalent to the desire for what Levinas calls the 'Most-High'. We recall also that it is the 'transcending diachrony', the 'refusal of conjunction', or 'the non-totalizable', that in also being 'infinite', still 'ordains me to the other' and provokes a 'responsibility against my will' for such alterity. The transcending diachrony, then, this element that leads him to think that he is engaged in a 'narrative' 'way of speaking', is exactly that which inaugurates the special state of responsibility to the other that grounds Levinasian ethics. There is a reluctance, however, on the part of Levinas to represent this arrangement. Does he feel he is guilty of the kind of figural gesture that might be regarded as representing 'some movement from the sensory to the nonsensory'?

For Levinas, language analysis and reading practices are irrevocably charged with, and influenced by, particular exegetical practices. A passage from his later work once again elicits how this influence plays itself out in his understanding of language:

> We wonder, in fact, if the idea of prefiguration, legitimate to the extent that it coincides with that of prophecy, does not alter, when it is raised into a system, the very essence of the spirit which Judaism installed. If every pure character in the Old Testament announces the Messiah, if every unworthy person is his torturer and every woman his Mother, does not the Book of Books lose all life with this obsessive theme and endless repetition of the same stereotyped gestures? Does the spiritual dignity of these men and women come to them through reference to a drama operating on a miraculous level, in some mythological and sacred realm, rather than from the meaning that this life, which is conscience, gives itself? Does the monotheist God haunt the roads of the unconscious? (Levinas 1990a: 120)

Levinas questions the raising 'into a system' of such essential spiritual components as 'prophecy'. For Levinas, the representation of prophecy, as recorded in the Old Testament, as Scripture, has come to take on the appearance of 'prefiguration', a notion that leads him to the critique of the notion of incarnational thought. Prefiguration is also central to Auerbach's canonical reading of narrative in terms of mimesis.

Presumably, it is this understanding of prefiguration that Levinas is wary of above. The sense of prefiguration implicit in Auerbach is integral to his notion of 'figura'. Auerbach's description of 'figura' draws from the Christian view of reality in late antiquity and the Middle Ages. As Richard Walsh explains, for this sense of 'figura', grounded as it is in 'biblical exegesis', 'the relations between remote events are understood as a series of figural anticipations and literal fulfilments that manifest, and are guaranteed by, divine providence' (Walsh 2003: 117). However, Walsh argues that 'versions of the same mechanism then inform the synchronic relation of the mimetic text to its historical milieu, and the diachronic relation of the worldview it encapsulates to past historical paradigms' (ibid. 117). Walsh believes that any purported hard and fast division between the narrativity of history and fiction is undermined when the background of Christian teleology is removed. Once removed, every event 'has the capacity to be not only itself, but also the fulfilment of an earlier event and the figure of a later one, resulting in a kind of unlimited semiosis' (18). This last notion would of course feed into post-structuralist descriptions of narrative.

Paul Ricoeur's phenomenological work on narrative also examines the notion of prefiguration. His employment of prefiguration draws from Augustine. Augustine writes of his own autobiography or self-narration: '[a]s the process continues the province of memory is extended in proportion as that of expectation is reduced, until the whole of my expectation is absorbed' (Ricoeur 1984: 20). For Ricoeur, the 'poetic act of emplotment' (21–2) replies to the 'enigma of the speculation on time' (ibid. 21). Like Levinas, Ricoeur believes that the major tendency of narratology must be to 'dechronologise' narrative, or to account for the surplus – Levinas's 'transcending diachrony' – that always remains after chronologization or temporalization (30). He argues that 'chronology does not have just one contrary, namely the achronology of laws or models. Its true contrary is temporality itself' (30). Ricoeur suggests that it is the reader who mediates and receives the temporality of lived time and narrative time in making sense of a particular narrative. Levinas does not clearly differentiate between the reader and the non-reading subject in terms of the 'temporality of lived time'. Ricouer, on the contrary, develops a vast schema that attempts to describe this temporality. He differentiates between muthos, 'the organization of the events' (33) and mimesis, 'imitation or representation' (33).

The question is, therefore, how does Levinas's unique conception of signification, prefiguration and diachrony play out themes of narrativity that are current in recent narrative studies and how does it influence his understanding of incarnation? One possible way of inspecting this is to look at the element of the figural that Levinas distrusts. Robbins argues that Levinas favours the 'perpetual recourse to the interhuman' (Robbins 1999: 47) over any representation of the 'movement from the sensory to the nonsensory'. Alain Badiou also reminds us that Levinasian ethics requires that the 'experience of alterity be ontologically "guaranteed" as the experience of a distance [...] the *traversal* of which is the ethical experience itself' (Badiou 2001: 22). Because Levinas makes little clear distinction between the time of narrative and the time involved in the 'transcendental dia-chrony' that absorbs subjectivity in signification, the ethic inherent in Levinas very often appears as a direct mapping of the narrative mode, or the mode of commentary, that he employs throughout his writings. Gershom Scholem regards 'commentary' as 'the first ranking form of Jewish creation' (Scholem 1997: 17):

> [O]ver the course of generations, commentary became the first ranking form of Jewish creation. In a society based on the acceptance of a truth which had been revealed in a written document originality could not be a central value. The truth is already known. We have naught to do but to understand it, and what is perhaps more diffi-cult, to pass it down. In other words: originality and the creative impulse which acted here did not declare themselves as such, but preferred to manifest themselves in a form which was less pre-tentious but in fact was no less creative – namely, that of commen-tary. (Scholem 1997: 17)

If our reading of characters in narratives is consistently regarded as prefiguring a 'truth' that is always already known, then we have surely turned our back on a whole range of theories of narrative. Even though Levinas questions such a prefigurative style of reading, does he replace it with a mode of commentary that regards the 'transcending dia-chrony' of narrative time as a horizon that directs the reader's approach to the text? Is it a horizon forever leading to a state of irremissible thrownness where responsibility transforms subjectivity into significa-tion, and, in turn, to the one-for-another integral to hostage-taking, never wholly relinquishing a reading strategy that subjects characters to the claims of responsibility. Moshe Halbertal argues that canonization, as the privileging or sacralization of a text or a series of texts above others, should not only be regarded as 'the addition of status to an accepted meaning but as a transformation of meaning itself' (Halbertal

1997: 11). In other words, even though Levinas challenges certain modes of linguistic analysis, his mode of commentary may find it impossible to shirk its responsibilities to such canonization.

Levinas, Merleau-Ponty and incarnation

Michael Purcell privileges 'incarnate existence' in his reading of Levinas. However, Levinas outlines his understanding of incarnation in his own reading of Merleau-Ponty. In the *Phenomenology of Perception* Merleau-Ponty describes a process of incarnation in language that is a fact of everyday existence. In admitting that language has an 'inner content' Merleau-Ponty argues that it does not express 'thoughts'. For Merleau-Ponty, language 'is the subject's taking up of a position in the world of his meanings' where the notion of world here refers to the fact that the ' "mental" or cultural life borrows its structures from natural life and that the thinking subject must have its basis in the subject incarnate' (Merleau-Ponty 2003: 225). When Merleau-Ponty comes to speak of the association between the 'subject incarnate', transcendence and language, there is very little direct correlation of this association with religious experience. The flesh and the body are fundamental for the kind of transcendence that Merleau-Ponty describes here. For Merleau-Ponty, the 'human body is defined in terms of its property of appropriating, in an indefinite series of discontinuous acts, significant cores which transcend and transfigure its natural powers' (ibid. 225). Merleau-Ponty makes little distinction between the nature of the transcendence involved in language exchanges and the kind of exchange constructed, for example, when an observer infers that one is meditating from the narrowing of one's eyes. Both fall into the category of 'giving significance' (226) and it is by means of this power of 'giving significance, that is, both of apprehending and conveying meaning' that man 'transcends himself towards a new form of behaviour, or towards other people, or towards his own thought, through his body and his speech' (226).

The 'subject incarnate' refers here, therefore, to a quality of natural life that appropriates 'significant cores' which then lead to further self-transcendence. There is little implication that the sense of incarnation implied for the 'subject incarnate' implicitly refers to the biblical incarnation narrative. There is no suggestion that the phenomenological employment of an incarnated subject references a hermeneutical strategy for life encompassed by what Paul Ricoeur refers to as the 'circle of the living word and the scriptural trace' (Ricoeur 2000:

132–3). Merleau-Ponty describes the kind of physical situation that arises in linguistic communication as a moment where language brings 'the body into play' in such a way that language 'allows itself to be invested with a *figurative significance* which is conveyed outside us' (Merleau-Ponty 2003: 225). The account of language set up here, where it is invested, in the physical communicative situation, with '*figurative significance*', does not draw from practices of textual commentary as in Levinas. The body is primordial for Merleau-Ponty and it is only against the backdrop of this primordial incarnated subjectivity that 'genuine communication' (ibid. 192) can arise. In 'genuine communication' 'the thing expressed does not exist apart from the expression' and 'the signs themselves induce their significance externally'. However, Merleau-Ponty once again refers to this kind of significance as 'incarnate significance' because 'existence realizes itself in the body' and because it is the 'central phenomenon of which body and mind, sign and significance are abstract moments' (192). The kind of incarnation described here, or the incarnative process implied, is taken up again by Merleau-Ponty in a section from *Signs* entitled 'On the Phenomenology of Language'. He describes a 'phenomenon of incarnation' (Merleau-Ponty 1964: 93) according to which in 'my experience of others' and even in 'my experience of speech [...] I inevitably grasp my body as a *spontaneity which teaches me what I could not know in any other way except through it*' (ibid. 93).

However, Claude Lefort argues that Merleau-Ponty's reliance on the notion of flesh is 'limited'. For Lefort, 'if we question the relation to one's own name', a quantity he later refers to as 'the representative of otherness', then 'we can no longer stay within the limits of the milieu of the flesh' (quoted in Johnson and Smith 1990: 12). Luce Irigaray, whose understanding of incarnation and impotence is examined in Chapter 4, also argues that Merleau-Ponty neglects the realities of language in describing '[a] speech that is always at risk', the 'speech of a subject who tries unceasingly to compensate for his incarnation in his language' (Irigaray 2004: 149). However, Gary Brent Madison stresses the fact that the flesh is an 'internal phenomenon' for Merleau-Ponty:

What the flesh 'means' is that, when I engage in reflection, I am *already* for myself an other. Because of this, otherness is inscribed in my very flesh. It is precisely because the flesh, which introduces otherness into me, is also 'my' flesh that there are for me *alter egos*, other *myselves*, such that I am always for myself the other of the other of me. (quoted in Johnson and Smith 1990: 33)

However, Levinas still cites problems in Merleau-Ponty's account of intersubjectivity that are, for him, symptomatic of the limitations of what he describes as 'incarnational thought'. Levinas describes Merleau-Ponty's privileging of 'the original incarnation of thought', (quoted in Johnson and Smith 1990: 56) in a version of intersubjectivity that Levinas regards as an 'anachronism' (ibid. 62), as 'a forgetfulness' (that he shares with Husserl) towards the 'even more mysterious' 'enigma of sensation-feeling' in the 'visual' (66) as opposed to the tactile. Levinas's heightened regard for the 'visual' inaugurates his interest in the 'face of the other' and the kind of 'incarnate existence' that Michael Purcell regards as so central to Levinas's privileging of ethics and intersubjectivity. It is noteworthy, then, that Michael Purcell's *Levinas and Theology* calls for a reading of Levinas that privileges 'incarnate existence', when it is precisely an account of incarnational thought – 'this anachronism [that] is precisely incarnation' (quoted in Johnson and Smith 1990: 55) – that alerts Levinas to the limitations in Merleau-Ponty's, and Husserl's, accounts of intersubjectivity.

The matter can be clarified somewhat by examining two brief essays by Levinas on Merleau-Ponty: 'Intersubjectivity: Notes on Merleau-Ponty' and 'Sensibility', published for the first time in English in 1990. In these essays, Levinas argues that the kind of 'embodied thought expressing itself' (quoted in Johnson and Smith 1990: 62) that he refers to through 'incarnation' is a 'modality of meaning that is older than that of the dualist metaphysics of Cartesianism or of the subject-object correlation that develops into transcendental philosophy' (ibid. 62–3). He describes this kind of thought as follows:

> What we have here is thought lived as extension [...]: extendedness belonging to the 'flesh of thought, to thought having flesh': it [this conception of thought] is not the intentional correlate of extension, no matter how closely interfused we might imagine it to be with extension. Thus there is, in the transcendental reduction of sensibility, the manifestation of a vicious circle, or of an anachronism – of a constitution presupposing, or already giving itself, the constituted. (in Johnson and Smith 1990: 61–2)

It is by associating this kind of thinking on the body, a kind that he refers to with the German term *Lieblichkeit* (corporeality) and that we have already come across in Derrida's reading of Husserl, with a kind of knowledge-based accounting for the human, that Levinas makes perhaps his strongest argument against the 'forgetfulness' of such incarnational thought:

Hence perhaps a certain priority given to the ambiguity of the sensible as [a form of] consciousness in which the mental element of the apprehension of things and the spatial element of the corporeal gestures of taking, in that same apprehension, go together. This is the original and originary [*original et originelle*] condition of the body proper, that status of the *Lieblichkeit,* solipsistic subjectivity and, in other people, the object 'invested with spirit'. But henceforth [there is a] priority of the flesh affirming itself in human spirituality and to the detriment of another ambiguity or ambivalence, that of the enigma of sensation-sentiment, which is played out in the passivity of the *sense affected* [*sens affectés*] by the sensorial, between the pure undergoing or suffering and eventual pain, and the *known* [*su*] of knowledge that remains behind as its residue or trace. (ibid. 65)

In 'Sensibility', therefore, the 'enigma of sensation-sentiment' that is neglected by Merleau-Ponty's and a whole philosophical tradition's privileging of the 'original incarnation of thought' (ibid. 56) is 'played out in the passivity of the *sense affected* [*sens affectés*] by the sensorial'. This enigma that alerts us to the 'ethical relation' that occurs 'between the pure undergoing or suffering and eventual pain, and the *known* [*su*] of knowledge that remains behind as its residue or trace' (65) is ultimately described, by Levinas, as an affectivity – 'secret structure or concretization of feeling' (65) – that carries within itself a 'waiting for God': '[s]hould we say a waiting for God in this anticipatory feeling of the absolutely other' (65). In other words, Levinas's move away from a philosophical tradition grounded on an 'original incarnation of thought' takes us, via a philosophical detour that urges a fresh appraisal of the philosophical notions of the visible, the ethical relation and difference, to another species of messianic eschatology that emphasises the 'call', the 'waiting' and the 'face' of the other, an other likened to God. The reader is then left wondering whether the dismissal of incarnational thought through a commentary on the use of flesh and incarnation in the philosophy of Merleau-Ponty and others, has, once again, taken us back to 'phenomenological religiosity' and to the problem of differentiating 'confessional' and philosophical writing.

Jill Robbins suggests that Levinasian alterity is particularly revealing of hidden elements in language and figuration because it 'render[s] explicit what Levinas calls 'the hidden resources' of the Judaic tradition' (Robbins 1999: 43), resources that have been, for Robbins, 'covered up by the negative and privative determinations of the Judaic within (Greco-) Christian conceptuality' (43). Michel Henry also is quite explicit in describing his later work in terms of a philosophy of Christianity. Henry shares Levinas's distrust of traditional accounts of representation, but he distances his material phenomenology from any concentration on representation in order to embrace the flesh's capacities for embodying 'suffering and joy'. Even though both Henry and Levinas recognize the failings of classical accounts of language and representation, Levinas builds his philosophy around radical alterity while Henry retreats to the close inspection of affectivity, suffering and praxis. Henry's material phenomenology relies on such a large glossary of terms linked to the daily conditions of life – suffering, joy, pain, auto-affection, labour, living, life, ecstasy, praxis – that he would be unable to formulate his philosophy apart from corporeity and according to the dimensions of the 'text', or according to the rigours of exegetical practice. These differences between the philosophies of Henry and Levinas, as mediated through their treatments of corporeity, have important influences on their work on religion.

Levinas also has a quite distinct understanding of difference that serves ultimately to reveal the oppositions that remain even when certain phenomenologies appear to be using a similar religious rhetoric, such as outlined above in relation to incarnation. The further one delves into the philosophical roots of the terms they employ to detail moments of self-revelation, either through the encounter with the other or through anguish and auto-affection, the more one realizes that their language must ultimately call on metaphorical or iconic terms such as 'call', 'waiting' or 'Life'. However, the somewhat messianic or mystical nature of these terms is lost as soon as they are divorced from the religious texts that haunt this phenomenological religiosity. Whereas Henry's notion of incarnation privileges synthesis and auto-affection, any notion of 'incarnate existence' that might be found in Levinas privileges difference:

> Is it not in the *difference* – the proximity of one's neighbour? In difference that, as proximity, can be reduced neither to an attenuated difference, nor to a partially abortive coincidence or assimilation, but a difference that (and this adds new meaning to peace) is tendered not by the psychism of intentionality and thematization, nor by a communication of information, but by non-in-difference, by responsibility-for-others; by *sentiment*, which originally is not 'intentional pointing towards values', but rather peace breaking apperception-consciousness? Is it not then an '*attuning oneself* to the other

– that is, a giving of oneself to him or her? To be sure, not all sentiment is love, but all sentiment presupposes or inverts love. The handshake is not simply the notification of agreement, but prior to that notification the extraordinary event itself of peace, just as the caress, awakening in the touch, is already affection and not information about sentiment. (quoted in Johnson and Smith 1990: 63–4)

Henry and Levinas would both agree, as we have seen, that any 'incarnate existence' should not include a 'psychism of intentionality' or an 'intentional pointing to values'. Levinas is here contesting Merleau-Ponty's symbolization of the handshake as an event that embodies authentic intersubjectivity. Levinas cannot accept Merleau-Ponty's thesis that proposes, for him, that 'I go from my hand to the other's hand, as if both hands belonged to the same body'; '[a]nd I did this without any reasoning by analogy whatsoever!' (ibid. 63). Using a language that speaks of the 'caress', 'affection' and 'sentiment', a language very similar to that employed by Henry in his later works, Levinas wants to privilege a moment 'prior' to Merleau-Ponty's 'handshake' that is not such a 'notification of agreement' and not bound up with 'information about sentiment'. The state of difference, the state of 'peace breaking apperception-consciousness' that Levinas privileges is prior to the tactile; it is the 'privation' that is 'the desire for the other'; it is an 'affectivity that carries within itself affection and love' (ibid. 65). The kind of 'incarnate existence' that Levinas promotes through difference appears very similar then to Henry's notion of auto-affection which can also be described in terms of a 'privation' prior to the contact with the other that also is an 'affectivity that carries within itself affection and love'. Henry employs the term auto-affection[8] to refer to both an individual's '[a]*ffection by self* (Henry 1973: 189) and to the essential movement of temporality. For Henry, time is not 'affected by a being' (ibid. 187), but instead by 'time *itself under the form of the pure horizon of Being*' (187). Henry's move to ground his philosophy on an account of auto-affection that incorporates both the individual's unique self-awareness and her being in time, distances Henry from Husserl's use of this term which Derrida critiques for its forgetting of time. However, it is now evident that the phenomenological religiosity that is evoked by Henry and Levinas around the notion of incarnation and other related terms that privilege the moment before the tactile encounter with the other, inaugurates a state of 'privation' or 'auto-affection', a state of 'appearing' or 'waiting' that is prior to the 'pure ontological moment'. The attempt to understand the ontological state described according to their particular 'confessional' or 'incarnational' rhetoric leaves us with a state of 'privation' that is already so infused with affection, passivity and peace that it can only call on the language of 'phenomenological religiosity' to properly describe this state. At a time when the notion of inter-confessional faith and linguistic hospitality is being viciously tested, it is timely to question our motivations for aligning ourselves with certain philosophical perspectives.

Revising incarnation: Agamben and Badiou

It is important to note how philosophers outside phenomenology, outside what Alain Badiou refers to as 'phenomenological religiosity', have questioned the importance of incarnation for a 'Christian imagery' (Badiou 2003: 65) through recent close readings of Paul. Badiou reads Paul as founding a 'Christian discourse' that bears an absolutely new relation to its object'; it puts in question 'another figure of the real' (ibid. 55), a figure that deploys itself through the 'revelation that what constitutes the subject in its relation to this unheard-of real is not its unity, but its division' (55). However, this is an internal division somewhat like the self-alterity Depraz describes by way of incarnation in phenomenology. For Badiou, 'it is of the essence of the Christian subject to be divided [...] into two paths that affect every subject in thought' (56); the subject is divided 'in itself' (58). Badiou tells us that the division is between death and life in the subject: 'Death and life are thoughts, interwoven dimensions of the global subject, wherein "body" and "soul" are indiscernible' (68). However, Paul urges the subject to move beyond the confines of this division in seeking grace and the life of spirit, a spirit not connected with soul. As with all of Badiou's philosophy, it is the event that is of prime importance. The event that defines the Christian imagery, in Badiou's reading of Paul, is the resurrection and not the incarnation, because, for Badiou, '*Paul's thought dissolves incarnation in resurrection*' [Badiou's emphasis] (74). Badiou's Pauline reading, his reading of the event, what correlates with Agamben's reading of 'messianic time' in Paul (Agamben 2005: 77), is oriented principally toward the future. Badiou wants to resurrect the subject from Law and tradition and a notion of sin that ensnares desire in an 'automatism of repetition' (ibid. Badiou 2003: 79). He, therefore, privileges the event; in this case, one as un-real as the resurrection, what will transform the subject into, what Paul describes as, a 'new creature' (Badiou 2003: 72). For Badiou, the life of the flesh or the 'subjective path of the flesh (*sarx*)' (ibid. 75), what the incarnation is too closely implicated in, for him, is regarded as the 'suspension of the subject's destiny' (63). Badiou argues that it is only through the event, what is forward-looking, that there can be 'an unqualified affirmation of life against the reign of death' (72) that the flesh always connotes. Badiou, therefore, clings to Paul's rendering of a distinct sense of praxis and materialism that shakes off all these trappings of tradition, law and mastery to give way to an empowering sense of universalism. Badiou's Pauline universalism is one grounded in activism that works on the 'idea that every existence can one day be seized by what happens to it and subsequently devote itself to that which is valid for all' (66). The figure of the resurrection, or the epitome of 'event', is then, more suitable for evoking the nature of this 'event' and for representing this belief that all subjects can attain en route to being reborn as 'new creature[s]'.

Giorgio Agamben's *The Time That Remains* questions whether this notion of universalism can be applied to the 'messianic instance' that he privileges in Paul, a moment that can be contrasted with Badiou's Pauline 'event'. Agamben questions Badiou's description of the Pauline 'event' in terms of a 'production of the Same' and an 'indifference that tolerates differences' (Agamben 2005: 52). We recall that the primordial event for Badiou here is the resurrection, what he regards as initiating universalism. Agamben argues that such concepts as 'tolerance' and 'production of the Same', in being legitimate, are yet alien to Paul. For Agamben, the 'transcendental' in Paul, what approximates to Badiou's rendering of 'grace', 'involves an operation that divides the division of the law themselves and renders them inoperative, without ever reaching any final ground' (ibid. 52). Badiou, we must remember, also regards Paul as working in opposition to Law with an intoxicating notion of 'grace'; it is 'the opposite of law insofar as it is what comes *without being due*' (Badiou 2003: 77). Agamben and Badiou also agree that it is the resurrection that is fundamental to Paul's teachings. Agamben argues that 'Paul's faith starts with the resurrection and he does not know Jesus in the flesh, only Jesus Messiah' (Agamben 2005: 126).

However, this is the point at which their readings diverge. They have very different views of the role of the flesh in Paul. As we have seen, Badiou's notion of the 'event' privileges grace as the opposite of the Law. However, Badiou's reading of the time of the event, what Agamben describes in terms of 'messianic time', is oriented to the future; Badiou writes that '[w]hat is called "grace" is the capacity of a post-evental multiplicity to exceed its own limit, a limit that has a commandment of the law as its dead cipher' (Badiou 2003: 78). Agamben also describes 'messianic time' in terms of what must ultimately look to the future, the kind of future a 'promise' always prefigures, but it must occur by way of an important backward glance. For Agamben, the 'messianic instance, which takes place in historical time and renders Mosaic law inoperative, goes back genealogically before Mosaic law, toward the promise. The space that opens up between the two *diathēkai* is the space of grace' (Agamben 2005: 122). Agamben differentiates between two kinds of law here: the law of faith (the new covenant or *kainē diathēkē*) and the Mosaic law of the commandments (the old covenant or *palaia diathēkē*). The space of grace that the 'messianic instance' unveils alters the new covenant, the new covenant that Paul revealed to the Corinthians. Agamben argues that this new covenant cannot be something 'like a written text containing new and divine precepts (which is how it ends up)'. The new covenant 'is not a letter written in ink on tables of stone; rather, it is written with the breath of God on hearts of the flesh. In other words, it is not a text, but the very life of the messianic community, not a *writing*, but a *form of life: hē epistolē hemōn hymeis este*, "You are our letter" (2 Cor. 3.2)!' (Agamben 2005: 122). The 'messianic instance' is bound up with a word that is also a 'form of life'. The covenant or agreement described here is to be duplicated and shared by subjects who do not renounce the flesh in their respect for grace. The desire to make of writing a 'form of life' is a concern that I have argued is important for Joyce and Proust, and it will be examined in this context in the following chapters.

One of Agamben's early essays, 'The Idea of Language', also expresses a willingness to believe in language as the 'thing itself' that absorbs the 'essential matter of human beings':

> Nothing immediate can be reached by speaking beings – nothing, that is, except language itself, mediation itself. For human beings, such an *immediate mediation* constitutes the sole possibility of reaching a principle freed of every presupposition, including self-pre-supposition. Such an *immediate mediation* alone, in other words, allows human beings to reach that *arkhē anypothetos*, that 'unpresupposed principle' that Plato, in the *Republic*, presents as the *telos*, fulfillment and end of *autos ho logos*, language itself: the 'thing itself' and essential matter of human beings. (Agamben 1999: 47)

Any new covenant, or new incarnation of word, must then be found in a 'form of life' that strives to attain a 'principle freed of every pre-supposition'. This principle can only be found when language is revealed as the 'thing itself', the 'immediate mediation' that is the 'essential matter of human beings'.

Chapter 2

Joyce and the incarnation of language

Joyce Studies and the language of difference

Joyce's desire to graft onto his words the actions of the living flesh proceeds at such a pace that one of his later *alter egos,* Jaun, responds to Issy's love letter by telling us that is he 'truly [...] eucherised to yous' (*FW* 461–2: 36–1). The word as flesh is offered as Eucharist to the reader, resuscitating the theme of transubstantiation that Stephen Dedalus has already employed to describe the work of the writer. Joyce's letter to Frank Budgen in 1918 also describes *Ulysses* as 'Among other things [...] the epic of the human body [...] In my book the body lives in and moves through space and is the home of a full human personality' (Budgen 1960: 21). In moving from phenomenology to literary narrative, however, it is important to examine the narrative forms Joyce employs in depicting an incarnation of language.

Joyce Studies has developed a fondness for examining Joycean language in the light of post-structuralist and deconstructive theories of alterity. Harold Bloom has summed up the differences between what he regards as 'Post-Structuralist Joyce', or 'French Joyce' (Bloom 2004: 1), and his own version of Joyce in terms of the character of Bloom, or Poldy. Bloom argues that there is a certain practice of 'creative misreading' that has given us, what he refers to as, 'French Joyce' (ibid. 4). For Bloom, this 'French' interpretive practice, or manner of reading Joyce, invests in a 'cultural belatedness' when it comes to discussing such archetypal figures of twentieth-century literature as Poldy. He argues that 'French Joyce' regards Poldy as a 'trope' and not as 'a supermimesis of essential nature' (4) and that 'the difference between Joyce and French Joyce is that Joyce tropes God as language' when, in fact, we must remember that 'Poldy was a humane and humanized God'. The crux of the argument rests on what conception of language one believes to be true for Joyce. Does it show any clear affinities for the theories of language outlined in Chapter 1? The notions of genesis and linguistic incarnation that are important for phenomenological accounts of language will be investigated here in the light of Joyce's determination to write the body and in the light of what critics have described as 'the unity of mind and body that Joyce insisted on in *Ulysses*' (French 1993: 64).

The roots of the Joycean conception of language can be traced to his early critical writings. In 'The Literary Influence of the Renaissance' Joyce recognizes the momentous advances made at the time of the Renaissance. In this period the 'human spirit' is, for Joyce, still struggling with 'scholastic absolutism' and a 'system of philosophy that has its fundamental origins in Aristotelian thought, cold, clear and imperturbable, while its summit stretched upwards towards the vague and mysterious light of Christian ideology' (Barry 2000: 187). With the Renaissance, the 'human spirit [...] heard the voice of the visual world tangible, inconstant, where one lives and dies, sins and repents' (ibid. 188). The important advance for Joyce is that humanity gives up the absolute and the 'cloistered peace' in order to understand and mediate the 'sensory power of his organism'. However, Joyce believes that the first wave of this desire to evoke the 'sensory' has, 'after three centuries', 'degenerated into frenetic sensationalism' (188): 'The sensory power of his organism has developed enormously, but it has developed to the detriment of his spiritual faculty. We lack moral sense and perhaps also strength of imagination' (189). It must be remembered, therefore, that Joyce did not envisage a writing of the body, solely in terms of the opposition that post-structuralism has privileged between text and the body. For Joyce, any privileging of the body in writing or any mediation between word and sense is worthless if the 'spiritual faculty' or the 'moral sense' is not also sanctioned. While Joyce sees himself as no 'literary Jesus Christ' (Ellmann 1982: 240), his desperate urgency to mediate the commingling of body, morality and spirituality, in writing, will make it impossible for him to dispense completely with the spiritual vocabulary learned in his university days that can sustain a transfer of meaning described in terms of a 'human analogue' for Incarnation.

Joyce is not alone in lamenting the loss of the subject's mediation of the 'sensory power of his organism' after the Renaissance. Michel Foucault describes this mediation in terms of the Renaissance's privileging of 'the living being of language' (Foucault 1994: 43). For Foucault, the organization of signs became 'ternary' in the Renaissance; resemblance was then bound up with the 'form of the signs as well as their content' (ibid. 42). However, after the Renaissance language no longer existed 'as the material writing of things'; its 'area of being' was now 'restricted to the general organization of representative signs' (42). In other words, one no longer asked oneself how it was possible to know that a sign designated what it signified. Now it was important to know how 'a sign could be linked to what it signified' (43); '[t]hings and words were to be separated from one another' (43). For Foucault, it is only literature that can restore this lost 'living being of language' (43) and that can find a way back from the Classical Age's privileging of the 'signifying function of language' to the 'raw being' of language (44). However, Foucault argues that even though literature has, from the nineteenth century onwards, rejuvenated this lost materiality, or 'raw being', language still does not appear as it did in the Renaissance. The difference, for Foucault, is that language can no longer sustain a belief in 'that absolutely initial, word upon which the infinite movement of discourse was founded' (44). Language must now accept its growth 'with no point of departure, no end, and no promise', with the help of a literature that traverses eternally 'this futile yet fundamental space' (44). Joyce is an important figure for this rejuvenation. However, in recognizing, and contributing to, the growth of language, he shares Proust's belief in the potential of language. In grounding the word's genesis in its mediation of the body and the body's desire in the mediation of the word, he shows the reader glimpses of what lies beyond the 'signifying function' of language.

Two of the formal features Joyce employs to achieve this end are 'stream of consciousness' narration and interior monologue. Joyce enthusiastically described the style of Edouard Dujardin's *Les Lauriers sont coupés* to Valery Larbaud: 'The reader [would be] installed in the thought of the main character from the first lines on, and it is the uninterrupted unfolding of that thought which, substituting completely for the customary form of narrative, [would] apprise us of what the character does and what happens to him'.[1] For Gérard Genette, interior monologue, or 'immediate speech', describes those instances in the novel where 'the narrator is obliterated and the character *substitutes* for him' (Genette 1988: 174). For Genette, it 'is not that the speech should be internal, but that it should be emancipated right away ('from the first lines') from all narrative patronage, that it should from the word go take the front of the "stage"'' (ibid. 173–4). Joyce moves from the free indirect speech, or stream of consciousness style of narration of all but the last chapter of *Ulysses*, to the 'immediate speech' or interior monolgue of Penelope, where the narrator is obliterated completely. The representation of Molly's interior monologue, free of a narrator or mediator, records the genesis of language in the thoughts of a half-conscious character, a brief interlude in Joyce's aesthetic evolution away from any discernible narrator or character and towards Wak*ese*. Joyce was eager to unsettle all received narrative strategies by making manifest more of the body in the word. In like manner, phenomenology's concern to describe how states such as immanence and auto-affection are made manifest to consciousness has privileged the body's role in mediating experience. However, post-structuralist and deconstructive criticism of Joyce has all too often focused on disembodied accounts of difference and alterity in bringing the fruits of phenomenology to bear on his work.

Derek Attridge's account of how 'deconstructive criticism' works on Joyce describes how such criticism unleashes the essential 'unrecuperable otherness' of 'Joyce's text':

> Deconstructive criticism would weave itself through the text being read, and weave that text through itself, and thread other texts through both, in a patient and careful movement of displacement and dissemination, at once exposing and destabilizing, however momentarily, the boundaries and hierarchies that have enabled the text to be pinned into (and to serve as a reinforcement of) an ideology or a metaphysic that denies it its specificity, its inexhaustibility, its unrecuperable otherness [...] This is why 'deconstructive criticism of Joyce' must be understood as Joyce's deconstruction of the critic's text as much as the critic's deconstruction of Joyce's text. (Attridge 2000: 26–7)

What is most interesting is that such criticism sees Joyce engaging in the deconstruction of the critic's text. The specificity of *Ulysses* or *Finnegans Wake*, a specificity momentarily freed of all 'boundaries', 'hierarchies' and ideologies, will enable these works to practise the same criticism that the critic practises on them. In other words, deconstructive criticism not only privileges an unspecified notion of 'otherness', but it also reduces much of the effect of Joyce's work to the effects of a style of criticism, a style, Attridge suggests, that 'would offer no insights, conclusions, or detachable propositions' (ibid. 26). However, it is unlikely that Joyce plotted the 'deconstruction of the critic's text'. For John Bishop, '[a]ll things in the *Wake* start here, "in the flesh" ' (Bishop 1993: 145); '[t]he primary unconscious meaning that Joyce, through Vico, discovers beneath all human language is the "meaning" of the human body' (ibid. 197). Attridge's suggestion, therefore, that deconstructive criticism sees in Joyce's work a 'simulacrum ... of the scientific model of cumulative knowledge' (Attridge 2000: 28) would then seem to be neglecting this fleshy 'meaning'.

The deconstructive and post-structuralist 'turn' in Joyce criticism has its roots in a celebration of alterity that very often fails to differentiate different versions of alterity between. The politics of otherness that has achieved a somewhat incongruous canonical position in literary and critical studies is partially the result of a by now somewhat defunct postmodern rhetoric, and of the application of deconstruction and Levinasian phenomenology to literary and cultural studies. While these have offered readers the opportunity to configure a rhetoric of otherness, and have allowed them to vicariously experience the thrill of ethical encounter that the narrative recounts, the privileging of otherness, most particularly the peculiar otherness that a text is regarded as conveying, is only effective once what is not other has been addressed and contemplated. To immediately flee to an ethics of otherness serves to condemn such an ethics to an uncertain future, and to ultimately project features of what is not other, of the familiar and the self-revelatory, onto the other. The location, space and markers of alterity will become so all-encompassing that alterity will become a badge of conformism that obscures the kind of distinct experience of alterity that a committed reading was to elicit in the first place.

Another strand of Joyce studies that may have influenced this ten-dency in criticism sees Joyce as representative of a 'poetics of Jewish-ness'. While Leopold Bloom's Jewishness, or Jew*ish*ness as Marilyn Reizbaum suggests, is an important factor in *Ulysses*, to regard this aspect of Joyce's work as a 'theory or pattern of meaning' (Reizbaum 1999: 2) that is synonymous with an explication of otherness and that comes to merge with otherness as it has been debated in ethical theory is to perhaps overdetermine one element of Bloom, not to mention Joyce. Steven Connor has suggested that Joyce is simply 'not Jewish enough' for 'some of his Jewish readers who are dissatisfied with his constructions of Jewishness' (quoted in Reizbaum 1999: 75). If we are to accept Reizbaum's observation that many of the themes produced in *Ulysses* 'are produced by a thematics as well as a poetics of Jewishness/ otherness' (ibid. 2) where any interrogation of such a poetics evinces 'a kind of anxiety about the possibility of an affirmative answer' (2) in regard to Bloom's Jewishness, then is there not also an anxiety in relation to positing Bloom as other? In other words, if we are to accept Bloom's Jewishness as being synonymous with otherness, where does that leave those influential ethical theories that also employ a rhetoric of otherness? How is the reader to differentiate between the relative merits of each variety of alterity?

Is there an unwillingness, then, to examine the precise nature of otherness as it is perceived in relation to Jew*ish*ness in Joyce, and as it is employed in deconstructive and post-structuralist criticism of Joyce? Ira Nadel suggests that '[i]n the understanding of language and its special status in a text, he [Joyce] emulates Rabbinic scholars and Talmudic students' (Nadel 1996: 9). This may be the case, but, as Marilyn Reizbaum correctly notes, there are 'a number of expressions' of the term Judaism (Reizbaum 1999: 3). Certain strands of Judaic interpretive style have very distinct conceptions of language and signification (as we have seen in Chapter 1) and they have transplanted these interpretive practices into their elaboration of ethical theories and discourses. While it must be accepted that Joyce had certain motivations in placing a Jew*ish* character at the centre of one of his works it does not necessarily follow that his 'understanding of language', to quote Nadel once again, implies that he 'emulates Rabbinic scholars', especially if a 'poetics of Jewishness' has come to be representative of, and to merge with, what critics such as Reizbaum regard as an ethic of 'otherness'. While Reizbaum may be correct in stressing Bloom's 'impossibility, doubly delivered by the alignment within him (despite detractors) between Jew and Irish' (Reizbaum 1999: 5), the positing of impossibility, hybridity and a 'constitutional resistance to definition' (ibid. 5) as benchmarks and motivations of Joyce's work may put the cart before the horse. Before the post-structuralist 'turn', Clive Hart also perceived a 'duality of being' in Joyce, one that he believes Joyce sought to represent, on the contrary, through intercommunication and communion. 'Duality of being' is, for Hart, perhaps the most important of all basic structural concepts in *Finnegans Wake*' (Hart 1962: 153), and Joyce 'finds a convenient technical term for all this – anastomosis'. Hart defines anastomosis as 'intercommunication between two vessels, channels, or branches, by a connecting cross branch', a trope having its origins in a symbolics of the Cross, and also derived from the 'connections between the arteries and veins, etc.; now of those of any branching system' (ibid. 154). Joyce puns both anastomosis and its etymological roots in 'veins' and the body in *Finnegans Wake*.

Marian Eide also privileges alterity in reading Joyce according to Levinasian philosophy. While Eide's work wishes to stress reciprocity over alterity and seeks to elaborate a Joycean ethic that 'examine[s] the character – or textual moment – in its habitat – or context' (Eide 2002: 3), Eide still begins by stating that '[e]thics as I am defining it, is an engagement with radical alterity, or difference, within the context of ultimate responsibility' (ibid. 3). For Eide, sympathy and communication are integral elements of the Joycean text, yet they must occur 'across incommensurable difference' and 'within the preservation of difference' (4). She argues that Joyce and Levinas put an 'emphasis on the dehumanisation of the subject' (5). However, surely Joyce gives, on the contrary, the most extensive and exhilarating account of the *re*humanization of the subject. Joyce gives himself over to the word, describing shared aspects of our inner being for a readerly consolation. As the voice of Shaun, who is now Jaun, he reminds the reader (as Jaun prepares to leave Issy with his 'darling proxy' Dave): 'But I'm not for forgetting me innerman monophone' 'my darling proxy behind for your consoleing' (*FW* 462: 15–17).

Joyce's preference for the representation of such paradigms as Vico's cyclical sense of history[2] invests his narrative with a structure more dependent on a Nietzschean-style eternal cycle of recurrence than on any thematics of radical alterity or 'unrecuperable otherness'. The dynamic of *Finnegans Wake*'s initially impenetrable prose works to such a principle. What initially draws the reader towards the work is the recognition of the familiar in the unfamiliar. The struggle to internalize truths found in seemingly impenetrable prose ultimately leads to a more lasting evaluation of self for the reader. In a letter of 1923, Joyce describes the procedures and plans for his *Work in Progress* to Harriet Weaver: 'these are not fragments but active elements and when they are more and a little older they will begin to fuse of themselves' (Joyce 1957: 204). Even the structure of *Finnegans Wake* is, for David Hayman, a 'nodal procedure' that displays Joyce's 'determination to build the *Wake* around the early sketches' which 'clearly enabled and conditioned the networks of echoing and interacting passages' (Hayman 1990: 41). Hayman describes how 'the book comes close to being cyclical' (ibid. 40). This is achieved, I suggest, through the workings of a governing structure that privileges how the recognition of the familiar in seemingly alien, polyglottal streams of word-thoughts offers the reader the potential for initiating a reunification of these variations on a theme. Proust's early notebooks share a similar interest: he works at 'discovering profound connections between two ideas or sensations' (Proust 1994a: 92). Joyce strains the received limits of interpretation not merely to leave to posterity an irresolvable gnomic conundrum, but so as to confer on the future of the intertext something that can always be mined for familiarity for just a little longer and applied to the reader's deliberations on her own life. He realized that if reading is reduced to an act of decryption or knowledge acquisition then it shares in the limitations of any act grounded on force.

Joyce's work makes the reader search not only for a narrative, but also for the reasons behind any personal investment in reading narrative. For Joyce, reading creates its own world – the book as world – and our approach to this world conditions how we interiorize its words and how they will be revived in us through our recollection of certain passages:

> [D]id it ever occur to you, *qua* you [...] by a stretch of your iber-borealic imagination [...] that you might [...] be very largely substituted in potential secession from your next life by a complementary character, voices apart. Upjack! [...] The next word depends on your answer (*FW* 486–7: 35–6).

Joyce puns 'next world' with 'next word'. The voice reminds the reader (and on this occasion Joyce may very well be addressing himself as well as the reader in shouting 'Upjack!') that the nature of her reading of the next word will depend on how the imagination has previously configured the self's progression towards its 'next life'. But the investigation of this 'substitution,' which is also a 'secession', or a voluntary withdrawal, possibly from some received religious means of self-examination, will result in a type of union. The subject will pass over to a 'complementary character', thereby even in death retaining something of its former self. In other words, even in this final and absolutist meeting, the meeting between death and the subject, Joyce still envisions a communion of sorts where something 'complementary' or something familiar will be found to unite with.

Joyce emphasizes the 'possibilities of transformation' (MacCabe 1979: 2) rather than any 'secret of disassociation' or 'radical alterity' that consistently appear as organizing motifs for language. The privileging of the body, evidenced in Joyce by the body that 'lives in and through' *Ulysses* was a common concern of many of the philosophers of the period. Henri Bergson's *Matter and Memory* sought to redefine perception and memory in terms of the physical moment of perception. Bergson felt that the contemplative and speculative aspects of perception were being privileged at the time at the expense of the affective or physical dimensions of perception.[3] Joyce also had an interest in Renan's *Life of Jesus* that led him to discover the work of a French Jesuit, Marcel Jousse. Jean-Michel Rabaté argues that 'Jousse's Jesus was a Rabbi teaching in such a way that his words would never be forgotten, exploiting all the resources of an *embodied* memory linked to the brain and the skeleton' [my emphasis] (Rabaté 2002: 133). Such an interest in detailing an embodied or incarnated aesthetic lies at the heart of Joyce's writing, appearing as early as the 'Trieste Notebook' where Joyce writes that 'The skeleton conditions the esthetic image' (quoted in Rabaté 2002: 133): '[p]erhaps more than any writer of this century, Joyce has forced criticism to acknowledge its theological nature' (Rabaté 1991: 1). Joyce's reader is like his character Nush, a 'carrier of the word' (*FW* 385: 5).

Genetic and archival criticism of Joyce stresses that the 'processes by which he [Joyce] wrote the book cannot be separated from other aspects of its meaning' (Groden 1977: 203). The collation, preservation and annotating of the Joycean archive extends the range of the metaphor that sees his work as a body, enacting a kind of textual transubstantiation of his writing processes. Michael Groden describes Joyce's drafting and redrafting of his notes, his 'compost of objects' (ibid. 202) as a schematism of correspondences and an 'accretion process' (102). His work also archives itself, recalling earlier incidents through an emphasis on the body. HCE finds himself 'cerebralised' (*FW* 292: 13) with a 'jetsam litterage' of 'convolvuli of times lost' (*FW* 292: 16). The Joycean body of work is a self-referential, intratextual palimpsest, that voices 'life's high carnage of semperidentity by subsisting peasemeal upon variables' (*FW* 582: 15–16), which I take to mean that the body of work keeps itself alive by enacting life's, or reading's, essential drive: the belief that a belief for reading further will be found. Groden argues that Joyce 'never entirely abandoned a set of aesthetic principles, even when new ones dominated his writing' (Groden 1977: 4). I argue that there is an interest in the 'incarnation of language' that is carried through into the later work. Poldy and Molly share only one conversation in their day, on the rather unlikely topic of metempsychosis. Stephen, who is haunted by the image of his dead mother, is thrown into a morbid questioning of patriarchy and incarnation: 'a voice heard only in the heart of him who is the substance of his shadow, the son consubstantial with the father' (*U* 252). Such evocative and soul-searching accounts of the body, and of its transubstantiation, incarnation and re-incarnation reveal much about Joyce's understanding of language.

Joyce's characters are works in progress, migrant elements, overburdened by meaning and semantic endeavour, yet 'subsisting peasemeal upon variables' (*FW* 582: 15–16) through 'life's high carnage of semperidentity' (*FW* 582: 15). Their questioning word-thoughts allow them to subsist. They are driven by the belief that their individual struggle to discover a personal meaning will present them with the possibility for further self-discovery. Their individuality is consistently haunted by images of that to which they are united through some process of creation: dead fathers, mothers and children. Their sense of themselves is discovered through a rigorous evaluation of the further possibilities that 'life's high carnage' can throw at them. Bloom returns at the end of his self-conscious odyssey to lie beside Molly, while Molly's interior monologue traces its own trajectory through her 'life's high carnage'. Her embodied self-examination convinces herself again of the reasons for their union. She revisits their shared encounters with new life and death. Her capacity for mediating and radiating sexual energy and affectivity still personifies inanimate objects as she recalls, in one breath, her only son's conception and burial: 'was he not able to make one it wasnt my fault we came together when I was watching the two dogs up in her behind in the middle of the naked street that disheartened me altogether I suppose I oughtnt to have buried him in that little woolly jacket I knitted' (*U* 926–7).

Joyce and phenomenology

Maurice Natanson has argued that literature conjures moments that describe the phenomenological reduction's 'abstention from complicity with the reality perceived' (Natanson 1998: 13). Maurice Merleau-Ponty's *Phenomenology of Perception*, as we have seen in Chapter 1 also relates perception and memory to the body in a radical fashion that parallels Joyce's motivations for experimenting with narrative form. Merleau-Ponty writes that ' "[g]ood form" is not brought about because it would be good in itself in some metaphysical heaven; it is good form because it comes into being in our experience' (Merleau-Ponty 2003: 19). Some pages later he takes up the idea again:

> Language certainly has an inner content, but this is not self-subsistent and self-conscious thought. What then does language express, if it does not express thoughts? It presents or rather it is the subject's taking up of a position in the world of his meanings. The term 'world' here is not a manner of speaking: it means that the 'mental' or cultural life borrows its structures from natural life and that the thinking subject must have its basis in the *subject incarnate* [my emphasis]. (Merleau-Ponty 2003: 225)

Joyce's work also enacts and connotes the potential for movement, or transformation, between mental life and 'natural life', between language and the body. Merleau-Ponty sees the novelist's task as one where he is 'not to expound ideas or even analyse characters, but to depict an inter-human event, ripening and bursting it upon us with no ideological commentary, to such an extent that any change in the order of the narrative or in choice of viewpoint would alter the *literary* meaning of the event [...]. It is in this sense that our body is comparable to a work of art' (ibid. 175). Joyce privileges this inter-human event, not by naturalistically detailing tics of conversation, but by plumbing the depths of interiority for a shared 'corporeity within'.

While it is unlikely that Joyce ever read any of Husserl's work in the libraries of Trieste, Pula or Paris, Husserl's conversion from Judaism to Christianity in 1886 did coincide with another Christian movement that William T. Noon argues was influential for the aesthetic theory of the young Joyce. The Neo-Thomist Scholastic revival at Louvain, led by Cardinal Desiré Mercier, launched its *Revue néo-scolastique* in the 1890s and in one of the earliest issues, 'one that Joyce most likely read' (Noon 1957: 20), Mercier writes: 'Art is the means of realising and expressing the beautiful, or more explicitly, art has as its aim to incarnate in a beautiful, sensitive form the ideal beauty, and to procure the pure joy for another through the contemplation.' This book argues that Joyce's aesthetic retains an interest in such a moment of incarnation throughout its various manifestations. Luciano Florindi argues that the two philosophers most representative of, what he describes as, the 'Two Faces of Scepticism' are Edmund Husserl and Desiré Mercier. It is therefore likely that Mercier's neo-Thomistic revival, elements of which Joyce incorporated into his early aesthetic theory, had close affinities with the philosophy of Husserl. Husserl's critique of psychologism, his development of what Florindi calls a 'purely conceptual approach to epistemology' and his acceptance of an 'anti-naturalist stand' (Baldwin 2003: 534), were shared in large part by Joyce. In one of Joyce's early reviews, 'Aristotle on Education', Joyce is concerned that the 'scientific specialists and the whole cohort of Materialists are cheapening the good name of philosophy' (Barry 2000: 80). Husserl privileges consciousness's manner of apprehending itself, a move that would spark the twentieth century's most influential philosophical movement, while Joyce's early criticism praises Giordano Bruno's 'vindication of the freedom of intuition' (ibid. 94).

The theme of genesis is important for both Joyce and Husserl. As we have seen, it was the topic of Derrida's master thesis on Husserl, written in Paris 12 years after Joyce's death, and Joyce's early work is also preoccupied with the genesis of the moment of heightened awareness, or epiphany, that is fundamentally a concern with language and is related to Joyce's understanding of fatherhood and conscious begetting as a 'mystical estate' (*U* 266). Joyce shows an interest in phenomenology in *Ulysses*. In 'Cyclops' Bloom is described as a 'distinguished phenomenologist' (*U* 445) and the narrator consistently contrasts his regard for the 'phenomenon' with the Citizen's grounding in history and nationalism. However, it is Joyce's understanding of perception and of the relationship between word and sense that is enabling of a reading of his work in relation to the main themes of early phenomenology. We recall that, for Colleen Jaurretche, 'Joyce sees *phenomenological* processes in terms of the medieval mystical tradition' [my emphasis] (Jaurretche 1998: 3). John Bishop has described the *Wake*'s 'huge shaping of literary anti-matter' as a 'kind of phenomenology of lack of mind' (Bishop 1993: 65) that prefigures of later phenomenological accounts of perception:

> Through its study of 'meoptics', the *Wake* is only anticipating the post-Wakean investigations of phenomenology and psychoanalysis in showing that our hero's seeing, even in its most dispassionate forms, is never a matter of purely passive Helmholtzian object-reception, but an actively chiasmic exchange in which his eyes seek out, frame, and light up objects of their own peculiar choosing. (Bishop 1993: 244)

Joyce's work also prefigures later writers in the phenomenological tradition who have developed a rhetoric of incarnation in rejuvenating Husserl's notion of the 'Living Present'.

Both Joyce and Husserl ground their presentations of perception and intersubjectivity in the body. Alphonso Lingis describes Husserl's understanding of consciousness in terms of an 'incarnation of consciousness' (Lingis 1970: 76). Even though Lingis acknowledges that Husserlian phenomenology is a philosophy that sought to discard any trace of naturalism, in defining intentionality as the 'purely ideal "movement" ascribing flux to identity, givenness to ideality', he argues that because 'corporeity appears impossible to conjure' in Husserl, it reappears as 'the incarnation of absolute consciousness' (ibid. 76–7). He argues that a philosophy of incarnate consciousness is not formulated by arguing that a body is a vehicle of consciousness, but by showing 'by internal examination of reduced consciousness a corporeity *within*' [Lingis's emphasis] (77). But how does Husserl evoke such a 'corporeity *within*? Husserl returns to his understanding of perception in the late work, *The Crisis of European Sciences*:

> If we pay attention now purely to the bodily aspect of things, this obviously exhibits itself perceptively only in seeing, in touching, in hearing, etc., i.e., in visual, tactual, acoustical, and other such aspects. Obviously and inevitably participating in this is our living body, which is never absent from the perceptual field, and specifically its corresponding 'organs of perception' (eyes, hands, ears, etc.). (Husserl 1970c: 106)

Lingis argues that it is precisely this manner of perceiving and of mediating intentionality that elicits the absolute corporeity. Consciousness is *localized* through its interaction with perception, thereby grounding intentionality, the fundamental motif of Husserlian phenomenology, in the body. For Lingis, Husserl argues, in *Ideen II*, that the 'localization of consciousness' is revealed *within* through states that Husserl names *Empfindnisse* (states of contact such as touch, pressure, heat, cold, etc.). This bodily grounding of consciousness and, therefore, of all that apperception reveals to consciousness, either through signs or through the perception of other bodies, occurs through these 'states of contact', states 'in which the distinction between subject and object, between the feeling "act" and the felt "content", is not yet discernible' (Lingis 1970: 79). It is this intimation of a momentary unmediated transition between body and consciousness, between sense and word, that is also elicited through the moments of self-revelation that Joyce assigns to characters who are more viscerally in touch with their bodies than any fictional characters before. It also speaks for the kind of readerly response Joyce strives to create through *Finnegans Wake* where the words, in embodying so many different meanings at once, appear to mutate almost organically, setting up a readerly analogue for the corporeity *within* and the 'states of contact' Husserl privileges.

In his 1925 Summer Session lectures entitled *Phenomenological Psychology*, three years after the publication of *Ulysses*, Husserl argues that 'the sole purpose' of his *Logical Investigations* 'was the establishing of an inner viewing which discloses the lived experiences of thinking hidden from the thinker, and an essential description pertaining to these pure data of lived experience and moving within a pure inner viewing' (Husserl 1977: 19). The Joycean project also formally creates in narrative a new fictional account of 'inner viewing'. Both writers were eager to separate their work from the psychology of the day. Husserl writes in *Logical Investigations*: 'we deny, however, that the theoretical discipline of pure logic, in the independent separateness proper to it, has any concern with mental facts, or with laws that might be styled "psychological"' (Husserl 1970a: 181). Joyce invents his own language of the unconscious, employing the greatest practitioners of the psychology of his day merely as raw material: 'm'm'ry's leaves are falling deeply on my Jungfraud's Messongebook' (*FW* 460: 20–1). The substitution of 'fraud' for Freud, the conjoining of Jung and Freud's names, and the reference to their writings as a songbook (*songe* being the German for song) suggests that Joyce had little time for their psychological theories. Indeed Jung wrote to Joyce in a letter dated August 1932: '[y]our book as a whole has given me no end of trouble and I was brooding over it for about three years until I succeeded to put myself into it' (quoted in Deming 1970: 583).

Joyce's early reviews also display an interest in what he calls the 'freedom of intuition' (Barry 2000: 94) and Husserl's eidetic philosophy privileges intuition's relation to the 'things themselves'. However, Husserl describes a particular understanding of intuition in the *Logical Investigations*:

> [W]e can absolutely not rest content with 'mere words', i.e. with a merely symbolic understanding of words, such as we first have when we reflect on the sense of the laws for 'concepts', 'judgments', 'truths' etc. (together with their manifold specifications) which are set up in pure logic. Meanings inspired only by remote, confused, inauthentic intuitions – if by any intuitions at all – are not enough: we must go back to the 'things themselves'. We desire to render self-evident in fully fledged intuitions that what is here given in actually performed abstractions is what the word-meanings in our expression of the law really and truly stand for. (Husserl 1970a: 252)

Of primary importance then, for Husserl, is that our 'fully fledged intuitions' will enable our word-meanings to adequately reference the 'actually performed abstractions' to be found in the 'things themselves'. Husserl's eidetic philosophy wishes to clarify our approach to meaning through both an openness towards 'fully fledged intuitions', and a scrupulous application of logical method to the 'things themselves'. Husserl realizes that our definitions of objects are primary in determining how we take those objects to be. Joyce also records 'actually performed abstractions', initially describing in a prose of 'scrupulous meanness' the epiphany of particular characters,[4] and finally, in *Finnegans Wake*, dispensing with character so the reader can 'peep inside' the 'cerebralised saucepan' of the 'illwinded good-fornobody' and see the 'jetsam litterage of convolvuli of times lost' (*FW* 292: 13–16). The subject's act of reading and interpreting is forced to reflect upon itself; the passages themselves become 'actually per-formed abstraction[s]' that must be worked through and tied to a momentary thread of narrative so that each reader differentiates some sense for herself.

Husserl's *Logical Investigations* also emphasizes two such elements of understanding: firstly, what he calls 'the *natural conditions* of our experience' (Husserl 1970a: 192) or the turn to 'the "things them-selves"' (ibid. 168), and secondly, 'inner evidence' or what he believes is 'nothing but the "experience" of truth' (194). Husserl's elaboration of a methodology for reduction as a specific philosophical practice can be interiorized to become a familiar aspect of behaviour for the indi-vidual so that perception and language create what is a rejuvenated sense of communion and unity for these aspects of the life-world. Some of Husserl's more 'lyrical' passages from the *Logical Investigations* can often appear as a kind of phenomenological account of aesthetic experience, similar to Stephen's speculations on perception and aes-thetic practice before the 'ineluctable modality of the visible'. In Husserl's 'Sixth Investigation' he speaks of 'utterances grounded on imagination' (Husserl 1970b: 679). He inspects those instances when we let our imagination 'run away' with us and 'employ ordinary state-ments, appropriate to things perceived, in giving a name to what then appears to us' (ibid. 679). He believes this process is the same as 'the narrative form in which story-tellers, novelists, etc. "express" not real circumstances, but the creations of their artistic fancy' (679). Husserl also devotes a section of his 'Second Meditation' from the *Cartesian Meditations* to what he calls '*The stream of* cogitationes: Cogito *and* cogitatum' [Husserl's emphasis] (Husserl 1970d: 31). We recall that Joyce's narrative style has become synonymous with a style described in terms of a 'stream of consciousness'.

Joyce has his main character, Bloom, profess a belief in 'universal love', and the later works take on a cyclical shape that stresses eternal recurrence and reunion.[5] Husserl also emphasizes a 'unitary *universe*' (ibid. 37) where the '*particular* realities that are meant [...] in some set or other of separate acts of consciousness' [Husserl's emphasis] (36), share a 'particularity' that is 'particularity within a unitary *universe*, which even when we are directed to and grasping the particular, goes on "appearing" unitarily' (36–7). All such particularity is grounded in his understanding of the 'correlational *a priori*'. Another section heading refers to '[*s]ynthesis as the primal form belonging to consciousness*' (39), where '[a]lways we find the feature in question as a unity belonging to a passing flow of "multiplicities"' (40). The coming together of particularities through a 'passing flow of multiplicities' describes the Bloomian mode of experience and, in turn, the reader's experience of reading *Ulysses* or *Finnegans Wake*.

In examining perception, Husserl describes how we perceive a blackbird:

'There flies a blackbird!' *What is here the act in which my meaning resides?* [...] Every chance alteration of the perceiver's relative position alters his percept, and different persons, who perceive the same object simultaneously, never have exactly the same percepts. (Husserl 1970b: 680)

The elements of chance and personal involvement described here recall Stephen's words to Cranly about the clock of the Ballast, that appears as a chance revelation to the 'man of letters' only when the context is right. Husserl accords his notion of the 'percept' similar 'epiphanic' qualities in his notes on the perception of a blackbird. For Husserl, the percept refers to 'a perceived thing as such'. He writes that between the percept and its expression lies the 'mediating act [that] must be the true giver of meaning' (ibid. 682). In other words, images conjured by the imagination as a response to some narrative, or from a description of perceptions, find their meaning in the act that unites the two through its 'intentional direction'. *Finnegans Wake* embodies all human faculties including perception and expression in a text that creates the reader as a mediator, between her own 'sensibility, sponsibility,' and 'prostability' (*FW* 189: 6–7) and the text's 'scribblative', 'defenceless paper' (*FW* 189: 9). Husserl's description of that which stands in as the 'mediating act' as 'the true giver of meaning' parallels Joyce's emphasis on language as mediating the body. Joyce makes the word itself, or language itself, the 'mediating act', what we have seen Giorgio Agamben refer to as the very 'idea of language'.

Derrida reads Joyce

In his introduction to Husserl's *Origin of Geometry*, Jacques Derrida argues that Joyce and Husserl share a 'common *telos*', namely, 'the positive value of univocity' (Derrida 1989: 104). Husserl's notion of 'linguistic embodiment' solves the problem of how the thematic 'ideal objects' of geometry are transformed into writing as 'ideal objectivity' (ibid. 161), and, in like manner, his conception of univocity relies on a notion of the 'properly animate body' (*geistige Leiblichkeit*) that constitutes, for Derrida, a 'refusal of history' (ibid. 101). Derrida argues that 'Joyce's project' (103), for which Husserl's is the 'transcendental "parallel"' (103), also relies on such univocity and, thus, on 'a certain anti-historicism'. However, even though both ultimately strive, Derrida argues, to constrain, or 'overcome', the 'unforseeable configurations' of plurivocity (101), Derrida admits that Joyce's desire to 'take responsibility for all equivocation' within the vast 'structural unity' (102) of his work does not impoverish 'empirical language' (103) like Husserl. The important point for this study, however, is that Husserl's desire to control equivocity and plurivocity is always related back to what Derrida refers to in terms of 'linguistic incarnations' (90) and what Husserl himself describes as a 'linguistic embodiment' where a passively 'awakened signification' in memory can be 'transformed back' into 'the corresponding activity' (164). I have argued that Joyce's project can be traced to a similar privileging of something akin to a 'linguistic incarnation'. Even when Derrida's notion of *différance* is introduced some years later in the essay 'Differance', the essay ends with a final description that recalls this linguistic incarnation: 'Such is the question: the marriage between speech and Being in the unique word, in the finally proper name. Such is the question that enters into the affirmation put into play by differance' (Derrida 1973: 155).

How do Derrida's readings of Joyce, then, elicit this problematic notion of 'originary constitution' or linguistic incarnation – what parallels Husserl's correlational *a priori* – between language and consciousness that he has found so troubling in Husserl? Derrida has written two long essays on Joyce: 'Ulysses Gramophone: Hear say yes in Joyce' and 'Two words for Joyce'. He also points out that '*La Carte postale* is haunted by Joyce' (quoted in Attridge and Ferrer 1984: 150) and has quipped '[a]nd yet I'm not sure I like Joyce' (ibid. 148). In 'Ulysses Gramophone' Derrida goes so far as to count all the 'yeses' in *Ulysses*, in claiming that '[n]othing is less a monologue than Molly's "monologue"' (Derrida 1992b: 299). In this long essay Derrida presents a persuasive argument around the nature of the word 'yes'. He employs numerous metaphors (telephone, gramophone, signature) to convince the reader that 'yes' is a performative, and that, therefore, Molly's chapter, which ends *Ulysses*, is not a monologue. Of course, what is at issue here is what is implied by the notion of interior monologue. Derrida's reading is, of course, grounded in the early account of signification found in *Speech and Phenomena*. Derrida is once again deconstructing any notion of language that privileges an intentional animation, a living voice that can communicate with itself in 'the absence of the world' or in the absence of the trace. Derrida writes that '*yes*, which names nothing [...] must be taken for an answer. It occurs after the other' (ibid. 265).

Once again, meaning is dependent on the relation with the other. As we have seen, this other can be located in the 'corporeity *within*, as Lingis, Henry and Depraz suggest. Later in the essay Derrida repeats this vanquishing of an auto-revelation, a *yesness*, from any originary site of interiority:

> But despite the umbilical scene ('navelcord' again), despite the archi-narcissistic and auto-affective appearance of this 'Yes - I' which dreams of massaging itself clean, all alone even in the caress itself, the *yes* addresses itself to some other and can appeal only to the *yes* of some other; it begins by responding. (Derrida 1992b: 301)

Derrida questions any *self*-performativity that *yes* might enact in monologue. He reads Molly's interior monologue as a performative that must first 'appeal to the *yes* of some other'. However, if Joyce is accepting of the type of 'corporeity within' or auto-affection that I examined earlier, then he might also be regarded as rescuing over to the aesthetic facets of the 'belief' and 'grace' that Agamben argues are important for performativity as it is conceived in relation to the 'The Nearness of the Word' (Agamben 2005: 136). Agamben argues that, for Paul, in every 'linguistic act' 'the word of faith rise[s] forth to go beyond the denotative relation between language and the world' (ibid. 134). Joyce had such faith in the artistic word. Agamben argues that in the 'experiences of the word' there is an 'essential' dialectic between the *performativum fidei* (the performative of the oath) and the *performativum sacramenti* (the penitential and sacramental performative) (135). However, Agamben argues that the former is 'today' being neglected in favour of the latter. The 'word of faith', then, for Agamben, exists as an 'absolute nearness of the word' that does not 'coincide with the performative value of a speech act' (136). Its power 'finds its *telos* in weakness' and this 'weakness' or impotentiality of the 'nearness of the word' is examined in the final chapter. The Joycean monologue invests in this kind of power in Molly's interior monologue, the only section in *Ulysses* where interior monologue is not 'embedded in a third-person narrative medium'. Derrida's foregrounding of 'interior monologue' in Joyce's work returns us to the philosophical questions examined in the last chapter in relation to what he cites as a problematic notion of 'linguistic incarnation'.

Joyce does not only present an unpunctuated verbal accretion of an inner voice so as to mimetically record in writing some preconceived notion of inwardness; he wishes to inaugurate a circuitry of reciprocation between the body of the reader and the body suggested in the words on the page, an incarnation of sorts. This is an incarnation later yearned for in *Finnegans Wake*, where his words more closely imitate thought-processes that desire their simultaneous material configuration: '[H]ow comes ever a body in our taylorised world to selve out this his [...] whereom is man, [...] nother man, wheile thishis he is asame' (*FW* 356: 10–14). Joyce and Derrida describe the genesis of language, the topic of Derrida's master thesis written in Paris 12 years after Joyce's death, with different emphases. For Derrida, Husserl's understanding of monologue or self-communication is flawed or 'naïve' because it privileges the connection between the voice of monologue and the 'living flesh' which is, for Husserl, 'intuitive and genetic'. In other words, signs are useless in monologue because it 'hears itself' (Lawlor 2002: 171). Since Derridean difference, what is primordial for him, is only found in the sign, such unity, such disregard for the nature of the sign in communication, is flawed. Derrida is of course correct to suggest that Joycean monologue is not merely a traditional conception of monologue, but the Joycean monologue has its own manner of appealing 'to the *yes* of some other'.

And perhaps we should leave the last word on Derrida's commentary with Molly:

I tried to draw a picture of it before I tore it up like a sausage or something I wonder theyre not afraid going about of getting a kick or a bang or something there and that word met something with hoses in it and he came out with some jawbreakers about the incarnation he never can explain a thing simply the way a body can understand. (*U* 893)

Incarnation and metempsychosis are persistent themes in the novel. Molly's words are open to the punctuation of the reader; they can be moulded according to 'everyone's personal experience'. Molly informs us here in her 'monologue' that the 'body can understand', and that it understands 'simply'. Molly intimates that she is aware of how the body understands in a manner very different to the manner Bloom employed to explain to her the meaning of the word metempsychosis in 'Calypso'. Choosing not to read Molly's words as monologue, based on a definition of yes as that which 'can appeal only to the *yes* of some *other*' (quoted in Derrida 1992a: 301) neglects the possibility of addressing a *yes* solely to oneself in a manner only the body can understand, in the 'simple' manner Molly understands. The above lines from Molly can also be regarded as humorously phrasing an incarnation as 'that word met something with hoses in it and he came out'. Reading Molly's words as monologue does not constrict the performativity or dialogic nature of the writing, but rather allows Joyce to express as never before the individual body as flesh in writing or 'excitable speech'. The reader takes up the role of communicant in the text, discovering and enacting a readerly 'auto-revelation' through what she realizes is the expression of a means for achieving such self-awareness. Reading thus receives 'through a portal vein' the 'dialytically separated elements of precedent decomposition' for the 'verypet purpose of subsequent recombination [...] [so they] may be there for you' (*FW* 614–15: 33–8), a process that leads Joyce to desire an ever greater commingling of word and body: 'Thi is Mi' (*FW* 607: 19).

Genesis and Incarnation

Harry Levin has argued that Joyce 'lost his faith, but he kept his categories' (Levin 1960: 35). His interest in the 'symbolic role of the word in liturgical acts' is transplanted into his later works. The evolution of his art gradually elicits a move away from Thomism toward a perspective on language that phenomenology can best account for. It is therefore to the phenomenological analogues for Joyce's religious 'categories' that we must now turn. His persistent interest in the epiphanic and revelatory potential of the word through which enlightenment fills the consciousness of some character is bound up with the philosophical theme of genesis. For Derrida, genesis is a fundamental problem in Husserl's early philosophy. In *The Problem of Genesis* he argues that the 'essential difference between phenomenological lived experience' and 'facticity in general' is that the former 'appears to itself' (Derrida 2003: 62). The manner in which meaning 'appears to itself' in consciousness is a fundamental concern for Joyce and early phenomenology. This capacity enables us 'to disengage ourselves from a perceptual present' and distances us from 'reality' (62). Interior monologue and stream of consciousness narration allow characters to reflect on incidents and objects recalled to consciousness, thereby distancing themselves from the world of objects through this capacity for reflection. However, Derrida points out in his early study of genesis in Husserl that any 'appearing to itself', any insight involving the running together of the 'perception of time' and the 'time of perception' – for it is the temporalizing of experience that is at issue here – necessitates *a priori* 'that an originary impression have some temporal destiny'. In other words, any recollection or retention, what is central to Joycean monologue and Proustian memory, in being recalled, is no longer solely a multiplication of the same, but is implicated in a temporalizing that implies a modification. As a result, the 'absolute originality' that the phenomenological moment of retention or recollection offers is, Derrida argues, '*already a synthesis* since it implies *a priori* a "retentional modification"' (ibid. 62).

Derrida faults the phenomenological recording of the *a priori* 'necessity of this synthesis' because the 'originary impression' is 'not sensation taken at the most elementary physiological level, but the originary impression in the immanent consciousness of time' (ibid. 62). In other words, Derrida's perception of this unacknowledged synthesis in the recalled originary impression between the time of perception and the perception of time does not mediate directly the 'sensation taken at the most elementary physiological level'; it does not mediate real lived experience. Absolute originarity, or 'originary constitution', would also appear to be pre-linguistic for Husserl in this instance. The synthesis invoked by absolute originarity is, therefore, integral to the Husserlian analysis of language that Derrida will focus on later. However, Derrida's commentary on Husserl's description of genesis comes to something of an impasse here because his readings of these fundamental syntheses and 'originary constitution[s]', in this early work, have not yet devised a means of working out precisely how the 'sensation taken at the most elementary physiological level' can be described. Derrida, as we have seen, will later describe this problem in terms of a 'linguistic incarnation' when he relates it to Husserl's account of language. It is chiefly a concern with the relation between the description of how meaning 'appears to itself' and the experience of the mediating body, or 'sensation taken at the most elementary physiological level', a relation Derrida has not yet worked through in his philosophy. Alphonso Lingis and Natalie Depraz describe this relation in Husserl in terms of a 'corporeity within', something that Derrida will later describe as a problem of 'linguistic incarnation'. Joyce and Proust account for this relation through their concern for the 'symbolic role of the word' that sees them relying on such figures as incarnation and transubstantiation. These narrative forms lyrically recount a stringent charting and recording of the processes by which the recollection of 'absolute originarity', an encounter, or 'previously unrealised disposition', is made to 'appear to itself'. Joyce and Proust employ *a priori* syntheses of their own. They do not posit intentional 'originary impression[s]' that discount 'sensation at the most elementary physiological level'.

Derrida argues in this early work that Husserl invests in a notion of 'originary constitution' whereby an *a priori* synthesis more 'fundamental' than 'lived experience' is implicit in the basic phenomenological reduction. This recalls the notion of linguistic incarnation employed in *Origin of Geometry*. We recall that Derrida sums up the problem as follows: 'Linguistic incarnation and the constitution of written or scriptural space, suppose, then, a closer and closer "interconnection" of ideality and reality through a series of less and less ideal mediations and in the synthetic unity of an intention' (Derrida 1989: 89 footnote). A similar 'interconnection' is in question here between the 'form' of the originary impression of the song or object, what Derrida calls the 'transcendental object', and the phenomenological retention where the originary impression must 'appear to itself'. Derrida argues that, because Husserl regards 'the pure content of sensation' as the 'correlate of an originarily intentional impression', passivity is introduced and 'the sensuous [...] datum of sound cannot [then] be constituted by the subject's activity' (Derrida 2003: 63). In other words, the subject's role in re-experiencing the impression is greatly diminished. The subject becomes little more than a mediator of a sense that has already passed through a double synthesis; the first synthesis being that implied in the notion of retentional modification where the recalled originary impression unites the perception of time and the time of perception, and the second being that integral to intentionality whereby the recalled originary impression must be regarded as the impression *of* some object or sound. However, in this early study Derrida distances phenomenology's unique manner of representing the 'appearing to itself' of the impression from any clear sense of corporeity. In reading through the development and ultimate dismembering of Joyce's notion of epiphany, I now want to examine how Joyce describes 'sensation taken at the most elementary physiological level' for an aesthetic end.

Transforming epiphany: from art to life

Joyce initially describes the genesis of language for the artwork through the workings of the notion of epiphany. He will discover that because the epiphany generally records the moment of enlightenment that describes the relation between the individual and the perception of an object, that it is incapable of recording the relation between the body itself and the meaning instilled in consciousness. The form of the epiphany does not allow for the manner of self-manifestation integral to revelation that occurs for the 'corporeity within'. The interior monologues and streams of consciousness of Bloom and Molly will impart to these characters the potential for a more durable and corporeal sense of communion, a potential Gretta and Gabriel cannot share since they are denied the possibility of interiorizing their epiphanic experiences for themselves and ultimately for each other.

William T. Noon reminds us that the Stephen of *Stephen Hero* 'speak[s] of art as an "incarnation" ' (Noon 1957: 27) in the sense that the Thomistic scholar Cardinal Mercier intends – '[t]he beautiful (artistic) form which human sensibility apprehends is presented as an "incarnation" of an otherwise humanly inaccessible "ideal beauty" ' (ibid. 20). Stephen talks about re-embodying the subtle soul of the image freed from 'its mesh of defining circumstances' (*SH* 78). The incarnation would take place, then, between the 'form' and its 'presentation'. However, even though the primary moment of apprehension and the subsequent 'presentation' is central to the theory of art that Stephen concocts from his 'applied Aquinas', and despite Joyce's belief in what was for him the central Thomist principle of art – 'to express or to incarnate the beautiful for an aesthetic end' (Noon 1957: 29) – Noon reminds us of some important distinctions between Aquinas and Joyce with regard to beauty.

Noon argues that Joyce's interest in the 'aesthetic arts' is an eighteenth-century invention and that it would have 'baffled' Aquinas (ibid. 18). However, an important difference is that while the early Stephen is committed to art as 'artistic process' (integritas, consonontia and claritas), the 'Thomist texts on art' are 'principally concerned with art as an intellectual virtue' (29). However, it is most likely that Joyce never wholly gave up the forms of artistic appreciation integral to his 'applied Aquinas'. Consonantia is, for Stephen, the 'rhythm of ... structure' (48), while, for Aquinas, it applies 'to the immanent procession of the Son from the Father within the Unity of the Divine Trinity, as well as to the immanent, dynamic presence of God in all creatures' (48). Claritas is also, for Stephen, 'the only synthesis which is logically and esthetically permissible' (53). These notions depart radically, then, from their Thomist roots. Yet Joyce's interest in those aspects of apprehension and presentation that epiphany foregrounds contributes to his privileging of a synthesis between form and presentation, or between 'the form of an object' and the constituting moments of revelatory experience. For Noon, a 'theory of literature' built on the Thomist texts on beauty would move to a 'solution of the question of content and style' where 'one should conceive of the words or the language as the formal, determining principle of embodiment' with the 'meaning or the poetic truth' being regarded as 'the potential' waiting to be actuated by the form' (53). Joyce, however, wants the 'determining principle of embodiment' to be intertwined with the form. Stephen's description of claritas elicits the early play with a Thomist 'theory of literature': 'The instant wherein [...] the clear radiance of the esthetic image, is apprehended luminously by the mind which has been arrested by its wholeness and fascinated by its harmony is the luminous silent stasis of esthetic pleasure' (*P* 179). However, this moment is a moment of the artistic process. The 'luminous silent stasis' must therefore undergo some process of communion with the word so that the moment can be recorded. This movement between the inner moment of revelation, self-affection or manifestation and the word is further brought to the fore with Joyce's move to the related notion of the epiphany.

Noon is correct to suggest that in *Stephen Hero* the epiphany is a 'precise concept' that applies to the 'meaningful, artless dramatization of inner, spiritual life through some particular bodily attitude or sign' (Noon 1957: 61). The emphasis is on the means through which 'inner, spiritual life' can be dramatized by the body. There is an important Joycean shift here away from the detailing of the manifestation of meaning integral to artistic inspiration and towards the detailing of the manifestation of meaning, through the 'corporeity within', for an understanding of life. The early notion of epiphany reveals how the body manifests or displays through a 'sign' or through perception some inner revelation that is important for the aesthetic. Stephen tells Cranly that the clock of the Ballast Office was capable of an epiphany, thereby implying that the individual can also have a moment of communion with the object as some previously unrealized disposition is made apparent through this revelatory experience; the object leaps out of its usual frame of reference. However, since this is also an important moment in the artistic process, it is only 'the man of letters' who can record these epiphanies with extreme care. Joyce himself kept what he referred to as epiphanies – little sketches of dialogue and short descriptive passages – that would later act as a genesis for a larger narrative.

Epiphany, therefore, has a double meaning: it refers to the moment of enlightenment for the individual and the recording of such a moment by the 'man of letters'. However, the latter has been privileged at the expense of the former. The elasticity of the term hides a neglected move in Joyce's own artistic progress. *Stephen Hero* and *A Portrait* describe how great art should be constituted. The lengthy diatribes on art intrude into our suspension of disbelief and we are thrown outside the events of these early novels to engage in our own speculation on the genesis of the artwork. In *Ulysses* Joyce retains Stephen, but the narrator is bitingly ironical of his early aesthetic theories. The 'new womanly man', Poldy, 'our hero', takes centre stage and Joyce can finally give up the urge to present us with seemingly authentic, aesthetic theories. *Ulysses is* the great artwork, as is *Finnegans Wake*; these works do not employ the subplot of a search for an authentic theory of art. The course of the aesthetic will no longer be treated as a theme in the writing for it is writing itself – language – that will consume Stephen's passion for aesthetic enquiry. We recall Giorgio Agamben's description of the 'idea of language' as the ultimate mediation: 'such an *immediate mediation* constitutes the sole possibility of reaching a principle freed of every presupposition, including self-presupposition [...] the "thing itself" and essential matter of human beings' (Agamben 1999: 47). The presentation of such a mediation is what Joyce now strives for.

However, Joyce's interest in the 'synthesis' and the communion integral to art that claritas and epiphany evoke for him has not been killed off. The privileging of the moment of revelation for the artist, the trained Scholastic, or 'the man of letters', and their means of contemplating its careful evolution, is parodied in *Ulysses* where 'our hero' is now content to browse through the Paul de Kock page-turners he buys for his wife. Joyce is now more interested in the less than idealized moment of revelation of the common man. The only means the writer has at his disposal to privilege and locate the movement of synthesis and incarnation is now between the common man, 'our hero', and how he interiorizes his perceptions. Bloom's perceptions and manifestations of meaning are our perceptions and manifestations. We are not only the 'authorized reader', we are the common reader of daily signs, as is Bloom. In being readers with and through Bloom, the site of revelation has now shifted to encompass the reader. Joyce establishes a connection between this philosophical meaning of epiphany as an insight given by the ' "trues coloribus resplendent" of an object', and the function of epiphany as a verbal strategy of art' (Noon 1957: 62). This connection must be interiorized for each character as a verbal strategy of life. Enlightenment and inscription will coalesce in the interior monologue of *Ulysses* and in the later Wak*ese*.

Even though critics have retained the notion of epiphany even to describe Joyce's late works,[6] Joyce achieves quite a dramatic aesthetic shift under cover of the epiphany from 'the actual experience of the spectator in life to the verbal act or construct that imaginatively re-presents this experience in the symbols of language, re-enacts it through illuminating images (though not purely luminous) for the contemplation of the imaginative mind' (Noon 1957: 77). The motivations for this shift in Joyce's work are prefigured in Stephen's fundamental artistic dilemma. Noon argues that he 'cannot integrate into his rationalizations about art the poetic sensibility which he experiences in the music of words' (ibid. 67). Joyce responds to this dilemma by killing off characters such as the early Stephen (although the name remains) and any opportunity for aesthetic posturing. Joyce's dramatization of 'his own story within the formal dimensions of an ironic narrative' (66) means that language itself, the form, in an unparalleled unravelling of every reader's 'corporeity within', must interiorize and then make manifest this passion for communion. Stephen's dilemma parallels Joyce's own frustrations with his means for describing his hero. Joyce's desire to chart the occurrence of sudden spiritual manifestations for the reader remains, as his interest in verbal correspondences, the symbolic function of language and the 'dramatic reprojection of imaginatively formed reality' (76) becomes further removed from the kind of everyday experience his first epiphanies recorded. His attention is drawn further inwards to inspect the correspondence between the word and the moral and the 'essential matter' of the sensible world.

For a Christian imagery the feast of the Epiphany celebrates the presentation of the infant Christ to humanity in material realization of the promise of Incarnation. Joyce is not the first artist to have been drawn to its potential. In *The Hidden Leonardo*, Marco Rossi describes

Leonardo da Vinci's unfinished painting *The Adoration of the Magi* as 'the first true representation of the Epiphany in the history of art' (Rossi 1977: 47). The representation of epiphany leads to an artistic revelation for both artists. *The Adoration of the Magi*, commissioned in 1481, was never completed. It is a complete departure from the ico-nographic treatments of the subject. The 'dramatic appearance of Christ among the Gentiles assumes a significance all the more striking due to its powerful naturalistic setting. Full play is given to the human passions' (ibid. 36). Rossi regards its 'naturalistic treatment of a reli-gious theme' together with its 'transformation of traditional fifteenth-century conceptions of mass, space, and perspective' as revolutionary. The unfinished sketch of the virgin and child at the centre of the painting is surrounded by a myriad of figures. The stately procession of three wise kings has been replaced by a setting in which Christ is presented amidst a crowd of swarthy, gesticulating bodies. Serge Bramly has argued that '[d]epicting the homage of the kings to the Holy Child meant rendering intelligible all that the birth of God's son represented. He wanted the viewer to grasp instinctively the con-sequences, the universal significance, of the event' (Bramly 1994: 161). Da Vinci's decision to depict the founding moment of Christian nar-rative in so naturalistic a setting parallels the motivations for Joyce's move away from epiphany. In the painting, the incarnated Christ, or the embodiment of revelation, does not appear solely to kings and wise men but to old men, quarrelling cavalry soldiers and young men who turn away from the momentous scene. Joyce also realized that revela-tion brings a self-awareness that is not only the preserve of the aspiring artist. The painting of the young man walking away from the scene in the foreground is often regarded as a self-portrait. If this is so, then Leonardo might be regarded as representing himself turning his back on a whole aesthetic tradition, and on his early artistic practices.

Leonardo da Vinci influenced the aesthetic theory of the young Joyce. In Joyce's early critical essay entitled 'Mr Mason's Novels', an essay on the novels of A. E. W. Mason, he begins by employing a carefully worked analogy between prose writing and the artistic prac-tice of Leonardo da Vinci:

[M]uch as they differ in their subjects and styles, are curiously illustrative of the truth of one of Leonardo's observations. Leonardo, exploring the dark recesses of consciousness in the interests of some semi-pantheistic psychology, has noted the tendency of the mind to impress its own likeness upon that which it creates. It is because of this tendency, he says, that many painters have cast as it were a reflection of themselves over the portraits of others. (Barry 2000: 91)

Joyce shares da Vinci's interest in the epiphany as a symbol for the 'tendency of the mind to impress its own likeness upon that which it creates'. Da Vinci argues in his *Treatise on Painting* that there is such an infinite number of forms and actions that the memory is incapable of preserving them all. The artist must, therefore, keep sketches of them as patterns and teachers. Joyce regards his own early epiphanies as his 'patterns and teachers' (Wallace 1966: 17). Leonardo writes in his treatise that 'the putting [of] several scenes in the same composition' (qtd. in Clark, 1993: 133), what Paul Valéry describes as Leonardo's attention to the 'brute unity and thickness of the world (Valéry, 48)', is of prime importance, and it is what Joyce now sought to achieve through the *immediate mediation of language.*

The resurgence of interest in a rhetoric of religion in contemporary critical discourse is also enabling of a reading of Joyce that emphasizes his manner of parodying religious language so as to enunciate a 'spiritual' aesthetic that works to privilege a character's self-awareness, or living 'manifestation of being'. Joyce models his early artistic sketches as epiphanies and *epicleti*,[7] enabling a rich religious intertext to be constructed about them. Stephen describes the aesthetic in terms of a necessary transformation, as 'an actuality of the possible as possible' (*U* 30), where a recorded moment of revelation is incorporated into the main body of writing. The death of the character that Joyce instigates towards the end of *Ulysses* and in *Finnegans Wake* necessitates the relocation of this aesthetic moment.[8] The 'authorized reader' becomes the mediation for the epiphany. The reader then becomes embroiled in Joyce's writing of 'the human body', or becomes *incarnated* in the moments of the text.

Hélène Cixous sees Joyce's symbols of communion and reconciliation inverting 'the relationship between interior and surface' so as 'to recover from holy objects their privileged profundity' (Cixous 1976: 608). She regards the epiphany as:

[A] revitalising devotion to the ordinary real. Joyce designed the plan of his works as a challenge to the enemy, reproducing in a structure composed of one single metaphor the unbearable situation which his writing was intended to destroy: the separation of soul and body caused by the national guilt-complex of Catholic Ireland. (Cixous 1976: 635)

Joyce incarnates the body in the word, and the soul in the body, by charting a seemingly unmediated relation between language and the body in self-communication, or in the 'corporeity within'. He rescues back into narrative a 'privileged profundity' through his incorporation of figures that describe transubstantiation, communion and incarnation. '[T]he separation of soul and body' is challenged through the application of these figures to apperception and auto-affection. The epiphany becomes a 'focus of metamorphoses, the meeting-point of *stasis and movens* where they unite for an instant, the brilliant reconciliation of contraries' (Cixous 1976: 676).

However, the 'philosophical insight' epiphany originally referred to has been neglected in Joyce Studies. In recognizing that Robert Scholes regards them as nothing more than 'trivial and supercilious' manuscript epiphanies (Scholes 1964: 73), I believe it is important to examine the 'philosophical insight' epiphany has been taken to describe in Joyce if only to rejuvenate some of Joyce's own 'privileged profundity'.[9] Morris Beja reminds us that it is not only the 'spiritual' that is being foregrounded through the epiphany: Joyce 'took a theological word and applied it to a literary tradition. By this clever device he was able to make use of suggestive spiritual meanings and connotations to help get across his own ideas' (Beja 1971: 71). Joyce has a distinct understanding of the 'spiritual':

> [W]henever he uses the word 'spiritual,' he seems to refer to the world of emotions, art, intuition – in terms of his aesthetic theory, all that cannot be analyzed (It is in the context of that theory that Stephen calls literature 'the highest and most *spiritual* art' [*P* 214, Beja's emphasis]). In Joyce's usage the word 'spiritual' need not have a religious reference, and the phrase 'spiritual manifestation' is more a figure of speech than an actual sign of religious feeling. (Beja 1971: 74)

For Beja, the epiphany refers to a 'manifestation, striking appearance, *esp.* an appearance of a divinity' (ibid. 71–2). Michel Henry regards the essence of manifestation as something that does not only occur sporadically for the individual; it is an original condition of Being:

> *The manifestation of Being, far from being able to be a simple consequence of the methodological work of clarification of phenomenology is rather its condition, as it is the condition of all possible manifestation of any being in general.* [Henry's emphasis] (Henry 1973: 137)

Zack Bowen questions whether '[at] the moment of revelation, experience is supposed to become transformed into truth' (Bowen 1981: 105). The reading of the epiphany as 'the moment of revelation' has privileged the notion of a brief encounter with some sacred otherness at the expense of the interrogation of an original and living occurrence with what Henry calls the 'manifestation of being'. Perhaps we can find the root of this omission in the accepted understanding critics have of Joyce's elaboration of the role of the artist. Even though Stephen's Thomistic apprehension of the beautiful does reveal certain aspects of Joyce's understanding of the epiphany, Stephen's discussion of the different forms of art, especially of the form Joyce himself practised most devotedly, namely narrative, regards the narration as incarnating or embodying the life, or this manifestation of being, of the artist: '[t]he narrative is no longer purely personal. The personality of the artist passes into the narration itself, flowing round and round the persons and the action like a vital sea' (*P* 180). It is only in describing the dramatic form, a form where for Stephen the 'mystery of esthetic [...] is accomplished' (*P* 181), that Stephen comes to regard the artist as 'refined out of existence' (*P* 181). William T. Noon regards Stephen's notion that the artist should be 'refined out of existence' as representative of the 'climax of Joyce's ironic development'. It is not the 'annihilation of the artist's personality' that Joyce himself sought, but the 'symbolic presentation of reality, be it the artist's personality or the personality of others or "the signature of things"' (Noon 1957: 67).

It is not only the momentary epiphany before an otherness that Joyce privileges, but the potential for sustaining an openness to the original 'manifestation of Being', a potential that moments such as those before the Ballast Clock can reveal to the subject. It is a state Joyce transferred to his experience before the word, where the narrative "twill carry on my hearz'waves my still waters reflections in words' (*FW* 460: 25–6) through the 'profound reciprocity' of a language of the body. Michel Henry argues that phenomenology must be concerned with the 'how', or the '*manner* [Henry's italics] in which reality manifests itself and must manifest itself to us' (Henry 1973: 56), and it is a similar process that Joyce's 'personnalitey' records.

Towards the end of *A Portrait* Stephen stares at the swallows and contemplates his prospective departure from home for the artistic life:

A soft liquid joy like the noise of many waters flowed over his memory and he felt in his heart the soft peace of silent spaces of fading tenuous sky above the waters, of oceanic silence, of swallows flying through the sea-dusk over the flowing waters.

A soft liquid joy flowed through the words where the soft long vowels hurtled noiselessly and fell away, lapping and flowing back and ever shaking the white bells of their waves in mute chime and mute peal and soft low swooning cry; and he felt that the augury he had sought in the wheeling darting birds and in the pale face of sky above him had come forth from his heart like a bird from a turret quietly and swiftly. (*P* 190)

While not included in the surviving epiphany collection this passage may be regarded as one of those 'many other epiphanies in Joyce's novels based on his own experience, but which were not first recorded in such manuscripts or for which we do not have copies' (Beja 1971: 84). Beja is right to point out that '[t]here is not one [epiphany] in which the "otherness" of the object is as significant as the revelation produced in the perceiver' (ibid. 78). In the above passage, we catch Stephen mid-revelation. The words of the description become part of the description itself; the vowels hurtle and lap, taking on the physical and material state of the waves that have caused his epiphany. It is not only the artist that might be perceived as 'refined out of existence' in this passage. Stephen has disappeared behind the loquacious flood of 'the soft peace of silent spaces' and 'the soft long vowels'. The repeated incantatory 'soft liquid joy' imitates both the returning 'shrill cries' of the nomadic swallows, and also imbibes the form of the stanza of the villanelle Stephen has just mouthed to himself. Amidst the flood of broad vowels and disjointed imagery, Joyce informs us that Stephen 'felt that the augury he had sought in the wheeling darting birds and in the pale face of sky above him had come forth from his heart like a bird from a turret'. Not only has the presentation of this moment of revelation imitated formally what has coursed through Stephen's body, but Stephen locates the origin, the genesis, of this 'augury' in himself as it 'had come forth from his heart'. And not only does the reader realize that the 'augury' was unconsciously motivated internally, the 'augury' also assumes the shape of that within which it was sought: it comes forth 'like a bird from a turret'. David Hayman reminds us that Joyce is 'making reality the vehicle for its own transcendence' or making the 'artist's ability to discriminate [...] nearly as important as his power to convey with precision not the impact of the event so much as its essential nature' (Hayman 1998: 638).

The epiphany has its genesis within individual characters. The reader's apprehension of some sudden 'spiritual' manifestation in a

character is the horizon, or exteriorization, of an unconscious disposition or manifestation of being that a character has harboured
inside. When Stephen decides to become a writer another 'spiritual'
manifestation, or epiphany, is described:

> The phrase and the day and the scene harmonized in a chord.
> Words. Was it their colours? He allowed them to glow and fade, hue
> after hue: sunrise gold, the russet and green of apple orchards, azure
> of waves, the greyfringed fleece of clouds. No, it was not their col-
> ours: it was the poise and balance of the period itself. Did he then
> love the rhythmic rise and fall of words better than their associations
> of legend and colour? Or was it that, being as weak of sight as he was
> shy of mind, he drew less pleasure from the reflection of the glowing
> sensible world through the prism of a language manycoloured and
> richly storied than from the contemplation of an inner world of
> individual emotions mirrored perfectly in a lucid supple periodic
> prose? (*P* 140)

Stephen desires an incarnated language; he thinks to himself, 'O! In
the virgin womb of the imagination the word was made flesh' (*P* 182–
3). Stephen intimates the direction his own aesthetic must take. He
does not accept any aesthetic mimesis which works to reflect 'the
glowing sensible world through the prism of a language manycoloured
and richly storied', but rather one that begins from within, from 'the
contemplation of an inner world of individual emotions' which are to
become 'mirrored' in a 'lucid supple periodic prose'.[10] Joyce's early
experiments 'to dramatize his own story within the formal dimensions
of an ironic narrative' (Noon 1957: 66) break down to a certain extent
in this passage. The authenticity of the aesthetic ideal presented here
momentarily blends authorial and third-person viewpoints. 'Are you
not weary of ardent ways' (*P* 183) is a line of a song that keeps revisiting
Stephen, and possibly Joyce, as both come to an artistic juncture. Joyce's desire to privilege and recount the 'ardent ways' of the 'personality
of the artist' (*P* 180) gives way to a desire, in *Finnegans Wake*, to extend
the word's 'personnalitey to the latents', or to describe the 'immediate
mediation' of 'language itself' through an incarnated language that
will 'carry on my hearz'waves my still waters reflections in words' (*FW*
460: 25). Bloom will take centre stage, as the Everyman capable of
revealing this commonplace, yet revelatory power of language. The
'philosophical insight' of epiphany records what Gadamer, in his

discussion of incarnation, refers to as 'the processual character of the inner word' (Gadamer 1995: 423).

There is an early epiphany that reappears a number of times in Joyce's later work:

> She comes at night when the city is still; invisible, inaudible, all unsummoned. She comes from her ancient seat to visit the least of her children, mother most venerable, as though he had never been alien to her. She knows the inmost heart; therefore she is gentle, nothing exacting; saying, I am susceptible of change, an imaginative influence in the hearts of my children. Who has pity for you when you are sad among the strangers? Years and years I loved you when you lay in my womb. (Joyce 1991: 194)

We recall Stephen's description of another feminine imaginative essence: 'O! In the virgin womb of the imagination the word was made flesh' (*P* 217). The imagination is a force that is irrevocably tied, for Stephen, to his memory and visions of his mother; the mother says through Stephen that she is 'an imaginative influence' in his heart. George Painter also argues that the memory of Proust's mother is so important for his work that she assumes the psychoanalytic figure of the 'Dread Mother' (Painter 1983: 626) for him, to the extent that his work is offered up to her in atonement for having 'killed his mother twice over' (ibid. 619). For Stephen, it is in this imagination, in this 'imaginative influence' that is his mother, that the 'word was made flesh'. Stephen must be both the incarnated embodiment of the imagination (his mother), and the means through which the word becomes incarnated. The artist must be both the product of the word and its means of genesis.

The 'technique' (Beja 1971: 70) of the epiphany also possesses an incarnating and imaginative power that returns itself to itself. Joyce returns, again and again, to specific 'epiphanies', allowing them to be 'susceptible of change' and 'an imaginative influence in the hearts' of his works. Morris Beja finds this epiphany recorded in Joyce's 'Trieste Notebook' under 'Mother': 'She came to me silently in a dream after her death: and her wasted body within its loose brown habit gave out a faint odour of wax and rosewood and her breath a faint odour of wetted ashes' (ibid. 103). It is found in a transformed state in Stephen's streams of consciousness in *Ulysses*. It describes a lingering sense of guilt that Stephen associates with matriarchy. It drives him towards an obsessive deliberation on the other side of genesis and incarnation, towards the consubstantiality of father and son: 'A *lex eterna* stays about him. Is that then the divine substance wherein Father and Son are consubstantial?' (*U* 47). In 'Telemachus' Stephen remembers his mother:

> Silently, in a dream she had come to him after her death, her wasted body within its loose brown graveclothes giving off an odour of wax and rosewood [...] Across the threadbare cuffedge he saw the sea hailed as a great sweet mother by the wellfed voice beside him. The ring of bay and skyline held a dull green mass of liquid. A bowl of white china had stood beside her deathbed holding the green sluggish bile which she had torn up from her rotting liver by fits of loud groaning vomiting (*U* 4).

Suzette Henke argues that Joyce subverts 'male authority' by amalgamating it with the 'semiotic pulsions of feminine desire' (Henke 1990: 8). She argues that he introduces the 'issue of feminine desire' through the 'context of maternal abjection' (ibid. 11). However, as I develop in Chapter 4 through the examination of impotence and impotentiality in Luce Irigaray and Giorgio Agamben, the 'imaginative essence' Joyce discovers in the maternal is not only a replacement for imagination as conceived through male desire. Joyce will later acknowledge how male desire, in acknowledging its impotentiality, can discover its own store of feminine 'imaginative essence', that can sustain the male subject in his new quest for a desire that remains 'immanent to itself'. In the redrafted epiphany above, Stephen is still too attached to the 'personality of the artist' as a rational state exempt from the workings of the body. This ideal continues to throw up 'heaps of dead language', as Joyce describes for an earlier version of Stephen in *A Portrait*, (*P* 150) that, under the protean dynamic of 'Proteus', are worked into his only experience of death, that of his mother. Her breath becomes an odour, the sea is hailed as a mother, and the 'ring of bay and skyline' that holds the sea as a 'dull green mass of liquid' becomes the 'bowl of white china' that held 'the green sluggish bile' of his mother. Nature is hailed as a 'great sweet mother' without such nature being aligned with the 'corporeity within' of the subject. Bloom will begin to show Stephen how to meld the two.

This transformative potential that Joyce embodies in his writing is only a mediation of the body's unique ability for being the genesis of such potential. It is this sense of embodiment and incarnation that Joyce has found writing can mediate and that he is able to present so completely in *Ulysses* through the interior monologue technique. The capacity for change and transformation invested in these early epiphanies becomes a rigorously worked trait and motivation of the Joycean aesthetic. The presentation of the importance of a susceptibility to change itself evolves to such an extent that finally the portmanteau words of *Finnegans Wake* even transfer the site of action, or agency of control, of the transformation onto the 'authorized reader'. Words in *Finnegans Wake* are transformed 'to mountainy mots in her amnest plein of language' (*FW* 333: 26–7) or to words with a new physicality through language's momentary forgetting of its fullness.

Hélène Cixous finds the above epiphany in 'Circe': 'Twenty years later, Joyce uses this dream [the original epiphany I have cited above] in "Circe" where the ghost of Stephen's mother appears in Bella Cohen's house in the form of a decaying body' (Cixous 1976: 29). The decaying body speaks to Stephen: 'Years and years I loved you, O my son, my firstborn, when you lay in my womb' (*U* 682). However, in this last meeting with his mother Stephen exonerates himself from guilt through an acceptance of the body's power to work on all, even the 'intellectual imagination' (*U* 682): 'They say I killed you, mother. He offended your memory. Cancer did it, not I. Destiny' (*U* 681). His acknowledgement of the body's power to bring its own end is rejuvenating. He cries after shattering the chandelier in the brothel: 'Damn death. Long live life!' (*U* 689). The feminine imaginative impulse that enables characters to discover meaning in their interactions with their world is always grounded on 'the contemplation of an inner world'. Jaun the Boast's last 'fireless' words (*FW* 469: 29), before he mutates into 'rural Haun' (*FW* 471: 35), see him reminiscing on his old schooldays and his examinations in the 'ologies' (*FW* 468: 2). The education that he regards as 'tootoological' includes an ironic presentation of incarnation: 'In the beginning was the gest he jousstly says, for the end is with woman, flesh-without-word' (*FW* 468: 5–6). For Joyce, the last word, the end, always is with woman, be it Molly or ALP, and his early schooling in catechism would have taught him that woman, as 'flesh-without-word', was denied some of the privileges allocated to man by that other Jaun, namely John the evangelist: 'the Word was with man'. In creating a new kind of writerly incarnation of flesh and word, Joyce reverses this hierarchy. As Alan Roughley reminds us, the 'privileging of the male over the female is continually overturned in Joyce's writings' (Roughley 1999: 81).

Killing off epiphany in 'The Dead'

Joyce also challenges the conventions of reported dialogue; his narratives move inwards in ever-increasing circles of monologue and in ever more encompassing streams of consciousness. Early in his writing, monologue is associated with perversions and the 'wild sensations' characters seek. We read that the monologue of the old pederast of 'An Encounter' gives the narrator the impression that he had learned something 'by heart, or that magnetised by some words of his own speech, his mind was slowly circling round and round in the same orbit' (*D* 18). Listening to the monologue the boy learns something about being penitent to others, he learns something about his relationship with his friend Mahony. Father Flynn's guilt at having broken a chalice leads him to talk to himself alone in his confession box, and Corley, who uses servant girls for money and sex in 'Two Gallants' speaks in 'long monologue[s]' (43) without 'listening to the speech of his companions' (*D* 45). Joyce gives us examples of how these monologues affect the listeners. Some kind of moral order, representing something of the moral history of Dublin, is upset in each case so that monologue might be considered appropriate for such characters.

Why does a writer who begins by recording snatches of dialogue in early epiphanies, and who originally assigns monologues to paedophiles, unhinged priests and self-absorbed scroungers come to privilege monologue and dispense completely with dialogue in the final sections of *Ulysses* and in *Finnegans Wake*? What little dialogue there is in *Ulysses*, naturalistic or otherwise, is either a satirical presentation of dialogic types as in Cyclops and Aeolus, dialogue for the sake of proving a theoretical point as in Scylla and Charybdis, or the wholly impersonal presentation of a dialogue that, we must believe, took place between Stephen and Bloom in Ithaca. Marilyn French writes that '[a]lthough Circe contains some dialogue, and Eumaeus a little, after that, reportage of actual speech will also disappear' (French 1993: 184). We know that for the Stephen of *A Portrait* the artistic progression moves from lyric to epic to dramatic forms, so as to embody the movement of the personality of the artist as something that 'passes into the narration itself, flowing round and round the persons and the action like a vital sea' (*P* 214) until it finally 'fills every person with such ideal force' that the personality of the artist 'impersonalizes itself'. But we also read in Joyce's letter of 1905 to Stanislaus that he is reaching 'prostrating depths of impersonality' (Ellmann 1975: 54). Impersonality refers to the state of 'having no personal feeling or reference'. At this stage Joyce had written all the stories in *Dubliners* except 'The Dead'. For the committed artist that Joyce was, 'impersonality' would seem to be the result of taking this early aesthetic ideal too much to heart. If a writer is forced to feel through his characters and if he is also removed from the location that he will endlessly write about, and from being able to record any further snatches of conversation from that location, it is very likely that introspection and monologue will play a bigger part in the writing. Memory is now the site from which all new snatches of conversation must draw. The creative inspiration that is found in the 'shout in the street' must now be found in the memory and in how the breaking out of understanding unravels itself in the 'inner voice'.

We begin to see how monologue will work in Joyce to leave characters clinging to patterns of repetition that are bound to the symbolization of history as circular. Joyce's own intention to recapture forever, the 'distant music' of Dublin and his prostrating depths of impersonality led him to the vast circular narrative pattern of monologue. As reported speech gives way to monologue, we read in 'Oxen of the Sun', 'The voices blend and fuse in clouded silence: silence that is the infinite of space: and swiftly, silently the soul is wafted over regions of cycles of cycles of generations that have lived' (*U* 541). Bloom and Molly share only one conversation in the book and it is on the unlikely topic of 'metempsychosis' or the 'transmigration of souls'. Joyce accepts that when conversation and physical contact are no longer the true harbingers of intimacy, that intimacy must be communicated by other means, by how repeated patterns of housekeeping, familiar acts of betrayal and bodily gestures are interiorized by such subjects.

For Joyce interior monologue is important as a literary technique that formally depicts important aspects of self-communication, what enables Joyce to develop his foregrounding of a cyclical understanding of life. Joyce leaves us with the impression, even in *Finnegans Wake*, that the subject's monologues and words to herself do impart a kind of knowledge:

What has gone? How it ends?
Begin to forget it. It will remember itself from every sides, with all gestures, in each our word. [...]
Have we cherished expectations? [...]
Our wholemole millwheeling vicociclometer [...] receives through a portal vein the dialytically separated elements of precedent

> decomposition for the verypetpurpose of subsequent recombination
> so that the heroticisms, catastrophes and eccentricities transmitted
> by the ancient legacy of the past, type by tope [...] anastomosically
> assimilated and preteridentified [...] may be there for you [...] (*FW*
> 614–5: 19–8)

Words have the capacity to allow life to 'remember itself', serving to
merge forgetting and remembering. The persistent digging down into
the text and the archive suggested in 'wholemole millwheeling' serves
up 'for you [the reader]' the 'dialiytically' (dialectically) separated
elements of 'precedent decomposition'. This suggests that Joyce's
book, the 'tetradomational gasebocroticon', receives through a 'vein'
(here again we have the text described in terms of a body) dying, past
elements for a 'subsequent recombination'. The phrase 'precedent
decomposition' also suggests that these elements of the past are
'assimilated' by the text, not to be composed according to some
authorial intentionality, but so as to decompose in being recombined
and assimilated. They set a precedent whereby they begin all over again
with their dying off. The fact that all truths become reified and com-
modified as 'trend[s]' and that perfect memories only ever imply that
something has been forgotten, leads the speaker to ask, 'Have we
cherished expectations?' The result of this self-learning and self-communication is a cyclical arrangement, or a 'subsequent recombination',
where the 'word', the 'type' and the 'letter' are 'anastomosically [and
we recall that Clive Hart regards anastomosis as Joyce's favoured trope]
assimilated' so that the same 'adomic structure', or incarnate substance, remains and awaits further readerly instances of the liberty of
'perusiveness' (FW 614: 24).

  'The Dead' marks a development in Joyce's handling of the presentation of enlightenment. In 'The Dead' Gabriel Conroy is caught in
a moment of hesitation as he contemplates what Gretta symbolizes.
Jean-Michel Rabaté regards the reader's '[a]esthetic pleasure' in
reading the epiphany as deriving from 'one's ability to prolong the
hesitation, a hesitation that is all the more palpable as we balance
between a profane and religious sense of the term' (Rabaté 2002: 129).
The development of the Joycean aesthetic presents us with a character
assuming this favoured position of the reader, caught in the epiphanic
moment of hesitation before the consideration of some object's relevance for a particular ego. 'The Dead' presents the reader with the
ironic dramatization of the capturing and contemplation of the
moment of revelation, a moment that in earlier stories possesses a

naivety and authenticity that brings denouement and closure to the tone of the narrative. Gabriel Conroy searches on a number of occasions for a suitable interpretation for what appears to him as a symbolic moment of perception:

> He stood still in the gloom of the hall, trying to catch the air that the voice was singing and gazing up at his wife. There was grace and mystery in her attitude as if she were a symbol of something. He asked himself what is a woman standing on the stairs in the shadow, listening to distant music, a symbol of. If he were a painter he would paint her in that attitude. Her blue felt hat would show off the bronze of her hair against the darkness and the dark panels of her skirt would show off the light ones. *Distant Music* he would call the picture if he were a painter. (*D* 211)

Gabriel is caught between 'trying to catch the air' that the voice is singing and trying to work out what his wife is a symbol of. Not only is Gabriel's artistic reverie based on a misconception, but his wife is also listening to a 'distant music' of a very different kind. Seized by the remembrance of Michael Furey, she has been transported to a time when Gabriel did not exist for her, to a time when he was *dead* to her. Ironically, it is in this moment that Gabriel, possibly for the first time, is able to perceive his wife as a symbol, disembodied and disincarnated of all familiarity and attachment to him, reduced to an inanimate element for the perusal of the artistic reveries of a teacher who sees himself, somewhat like Bloom, as a 'bit of an artist'. The narrative voice, the third-person narrator, recognizes the characters' deaths to each other at this time. Gretta is never again called by her name by the narrator from this point; she becomes a universal 'she', assuming some of the symbolic attributes that Gabriel had attempted to consign to her.[11] Gretta has also become dead to the world around her; we read that 'Gabriel watched his wife who did not join in the conversation' and that '[s]he was in the same attitude and seemed unaware of the talk about her' (*D* 213). Upon leaving the house Aunt Julia says 'O, goodnight, Gretta, I didn't see you' (*D* 213).

In 'The Dead' dialogue and conversation are beginning to kill themselves off. Gabriel thinks to himself that his attempt to communicate something to the dinner guests is 'sure to fail', just as his exchanges with Lily have failed; his 'whole speech [...] was an utter failure' (*D* 179). The intent to listen to the voice begins to be separated from any marker of identity; listening to Aunt Julia, Gabriel realizes that 'to follow the voice without looking at the singer's face, was to feel the excitement of swift and secure flight' (*D* 193). At dinner, as Gabriel 'takes no part in the conversation', he asks the guests 'to forget his existence' and as Joyce moves away from reported speech with the close of *Dubliners*, Gabriel's desire to look for meaning in symbols means that 'one by one they were all becoming shades' (*D* 224). Having asked himself what Gretta as 'a woman standing on the stairs in the shadow, listening to distant music, is a symbol of', she dies a symbolic death for the narrator.

Ironically, Gabriel's search for revelation in his attempts to symbolize the 'grace and mystery' in Gretta's 'attitude' (*D* 211) also marks the moment of Gretta's separation from him. She has become transfixed by the memory of her dead lover. Nouri Gana sees an element of prosopopoeia at work in the story (Gana 2005: 159–78). Paul de Man describes prosopopoeia as the 'trope of autobiography *par excellence*' (de Man 1984: 76) and there are autobiographical elements in the story. Stephen Spender reads all of Joyce's works as autobiography: '*The Portrait of the Artist as a Young Man* is the first volume of a great self-absorbed autobiographic work, which is treated objectively in *Ulysses*, and which, finally, in *Finnegans Wake* transcends itself and passes into the universal, disintegrating in the process'.[12] Kevin Whelan argues that 'the betrayal of Gabriel by Gretta [...] mirrors Joyce's own fear of betrayal by Nora' (Whelan 2002: 82). Prosopopoeia refers, then, to the personification of an abstract or absent thing. It is employed, de Man believes, in passages 'in which the dead speak'. Because it 'posits the possibility of the latter's reply and confers upon it [the dead] the power of speech', it harbours a 'latent threat'. It 'prefigures our own mortality' and our own 'actual entry into the frozen world of the dead', since 'by making the death speak, the symmetrical structure of the trope implies, by the same token that the living are struck dumb, frozen in their own death' (de Man 1984: 78). Even though de Man's reading of trope relies upon a distinct post-structuralist leaning, it gives a persuasive thematization of death in the story. Why is Joyce so eager in this story to make 'the death' speak? As there is no clear personification of Furey, he can be taken to symbolize a 'vibrant, passionate life which has vanished' (Whelan 2002: 70), as Whelan suggests, or he can be taken as symbolizing the communicative dead end that reported speech always prefigures for Joyce. For Joyce and Proust, the 'real voyage of discovery' is a voyage inwards, and Joyce requires a new narrative form for mediating self-communication before he can stave off this dead end. Michael Furey haunts the story, prefiguring the 'mortality' of Gabriel and all the reader sees through him. Nouri Gana argues that characters, lured by prosopopoeia's 'promise of reuniting' with the dead 'fall prey to the pretension of the trope to cure, and are thus victimized by its fundamental impotence' (Gana 2005: 160).

Gabriel and Gretta are literally 'struck dumb, frozen in their own death' through their encounter with death. Gabriel has been unconscious of how he has seen death everywhere. In realizing that it is better to 'pass boldly into that other world, in the full glory of some passion, than fade and wither dismally with age', Gabriel is impotent when it comes to finding a locus for this 'passion'. The passion he works himself into for his wife is 'ludicrous' 'lust' and the passion he works himself into for his speech has only found him 'orating to vulgarians and idealising his own clownish lusts' (*D* 221). Joyce also realizes the short story's limitations for housing his writerly 'passion' as he passes 'boldly into that other world' of interior monologue and stream of consciousness narration. Gabriel and Gretta are denied the communicative outlet these forms allow despite Gabriel's literary pretensions. Confronted by the memory of Furey, who gave his life for love, and by the ludicrousness of his own monologues on love, Gabriel learns that intimacy is bound up with misunderstanding. But whereas Joyce will strive to shape the forms of that 'other world' in narrative experimentation, Gabriel's frustrated energies leave him suffering the same fate as the outmoded artistic forms he applies to his surroundings. Gretta has died to Gabriel and Gabriel feels himself fading into a 'grey impalpable world' (*D* 225). At the end of their day, Gretta and Gabriel lie beside each other in bed, prefiguring the last moments of Molly and Bloom, yet their crisis seems greater. While there has been no 'betrayal', their identities, that fade before their story can, appear incapable of embodying the invasive yet rejuvenating 'passion' of the interiorized, monologic 'form' that gives Bloom and Molly such consolation and such seemingly immortal durability.

Gabriel's misreading of his wife's symbolic behaviour is described in terms of stellar explosions: '[m]oments of their secret life together burst like stars upon his memory. A heliotrope envelope was lying beside his breakfast-cup and he was caressing it with his hand' (*D* 214). Richard Ellmann reads Gabriel's recalling of instances from his love's history – the stars bursting upon his memory – as ironic because the 'sharp and beautiful experience was, though he has not known until this night, incomplete' (Ellmann 1972: 261). The correlation of the use of trope (in this case the metaphor of stars for memories) and a notion of incompleteness recalls the gnomon motif from 'The Sisters'.

It has led many readers to regard the stories as puzzles that must have some missing part restored to the 'incomplete' presentation of revelation by the reader. Jacques Derrida has extended this parallel between planetary motion and trope. He argues that metaphor 'means heliotrope, both a movement turned toward the sun, and the turning movement of the sun' (Derrida 1982: 251). For Derrida, the sun is the sensible signifier *par excellence* and, therefore, also metaphor itself. Derrida regards phrases such as the sun is 'the brightest star that moves about the earth' (ibid. 250) as possessive of an element of incomprehensibility because when the sun sets we must go on past experiences: 'Heliotropic metaphors are always imperfect metaphors. They give us too little knowledge because one of the terms directly or indirectly implied in the substitution (the sensible sun) cannot be properly known' (250). Joyce prefigures such linguistic speculations.[13] In these sections from 'The Dead', Gabriel is caught in a moment of uncertainty as he asks himself what Gretta symbolizes; there is some aspect of the comparison that he has 'too little knowledge of' at the time. Through his attention to symbolism he is blind to the subject's inability to be contained by figure, a resistance that makes the imperfection of metaphor so enthralling. Gabriel is unwilling to invoke metaphor. This would require an admission that 'one of the terms' implied in his substitution (Gretta) 'cannot be properly known'. As we learn later, Gretta is not 'properly known' by Gabriel. Gretta can only ever be a symbol for their imperfect planetary orbit about each other, and for their infinite potential for misunderstanding each other. His realization that his sense of language is limited is paralleled by Joyce's realization that the symbolization he has assigned to intersubjectivity, through his Thomistic understanding of the artwork, is also limited.

Gabriel's misreading of Gretta and his flirtation with symbolism almost leads him to violence: 'If she would only turn to him or come to him of her own accord! To take her as she was would be brutal. No, he must see some ardour in her eyes first. He longed to be master of her strange mood' (*D* 218). All the components of an evening that had led Gabriel to imagine that his love must be symbolized in some way are now merely variegated aspects of death. Gabriel remembers the 'haggard look' upon Aunt Julia's face and imagines 'sitting in that same drawing-room, dressed in black' (*D* 224) at her funeral. Even the language that describes his final moments begins to 'fade and wither' (*D* 224). His soul swoons, or faints, slowly as he looks at the snow 'falling faintly' and as he senses the descent of the 'last end' of 'all the living and the dead' also 'faintly falling' (*D* 225). As sleep approaches, he falls faintly to his own 'last end', leaving language itself as a pale, repetitive image of itself. Joyce's movement away from reported speech and dialogue towards stream of consciousness narration and interior monologue will enable him to assert control over the representation of intersubjective communication, a control that may have eluded him in the short story form. In 'The Dead' Joyce asks the epiphany to kill itself off; all epiphanies in the story are either based on misunderstandings or on images of death that finally reduce everything to 'a grey impalpable world' (*D* 225). The presentation of a seemingly unmediated transformation between word and sense that transforms passion into a manifestation that can be shared is denied the Conroys due to the restrictions of naturalistic dialogue.

Molly and Bloom are less capable of such misunderstandings even though they share only one conversation. Bound to each other in the one flesh of wedlock their moment of greatest sundering occurs just after four in their day. They do not ask themselves what they symbolize for each other. Instead, they are painfully aware of the fleshy, corporeal moments of each other; at times each bodily experience is charged with the memory and sense of the other. The streams of consciousness that reveal their thought patterns to the reader give them over repeatedly to each other; their respective corporeities within are capable of unions across space because the idiosyncrasies of their corporeities without have become consubstantial with their own flesh. We recall that in a letter to Nora, Joyce describes them as possessing 'one flesh' (quoted in Maddox 1988: 169). Bloom also traces so much of what he experiences through his body back to Molly: 'Tiresome shapers scraping fiddles [...] sawing the 'cello, remind you of toothache. Her high long snore' (*U* 349). Their incarnations for each other, evident in their intermingling narrative threads, privilege the 'passage from the corporeal sensible to the conscious lived sense' (Depraz 1995: 275) that Natalie Depraz finds in Husserlian intersubjectivity. Their intersubjectivity is also accepting of alterity, but of an alterity found *within* through the painful and rigorous self-communion their day brings.

In 'Sirens' Bloom's first-person streams of consciousness give way to a consistently truncated and forgetful third-person narrator's voice that describes the same instances repeatedly during the coupling of Molly and Blazes. In these painful moments for Bloom, the reader feels that her access to Bloom's thoughts is being curtailed; their recording assumes the voice of a distracted narrator who struggles to prevent himself aimlessly following where his thoughts lead him. Bloom's attempts to monitor and curtail his thoughts merge with the narrator's voice: 'Bloom ate live as said before. Clean here at least' (*U* 349). And earlier: 'By Bachelor's walk jogjaunty jingled Blazes Boylan, bachelor, in sun, in heat, mare's glossy rump atrot [...] on bounding tyres: sprawled, warmseated, Boylan impatience, ardentbold. Horn' (*U* 347). Bloom could only see Boylan's journey to Eccles Street in his mind's eye as he sits eating in the Ormond, and yet the description is laden with contracted double meanings that prefigure the later coupling with the 'warmseated' 'glossy rump' of 'sprawled' Molly. Like Bloom and his dinner partner Goulding, Molly and Bloom are 'married in silence' (*U* 347). However, the words and music and the 'whats's behind' (*U* 354) of Simon Dedalus's rendition of 'All is lost now' offer Bloom some respite – 'they listened feeling that flow endearing flow over skin limbs human heart soul spine' (*U* 352) – the sensations sending them into fond reveries: 'touching their still ears with words, still hearts of their each his remembered lives' (*U* 353).

Bloom and Molly share a 'kind of language' across the space between them. The words and music of their lives together are remembered through the medium of music, sending Bloom into ineffable states of auto-affection, where all sensations and mysteries work to coalesce: 'skin limbs human heart soul spine'. Transported to a state of '[t]enderness' the words and music of Molly's and Boylan's lovemaking meld with the transfixing word-sensations Bloom receives from the music: 'Tenderness it welled: slow, swelling. Full it throbbed [...] Throb, a throb, a pulsing proud erect' (*U* 354). Yet interspersed with these descriptions Bloom realizes that what is important is not the words and the music of their lives together, but 'what's behind' (*U* 354). Transported, once again, by the music, the harmonics of their interiorized climaxes (Bloom with himself, or possibly with Molly across space, and Molly with Boylan) merge as one great expression of love for Bloom. It is Bloom's ability to believe in love and not '[f]orce, hatred, history, all that. That's not life for men and women' (*U* 432) that enables him to sense the 'language of love' through the sensations and reveries the music instils, to give in to the 'passage from the corporeal sensible to the conscious lived sense' that consistently leaves him with a '*ray of hope*':

Bloom. Flood of warm jimjam lickitup secretness flowed to flow in music out, in desire, dark to lick flow, invading. Tipping her tepping her tapping her topping her. [...] Tup. The joy the feel the warm the. [...] Flood, gush, flow, joygush, tupthrop. Now! Language of love. – ... *ray of hope* ... (*U* 354)

Such moments of contact and empathy across space through a state of self-alterity within that Molly sustains for him are possible for Bloom because of Joyce's move beyond epiphany to stream of consciousness narration. Later in the Joycean evolution, in *Finnegans Wake*, it is the reader who will be asked to fill Bloom's shoes.

Incarnating Shem the Penman

Due to its density, obscurity and impenetrability, *Finnegans Wake* remains a text that criticism appears more willing to dissect empirically, than investigate thematically. It remains impervious to the customary reading approaches devised by post-structuralism and deconstruction because there are no normative elements against which deconstruction can claim to decipher lacunae that then turn these normative elements on their head. For John Bishop, '[i]mpossible as it may be to fathom [*Finnegans Wake*] as an obscure totality, even at the level of a page [...] particles of immanent sense will stand out from the foil against which they are set, in turn to suggest connections with others' (Bishop 1993: 27). The 'Shem the Penman' episode parodies various means of incarnating the word and even Joyce's longing to 'write himself into the body of the text' (Henke 1990: 1).

Shem the Penman's portrait, section 1.7, is a revealing section for beginning a reading of *Finnegans Wake*. It describes both a writer and the process of writing, and possesses autobiographical detail; indeed *Finnegans Wake* is the closest Joyce comes to autobiography. Joyce reiterates in this section his conception of language and writing as processes inextricably tied to articulations of the body, a parallel that he viscerally realized throughout his own writing career; eye operations very often dictated the pace of his writing[14] and he described the words of the *Wake* as coming like 'drops of blood' (Joyce 1957: 295).[15] In the Shem the Penman episode from the larger dreamscape of the book, Shem's identity is important. The section begins: 'Shem is as short for Shemus as Jem is joky for Jacob' (*FW* 169: 1). The name Shem is, therefore, somewhat interchangeable with Jem, and both are short for Shemus. Jem, of course, cannot be short for Shemus as it bears little resemblance to this longer name. Changing the longer name to Jemus gives us a name that perhaps Jem, and also we must remember Shem, might be short for. Jemus is quite close to Jesus, the figurehead of the Christian faith, and Jacob, the name that is also connected 'jokily' to Jem, and therefore Shem, is the father of the Israelites and a patriarch their Judaic faith. A note of authorial duplicity is sounded with the allusion to Jacob, a biblical figure and twin who came from the womb clutching the heel of his brother Esau. Jacob later persuaded his father Isaac that he was the firstborn.

With the figure of Shem, therefore, Joyce manages to reference both the figure of the universal writer, the 'penman', and two of Western religion's most important figureheads (who, for believers, straddle incarnation in their own unique way), thereby deftly encompassing writing's connection to the body and the traces of a religious intertext in his narrative. A genealogy of interpretation and a genealogy of the body are conjoined to offer an incarnated narrative that elicits how interpretation theory and theories of the body are inextricably tied to a system of tropes inherited from scriptural exegesis. Shem's portrait is the portrait of a complex persona, one that Joyce gradually unfolds, informing us that by '[p]utting truth and untruth together a shot may be made at what this hybrid actually was like' (*FW* 169: 8–10).

The opening section commences with a lengthy list of Shem's physical attributes: Shem has among other things 'a blind stomach', a 'deaf heart', 'a loose liver', and 'two fifths of two buttocks' (*FW* 169: 17–18). The synaesthetic quality suggested here by the universal writer's physical condition extends Joyce's cyclical and pansensual depiction of writing and language. One of the first important incidents of Shem's life is when he composes 'the first riddle' of the universe for all his 'brothron and sweestureens' (*FW* 170: 4). The riddle asks 'when is a man not a man', and seeing that Shem appears to embody, among others, both the universal writer, the man whose legacy extends beyond the life of a single man, and Christ, the incarnated man-God, it is a question that colours much of the section. We learn that Shem is a plagiarist and a 'low sham' (*FW* 170: 24). When we hear him described as 'an Irish emigrant the wrong way out' (*FW* 190: 36) and as a young teenager who is covetous of his 'neighbour's word' (*FW* 172: 29–30), Shem begins to take on the shape of the Joycean autobiographical self that we have found mediated through the young boy of 'The Sisters' and Stephen Dedalus. We come to realize that the narrator/dreamer of the text is addressing both subject and object of the writing process, both author and character.

Towards the end of the section, however, Joyce will tire of this literary device; he introduces a non-character named Justius who assumes both the persona of author speaking to his text and of God speaking to his somewhat petulant Son: 'Stand forth, Nayman of Noland (for no longer will I follow you obliquelike through the inspired form of the third person singular [...] but address myself to you' (*FW* 187: 28–31). At this point Joyce's third-person, narrated retelling of the life of a character made to represent, at the very least, two archetypes for mediating incarnation and embodied meaning, namely the incarnated Son of God and the figure of the universal author, is interrupted by a narrative voice that wishes to question both the artifice of this narrative mode and the artifice of these other belief systems. We are made to question the means through which a narrative, no matter how rigorous and corporeal its description of a character, works to sustain a sense of believability before it is disrupted by the introduction of a different narrative voice. Joyce, of course, is at the threshold of narrative here; he pre-empts any move to draw analogies between his text and another narrative or belief system. He is not content to allow his narrative to be an allegory or vehicle for another code of beliefs. All attempts to suggest that Joyce is here creating a character that stands in for Jesus, Jacob, the universal writer and Joyce himself are interrupted at this point. Joyce questions the notion of body that we seek to assign to his writing. He has progressed from seeing his work as 'an epic of the body' and has moved to a reconfiguration of the body in *Finnegans Wake.* Deleuze and Guattari argue in *Anti-Oedipus* that 'the question of a being superior to man and to nature does not arise' (Deleuze and Guattari 2004: 78) for the 'body without organs'. The 'body without organs' is a model of the body they elaborate in order to contest Freudian psychoanalysis's reduction of the body to an Oedipal body; the 'body without organs' repels the 'desiring-machines' that Deleuze believes bodies become under Freud. Freudian conceptions of the body have affected the family relationship that also lies at the heart of Christianity. The customary story of incarnation depicts the synthesis of 'Man-God' as a synthesis of 'negative disjunctions of the derived reality', a reality that must be based on some 'original reality of Man-God' (ibid. 77). Deleuze's 'body without organs' works instead to 'an inclusive disjunction that carries out the synthesis itself in drifting from one term to another and following the distance between terms' (77). As Deleuze suggests, it is more a question of 'usage' than of meaning for the 'body without organs'.

Joyce sets up something similar in the Shem the Penman section. The creation of a character in narrative who represents both the figure of the universal author, the Christ-figure and the figure of Jacob, must be in someway presented as self-creating. Its self-'usage' is an important aspect of its nature and it is no longer sufficient to describe this non-character's nature in a consistent stream of third-person narration. The irruption of the voice of an authorial and God-like figure into a narrative that we have already accepted as a dream, as a manifestation of the unconscious, works to reconfigure the relationship between creator and created, author and text, and reader and response. Before this interruption, we learn that Shem has written all over his body, and if Shem is already the word incarnate in its religious and authorial senses, then this act is representative of the Son, or the character of a narrative, dispossessing his creator, or Father, of His power only to claim it as his own. We learn that he

> [W]rote over every square inch of the only foolscap available, his own body, till by its corrosive sublimation one continuous present tense integuement slowly unfolded all [...] cyclewheeling history [...] reflecting from his own individual person life unlivable, transacci-dentated through the slow fires of consciousness into a dividual chaos [...] common to allflesh, human only, mortal) [...] This exists that isits after having been said we know. (*FW* 185–6: 34–9)

The narrative of Shem does not only seek to lay claim to the powers that have created it through the irruption of an authorial voice that speaks to the character, but Shem also seeks to 'corrosively' sublimate, or imbibe, the act of writing into his very person. Shem's writing on his body with his body that is already the word incarnate acts as a pastiche of creation. Shem's 'body without organs' becomes a pure body of writing enwrapped by 'one continuous present tense integuement' or skin, a body that reflects 'from his own individual person life unli-vable'. The body as writing is the body without organs that reflects both 'life unlivable', or life as customarily understood, and also life un*liva-belle*, or life not lived beside the Liffey, a daily life Joyce can now only write about and imagine. Even though the narrator/dreamer perceives this life as becoming a 'dividual [or divided] chaos' through conscious reflection, it is still a state 'common to allflesh', a state that necessitates the familiarity of the body. The final line offers an account of existence that connotes both existential and Cartesian proclamations; it writes of what 'exists' 'after having been said we know', or after having been mediated by speech and a will to knowledge. Joyce's punctuation and word order juxtaposes ontological theories that have come to rely more and more on rhetorical and 'literary' language.

The description of Shem's writing also assumes the qualities of a language of the body, an incarnated language, as Shem's description becomes more autobiographical for Joyce. We learn that Shem's 'growing megalomane' of a 'loose past' (*FW*179: 21) was spent 'making believe to read' his 'usylessly unreadable Blue Book of Eccles', or what sounds suspiciously like Joyce's *Ulysses*, a book that revolves around the Blooms' home at Eccles Street. Shem's memorizing of his words in a rare stage appearance also becomes a painful and curtailed affair, hindered by bodily limitations, and we recall that Joyce's work on *Ulysses* and *Finnegans Wake* was frequently hindered by physical ailments. Joyce writes to Ezra Pound in April 1917: 'If I am a bad reader I am a most tiresome writer – to myself, at least. It exhausts me before I end it' (Joyce 1957: 101). Shem's experience with the word is equally tiresome. Due to the

> [M]urky light, the botchy print, the tattered cover [...] the fumbling fingers, [...] the lieabed lice, the scum on his tongue, the drop in his eye, the lump in his throat, [...] the itch in his palm [...] the grief from his breath, [...], the tic of his conscience, [...] the gush down his fundament, the fire in his gorge [...] he was hardset to mumorise more than a word a week. (*FW* 180: 17–30)

What is noteworthy here is the subtle move from the textual hindrances, the 'botchy print' and the 'tattered cover', to the physical hindrances, such as the 'lump in his throat' and 'the wail of his wind'. The textual work is represented as an extension of the work of the body. We move from the print, the cover and the page, to the eye, throat and palm of the writer via the lice, fleas and scum that form some intermediary variety of life between the text and the body. We are not asked to regard the text and the body, the written word and the body, as radically different, or as resting on an interpretive style that privileges concepts of radical alterity, but instead as cyclically integrated into each other, intertwined by the base, yet thriving, forms of life that are nourished by our decay. Joyce even extends this reading of the body, and its autobiographical detail, to Shem's trials with the publishers: '[W]hen Robber and Mumsell [...] boycotted him of all [...] romeruled stationery' (*FW* 185: 1–5) he 'made synthetic ink and sensitive paper for his own end out of his wit's waste' (*FW* 185: 6–8). 'Robber and Mumsell' are Grant Roberts and Maunsel, the publishers under whom Joyce suffered so many grievances while trying to publish *Dubliners*. The pun on pulpit, pulp and pubic with the phrase 'pulpic dictators' further articulates Joyce's insult towards them. The publishers' 'legal advisers' are referred to as 'Codex and Podex', a phrase that once again emphasizes Joyce's correlation of body and text, codex being a type of manuscript and podex referring to the posterior. Joyce/Shem is then forced to make 'synthetic ink and sensitive paper' as an end in itself. His exacerbation extends beyond the popular idiom 'at wit's end', to the point where 'his wit's waste' must lead instead to further writing and creative endeavour. The limits that physical endurance possess for dealing with pain have forced Joyce to find his catharsis, or his 'kathartic ocean', in the creation of a writing of the body, of a writing that is both sensitive and an amalgam, or synthesis, of diverse physical features. Joyce is not content to regard himself as being at his wit's end; he must instead direct his energies into the creation of an artwork that can both absorb and create a symbiotic writing.

The final passages from this episode see the omniscient voice of 'Justius' addressing the figure of the universal writer, and, once again, drawing parallels between the writer and the God-Man, or Christ. The writer is 'excruciated' to the 'cross' of his 'cruelfiction!' (*FW* 192: 18–19). The figure of the universal writer, Shem the Penman, also invokes the spirit of a transformed Shakespearean intertext. Justius retorts: '[d]o you hear what I'm seeing hammet?' (*FW* 193: 10–11). He wants to know whether the penman will for the laugh of 'Scheekspair' help 'mine with the epithet?' (*FW* 191: 2). The name of Shem gradually morphs into the bard's greatest dramatic character: Shem the Penman becomes 'Pain the Shamman' (*FW* 192: 23) and Shamman becomes 'hammet' (*FW* 193: 11), a name very close to Hamnet, Shakespeare's son. Joyce's final artistically challenged character, one in whom all literary personas merge, even arrogates Hamlet to himself, possibly the most enduring character of his greatest literary rival. The same omniscient voice then assumes the name 'Mercius', and through this voice Shem becomes Cain, the son of Adam. Mercius, the Adamic father, the 'branded sheep' (*FW* 194: 13) before the 'windblasted tree of the knowledge' (*FW* 194: 14–15) gradually introduces the female voice of 'gossipaceous' Anna Livia, the subject of the washerwomen's gossip in the next section. Shem's authorial 'longsufferings of longstanding' (*FW* 184: 1), his plagiarist 'selfwilling celebesty' (*FW* 191: 17), shows up the cult of the writer, the ideology of writerly authority in Western literature, and religious discourse's strategy of confiscating the Word, for the treacherous discourses they are. All three must finally succumb to the gossip of some washerwomen.

The patriarchal voice of Western writing, its logocentric architectonics of deception and violence, must, time and again, give way to a matriarchal and feminine voice. Joyce spent his latter years attempting to comprehend the 'curious abbreviated language'[16] of his daughter Lucia, a language he feared Western medicines would cure: 'It is terrible to think of a vessel of election as the prey of impulses beyond its control and of natures beneath its comprehension and, fervently as I desire her cure, I ask myself what then will happen when and if she finally withdraws her regard from the lightning.'[17] Joyce may have sought to present the speech of such a feminine 'vessel of election' as a narrative of 'lightning' to counteract the dominant intertext of patriarchal writing with which much of his early work had struggled. The Shem the Penman episode marks a last attempt to wrestle with, and mould into one large narrative configuration, all the dominant voices of Western writing: Hamlet, Jesus, Jacob and Joyce. It informs the reader of the potential infidelities of such writing and restores the reader to the news of the 'great big world' (*FW* 194: 23–4) and the 'babbling, bubbling' (*FW* 195: 1–2) language of the washerwomen that Joyce directs to 'Flow now' (*FW* 206: 27).

Shaun carries his brother's message. His tireless efforts to deliver the letter he believes to be written by his brother ultimately become so embroiled in the detail of their various failed deliveries that the message becomes lost in the context. Shaun is the embodiment of the process of transmission. Even though Shaun's attachment to the message he carries might be regarded as binding him to the word as closely as Shem is bound to it, his denigration of Shem's 'penmarks' in favour of his own 'slanguage' results in his condemnation of all writing: 'Every dimmed letter in it is a copy [...] The lowquacity of him! [...] Thaw! The last word in stolentelling! [...]' (*FW* 424–5: 32–3). Thot, the god of writing, rendered here as 'Thaw', is credited with the 'last word in stolentelling'. Joyce is referencing the speech/writing dichotomy that lies at the heart of deconstruction and that also, once again, recalls Husserl's descriptions of indication and expression. Derrida's *The Post Card* credits Joyce with recognizing the importance and primordial nature of transmission:

In the beginning, in principle, was the post, and I will never get over it. But in the end I know it, I become aware of it as of our death sentence: it was composed, according to all possible codes and genres and languages, as a declaration of love. In the beginning the post, John will say, or Shaun or Tristan, and it began with a destination without address, the direction cannot be situated in the end. (Derrida 1987: 29)

And it is in recognizing the established nature of the transmission lying at the heart of philosophy, where to write is to leave oneself open eternally to interpretation and where to have spoken is to have saved oneself the 'distance' involved in writing, that Derrida comes closest to expressing a desire that is also found in Joyce:

> [D]istance myself *in order* to write to you. If now I am still sending you the same card, it is because I would be willing to die, to enclose myself finally in a single place that is a place, and bordered, a single word, a single name. The unique picture then would carry off my immobile, extended body, then slowly how you will have sent me away [...] [Derrida's emphasis] (Derrida 1987: 28)

However, Shaun is fearful of such a state when he is mindful of the prospect of him becoming a writer. He seems to want to avoid the 'distance', possibly the 'self-distance', that is required of one in order to become a writer. He is being cajoled and coaxed into writing by the voices of the public who flatter him so they can receive some written form of the message that he must deliver. They fancy that he is so 'strikingly brainy' and 'well lettered in yourshelves as ever were the Shamous Shamonous' (*FW* 425: 5–6). In being a carrier of the message, he is exempt from the responsibilities of writing. He is an embodiment of what phenomenology describes as the *phōne* or the living voice. He gives his reasons for not writing, seeing it merely as 'show', as he replies to their pleas that he take up the pen:

> [Y]ou can keep your space and by the power of blurry wards I am loyable to do it [...] it is an openear secret, [...] I'd pinsel it with immenuensoes as easy as I'd perorate a chickerow of beans [...], the authordux Book of Lief, would, if given to daylight, [...] far exceed what that bogus bolshy of a shame [...] is conversant with in audible black and prink. [...] Acomedy of letters! I have them all, tame, deep and harried, in my mine's I. (*FW* 425: 12–26)

The book Shaun would write, if he was so inclined, would be the 'Book of Lief'. He would refrain from the 'show' of Shem's writing in favour of a transcription of his 'mine's I' that would reveal something of 'his blood'. The 'mind's eye' has become 'my mine's I', suggesting a kind

of monologue that makes little distinction between solitary representation – the interiorization of the 'I' – and consciousness's capacity
to conceive of this representation as one with its sense of its self, and
with the possessions this sense of self is bound up with – 'my mine's'.
Joyce's comic depiction here of the opposition between writing –
'Acomedy of letters' – and speech and its 'opeanear secret[s]' will end
up collapsing in on itself, leading him to weave between the 'living
speech' of two washerwoman and the monologic, incarnated language
of ALP.

Chapter 3

Proust and the incarnation of language

The translation of Proust: metaphor's lost time[1]

The translation of Proust would be of the utmost importance to his
narrator who, it must be remembered, is careful to opt for Galland's
Arabian Nights over Mardrus's translation (Proust 2002d: 235). In
focusing, in this chapter, on the more 'inward-looking' sections of *À la
recherche*, and, in the next chapter, on Proust's understanding of 'sexual
inversion', it is important to note the changes translators have brought
to the Proustian equation. In 'Notes on Literature and Criticism' the
young Proust laments not using his distinct 'gift' for 'discovering
profound connections between two ideas or sensations' (Proust 1994a:
92). Some years later, in an essay entitled 'Contre l'Obscurité', Proust
again speaks of how a poet can rejuvenate 'un mot en le prenant dans
une vieille acception, il réveille entre deux images disjointes des harmonies oubliées' (Proust 1994b: 89). The bridging of the space
between objects and the memories they conjure motivates the metaphoric movement of Proust's aesthetic. The Proustian metaphor
strains the received limits of figurative analysis. The narrator of *À la
recherche*[2] consistently contemplates the proper course of tropological
movement, thereby parodying any interpretation of figure by the
reader or critic. The more the reader seeks to follow the course of the
rigorous delineation of metaphoric transformation (something Proust
frequently explains with the aid of metaphors) the more she further
extends the work of these metaphors she is reading.

The reader's analysis of metaphor becomes a metaphor for the work
this narrative voice is contemplating and unravelling. The Proustian
narrator laments our lack of introspective rigour, suggesting that 'we
find it too demanding a task to try to perceive the little furrow that the
sight of a hawthorn or a church has made in us' (Proust 2002f: 200).
We increase the distance between 'the personal root of our own
impression' (ibid. 199) and its stimulus in continuing to read the
Proustian narrator's efforts to bridge this distance for himself. In

reading the narrator's analysis of metaphor we come to enact Proust's metaphor, ever more ensnared by it the more we seek to localize it for analysis. As the Proustian narrator endlessly deliberates on the proper course of the aesthetic, and the metaphors it employs, so do we endlessly read between the lines of the narrator's metaphors for glimpses of Proust's aesthetic motivations.

Paul de Man's careful reading of Proust suggests that 'by generalising itself in its own allegory, the metaphor seems to have displaced its proper meaning' (de Man 1979: 72). However, even though the deliberations of Proust's narrator can be regarded as acting as an allegory for reading, to encompass reading in any specific trope disregards the extent to which reading influences and forms our understanding of tropes. Proust does not only seek to displace metaphor's 'proper meaning' or seek to invest 'in the allegorical narrative of its own deconstruction' as this can imply that there is a prescribed amount of semantic innovation that can be exploited, objectified, and removed from the practice of analysis. This section incorporates the alterations of the new translations into the work of Proust's metaphors and language. Each translation voices the contemporary state of the reception of language. Each new translation is marked not only by the creative strain of the individual translator but also by the wider institutional strain of the contemporary state of language. The new translations, therefore, bring our attention to what has been lost by language in the intervening time, or in other words, the new translations introduce another species of 'lost time' to the work of Proust.

The new translations of *À la recherche*, the first since criticism's assimilation of the rhetoric of post-structuralism and deconstruction, display important changes in both the reception of Proust and of figurative language. These new translations elicit how metaphor's work is never completed. Metaphors, 'the rhetorical equivalents of the Proustian real' (Beckett 1999: 88), bring us into contact with what Paul Ricoeur refers to as a 'surplus of meaning' (Ricoeur 1976: 45). Metaphor's unique figural mode works through its almost dialectical play with the method of its analysis. Distinct periods of literary criticism have assigned distinct forms to the workings of metaphor. Ricoeur has suggested that 'metaphor does not exist in itself but in and through an interpretation' (ibid. 50). In contrasting metaphor with symbol he tells us that symbol, for the literary critic, what Modernist writers such as Proust and Joyce began their writing careers as, 'refers to something like a vision of the world, or a desire to transform all language into literature' (54). The word 'vision' connotes the interpretive radiance or *claritas* of the early Joycean aesthetic and of Gabriel Conroy's artistic worldview. Proust's attention to harmonies of resemblance works to conjoin 'disjoined images'. As we have seen earlier in reading 'The Dead', metaphor is more difficult to unravel than symbol. The symbol is, as Umberto Eco informs us, 'the sudden apparition of something that disturbs the course of a previous narration' (Eco 1984: 161). The reader of *À la recherche* is rewarded by giving her attention to the 'critical' nature of the literary writings of Proust, thereby implicating Proust, as literary critic, in the analysis of his own metaphors.

In suggesting that the metaphor has a distinct artistic relevance and importance for Proust, I am only taking him at his word. In his preface to Morand's *Tendres Stocks*, appearing in the *Revue de Paris*, under the title 'For a Friend: Remarks on Style', the only direct remark Proust makes about Morand as a writer is critical of Morand's use of metaphor (Carter 2000: 737). Proust writes that Morand's metaphors always fall short, saying that a 'good metaphor must seem inevitable: water boils at 100 degrees centigrade; near misses do not count' (ibid. 909n). In his article 'On Flaubert's Style' we also hear that Flaubert's use of metaphors and analogies did not measure up to Proust's own standards for writers. William C. Carter writes of Proust's belief that 'metaphor alone can give a kind of eternity to style and there is perhaps not in all Flaubert a single beautiful metaphor' (ibid. 717). Proust informs us that Flaubert's 'entire theory of art' was based on the phenomenon of involuntary memory, a phenomenon that contributes to the presentation and form of Proust's foregrounding of metaphor.

Proust's narrator reveals the frequently neglected cause of figurative language. The narrator tells Charlus that churches are only symbols that have 'for a moment given fixed form to human truths' (quoted in Carter 2000: 665). Whereas the narrator can refer to the symbol as possessing a 'fixed form', the metaphor is consistently more elusive. The metaphor reveals, as Proust's narrator informs us in employing the distance between the Guermantes way and the Méséglise way to describe cognitive distances, 'those distances of the mind which not only moves things away from each other, but separates them and puts them on different planes' (Proust 2002a: 136). Given Proust's disbelief in any notion of 'the eternity of human works' (Carter 2000: 666), or in an 'originality of form' (ibid. 791), it is in the 'impression or idea to be translated' (qtd. in Carter 791) that his narrator's deliberations on art and writing find the essence of metaphor. His discussions of metaphor refer to an 'eternity of style' that also reveals essential 'human truths'.

Proust's intentions, through writing, become ever more closely aligned with a sense of living. The narrator's description of what he hopes his 'book' might achieve becomes embroiled in words which refer to the author in heliocentric terms and the book as a laboratory for handling 'life': 'Combien me le semblait-elle davantage, maintenant qu'elle me semblait pouvoir être éclaircie, elle qu'on vit dans les ténèbres, ramenée au vrai de ce qu'elle était, elle qu'on fausse sans cesse, en somme réalisée dans un livre!' (Proust 1999: 2389). Moncrieff's translation reads:

> How much more so it appeared to me now that I felt it possible to shed light on this life which we live in darkness and to bring back to its former true character this life which we distort unceasingly – in short, extract the real essence of life in a book. (Proust 1932b: 1112)

Patterson's translation begins: 'How much better *life* seemed to me now' [my emphasis] (Proust 2002f: 342). The narrator has just been deliberating at length on 'cette idée du *Temps*', the phrase which begins the paragraph this extract is taken from. As readers we can never be sure whether it is 'cette idée du *Temps*' or life that it has been decided is to be illuminated or clarified by the narrator from this point. The new title, *Finding Time Again*, however, might hint that it is 'cette idée du *Temps*' that is to be clarified, something that undoubtedly for Proust is inextricably intertwined with any examination of life. However, it is the explicit inclusion of the word 'life' in the new translation of this passage that denies the reader some of the mystery involved in reading the original French.

Is it an example of the new translations' intentions to 'clarify' the circuitous nature of Proust's style, of the Proustian metaphor? Proust always suggests that life will be extracted from the book so as to restore 'this life' to its 'former true character'. Reading, therefore, becomes a process in which the readers of Proust are given 'le moyen de lire en eux-mêmes' (Proust 1999: 2390): 'the means of reading in their own selves' (Proust 1932b: 1113). Readers read in their own selves and, in so doing, extract the 'former true character' of this life. The narrator asks the readers 'mais seulement de me dire si c'est bien cela, si les mots qu'ils lisent en eux-mêmes sont bien ceux que j'ai écrits' (Proust 1999: 2390). Again we have an important difference in the translation of this metaphor of reading for self-examination. Moncrieff translates: 'tell me if it is as I say, if the words they read in themselves are, indeed, the same as I have written' (Proust 1932b: 1113), whereas Patterson translates: 'tell me if it was *right*, if the words they were reading in themselves were really the ones I had written' [my emphasis] (Proust 2002f: 343). Patterson's depiction of the metaphor where readers find in the narrator's future project 'le moyen de lire en eux-mêmes' with the notion of 'right' taints the prospective reading with traces of a 'correct reading'. Moncrieff's 'tell me if it is as I say' instead opens out the prospective reading and enacts the very process the metaphor suggests for a reading of a work yet to be completed. Reading Moncrieff's translation we are more able to *read in ourselves* without wondering whether we are right or wrong. It allows, here, an individual response to Proust's words so that *similar* words, not necessarily the very same words (something intimated by Patterson's translation of this passage), can be found within ourselves for reading our own particular deliberations.

For Proust's narrator, a discrepancy would only arise, not through any fault of the narrator/writer-to-be, but because the 'reader's eyes would not be of the type which my book would "fit" for comfortably reading in one's own self' (Proust 1932b: 1113). It thus appears that a distinct congeniality, complicity of ideals, or perfect 'fit', must be presupposed for a reading of one's own self. The overarching metaphor is one between the author-to-be and the reader. One might suggest that the reader who replies 'Yes, it is as you say' most earnestly and with most conviction would be the author himself. Approaches to writing that emphasize reading's extraction of a 'former true character' of 'life' return us to the notion of the 'congenial reader', and to the guiding Proustian metaphor mapping the contemplative narrator onto the reader. The author's referencing of the intention of his novel comes ultimately to account for the reader in terms of his own self, and thus places the reader and the 'curious composites' of the indifferent 'this life' under the aegis of a burgeoning metaphor between reader and writer.

The self-reflexive reading of self and text in figurative language and specifically in metaphor has received much attention among contemporary moral theorists. Sabina Lovibond writes in *Ethical Formation* of a recent evolution and 'linguistic "turn"' (Lovibond 2002: xi) in virtue ethics. Lovibond describes one theoretical device virtue ethics can employ in this linguistic turn, namely the 'figure of the virtuous (or "practically wise") *person*, who represents a condition of ideal sensitivity to the claims exerted by different sorts of value' (ibid. 13). In like manner Proust's narrative strategy, where readers are given the 'means of reading in their own selves', and yet must 'fit' to the author's words, also employs the 'theoretical device' of the 'virtuous person', recalling the metaphor of the virtuous narrator/reader. The comparison of discursive strategies in Proust and recent ethical theory suggests that contemporary moral theories are learning to accept the therapeutic and introspective value of the transference involved in any reading of figurative language. It may also suggest that the 'practical reason approach to ethics' has evolved and taken cognisance of the patterns of response that allow us to understand one another, patterns which, in being distinctly 'uncodifiable' (ibid. 31), are customarily regarded as literary or figurative.

Lovibond tells us that the virtuous person has 'a *distinctive way of seeing* situations' [Lovibond's emphasis] and that 'this way of seeing is *objective* in that those who become party to it are thereby alerted to genuine features of the world'. This way of seeing does not depend on an individual's 'contingent interests' but is '*motivated*' by her 'grasp of the not merely instrumental value of those patterns of conduct' (ibid. 13). In other words, the realization that a way of seeing 'ethical for-mations' can motivate ethical action is an important consideration in the practical reason approach to ethics. While Lovibond writes that individuals can 'become party' to such a way of seeing, she does not elaborate on how this might occur. This is where Proust's metaphors are important. Proust's narrative takes us through metaphor after metaphor until we are finally told, near the end, that the writing that is to be done must act as 'le moyen de lire en eux-mêmes'; it must enable the reader to perceive that there might be a correspondence between the reading of all these metaphors (which as I have stated foreground the metaphor of reader as reader of herself) and the self-examination that has enabled her to unpack their intentions. If we do not translate this medium generously and if we do not allow for the separate spaces implied by the correspondence between self and book that gives us the metaphor of reading for self-examination we limit the particular 'way of seeing' that Lovibond tells us can motivate a rejuvenated practical reason approach to ethics. If we do not elaborate 'une de ces distances dans l'esprit qui ne font pas qu'eloigner, qui séparent et mettent dans un autre plan' (Proust 1999: 114) then we are less likely to perceive the conditions of possibility of that reading that must accept the difference between reading and self-examination in order to charge the metaphor of this difference's bridging with such emotion.

Proust's narrative presents the reader with a nostalgic traumatism, a 'sober reflection on the past, which may enable us to safeguard the future' (Proust 2002b: 395), and is therefore easily co-opted by ethical theorists. Cora Diamond argues that there is an 'excessive emphasis on

moral *vocabulary'* (quoted in Lovibond 2002: 34) in ethical theory.
Proust's narrator is very aware of this tendency; he questions the 'moral
duty imposed on me by the impressions I received from form' (Proust
2002a: 179). Diamond questions the relationship also:

> If we want to see what moral thinking is, we need to be able to look
> away from the case of 'moral propositions', and to free ourselves
> from the idea that goes easily with exclusive focus on that case, of
> sentences as about moral subject matter through the presence in
> them of moral words. (Lovibond 2002: 35)

Diamond is against the embrace of a 'moral vocabulary' in ethical
theory. Her argument acknowledges the need for a greater emphasis
on the 'thought experiment' in ethical theory, and a move away from
what Lovibond refers to as 'an undue emphasis on the business of
spelling things out' (ibid. 35). I have suggested here that the new
translations of Proust might do exactly that, they might 'spell out' the
formal and figurative motivations of Proust's narrator. Any use of
language must not shrink from the peculiar ability of such language to
be institutionally received as a 'vocabulary'. The very fact that certain
ethical discussions are being questioned due to their propensity for
harbouring 'moral vocabulary' might rather be suggestive of how
ethical theories share an affinity for figurative language. Proust's
emphasis on the continued contemplation of aesthetic invention and
reception rather than on any 'fixed form' of the artwork, or an 'originality of form', enables moral theories to realize that the presence of
'moral words' does not necessarily imply 'moral thinking'. The translation of Proust's understanding of signification works, therefore, to
influence other disciplines.

The new translations, through their alterations and omissions, both
extend the range of the Proustian narrative and the range of the critical analysis and reception of metaphor. No other writer has so
explicitly sought the representation of the loss of time, its regaining
(something still eluding the English title) of itself, and its revelation of
eternity. Gilles Deleuze's *Proust et les signes* divides the Proustian Time
into four *lignes* of time to which correspond four species of sign. His
analysis, coupled with the Proustian narrator's words that 'the writer's
task and duty are those of a translator' (Proust 2002f: 199), alerts the
reader to the distinct nature of the relationship between metaphor and
its analysis, between writing and translation. Deleuze further divides
the essential distinction in Proust between time lost and time regained:

C'est que le temps perdu n'est pas seulement le temps qui passe, altérant les êtres et anéantissant ce qui fut; c'est aussi le temps qu'on perd (pourquoi faut-il perdre son temps, être amoureux, plutôt que de travailler et de faire œuvre d'art?). Et le temps retrouvé, c'est d'abord un temps qu'on retrouve au sein du temps perdu, et qui donne une image de l'éternité; mais c'est aussi un temps originel absolu, véritable éternité qui s'affirme dans l'art. (Deleuze 1976: 26)[3]

The English translation of Proust has been losing time. The new translations give the most dedicated annotator of metaphor another chance to be reinvented in English. It is possible to align Deleuze's *lignes* of time with the original Proust manuscript and its translations. The original French manuscript, what English readers must imagine as the essence of the Proustian odyssey, acts as a time that one regains through a reading of the new translations. The translation of Proust and the four narrative times, each closely aligned with a species of sign, reveals yet another time; the time that translation elicits as having been lost. The changes any new translation of Proust both produces and requires for its coming to be, are changes already predicted by the narrator. Since the narrator is consistently prospecting a book that has yet to be written, a book that relies upon the metaphoric understanding delineated in the narrative, any changes to the wording and sense of these deliberations on metaphor and the aesthetic also alters the artwork that the reader regards the narrative as working towards. The four time schemas cited by Deleuze all work within the time of language and the sign in general, within the time that translation will elicit (through its re-presentation of these four times) as having passed. Only the translations, the re-presentations of the Proustian narrator's deliberations on time and language, will elicit, through their omissions and alterations, the inter-textual and institutional time that has passed and that ultimately assigns the space for translation.

Lydia Davis's *The Way By Swann's* presents us with a new reading of Proustian memory, one that at least on one occasion translates memory as inherently violent. The broad metaphor that gives us the personification of memory through its capacities for sensual living, its taste and smell, is fleshed out with a simile. The narrator likens smell and taste to souls wishing on the death of all material objects. He presents us with what is, for Davis, a violent description of memory, one that is reliant on the 'impalpable droplet' that contains the vast 'edifice of memory':

But when nothing subsists of an old past, after the death of people, after the destruction of things, alone, frailer but more enduring, more immaterial, more persistent, more faithful, smell and taste still remain for a long time, like souls, remembering, waiting, hoping, on the ruin of all the rest, bearing without giving way, on their almost impalpable droplet, the immense edifice of memory. (Proust 2002a: 49-50)[4]

Scott Moncrieff's original translation gives the reader a very different account of memory in this section. Memory is for him not regarded as a destructive force. '[L]'edifice immense du souvenir' is translated as 'the vast structure of recollection', and the souls are *'waiting and hoping for their moment'* [my emphasis]' rather than hoping for the destruction, or 'ruin', of 'all the rest'. Moncrieff also speaks of the metaphor of souls for smell and taste as possessing an 'essence', a word Davis has removed (Proust 1932a: 36). Terence Kilmartin's 'revision' of Moncrieff's edition, working from the 1954 Pléiade edition, also keeps the word 'essence' here and it does not present the souls of smell and taste as waiting or hoping on the 'ruin of all the rest' either.[5] The changes here are representative of distinct changes to the nature of metaphor and, therefore, memory in the new translation. Moncrieff's original translation reads:

But when from a long-distant past nothing subsists, after the people are dead, after the things are broken and scattered, still alone, more fragile, but with more vitality, more unsubstantial, more persistent, more faithful, the smell and taste of things remain poised a long time, like souls ready to remind us, waiting and hoping for their moment, amid the ruins of all the rest; and bear unfaltering, in the tiny and almost impalpable drop of their essence, the vast structure of recollection. (Proust 1932a: 36)

The new translation's refusal to speak of 'essence', and its presentation of a harmful and vengeful motivating memory, may then elicit language's assimilation of a post-structuralist negative epistemology in recent decades. Paul de Man, as I have suggested, reads the novel as the 'allegorical narrative of its own deconstruction' (de Man 1976: 72). Gilles Deleuze's *Proust et les signes* also assigns a necessary violence to the signs of Proust and in 'Violence and Metaphysics' Derrida argues that there is no phrase which 'does not pass through the violence of the concept' (Derrida 2002a: 185). Deleuze argues that Proust opposes 'la double de "contrainte" et de "hasard" ' to 'l'idée philosophique de "méthode" ' (Deleuze 1976: 25). Deleuze goes on to state that Proust must do this because 'la vérité n'est jamais le produit d'une bonne volonté préalable, mais le résultat d'une violence dans la pensée' (ibid. 24). The new translations may unconsciously mediate post-structuralism's ascription of a necessary violence to the sign, what is ultimately carried over, therefore, into Marcel's aesthetic deliberations.

The new translation of the final volume, *Finding Time Again*, also has some curious omissions and alterations. In a late section the narrator informs us that 'truth will begin only when the writer' employs a distinct notion of semantic transformation. The rumination on metaphor's connection with truth is followed only in the Moncrieff translation by an important commentary on literature:

> The literature that is satisfied merely to 'describe things', to furnish a miserable listing of their lines and surfaces, is, notwithstanding its pretensions to realism, the farthest removed from reality, the one that most impoverishes and saddens us, even though it speak of nought but glory and greatness, for it sharply cuts off all communication of our present self with the past, the essence of which the objects preserve, and with the future, in which they stimulate us to enjoy the past again. (Proust 1932b: 1009)

This section does not appear in the new translation or in Jean-Yves Tadié's revised French edition. It is an interesting omission as it is a passage voicing the implications for literature of a figurative style not merely content to 'describe things'. The narrator's deliberation on metaphor in this passage is altered in the new translation by the omission of this section. The motivations for employing metaphor are more pronounced in this section in the Moncrieff translation through the retention of this critical commentary on 'literature' that merely 'describe[s] things'. Marcel's critical understanding of writing and literature is clearly revealed here. The omission is made particularly ironic by the fact that Marcel admits at the end of this section that 'the writer's task and duty are those of a translator'.

Another section from the new translation of *Le Temps retrouvé*, Ian Patterson's *Finding Time Again*, presents us with the narrator deliberating, once again, on the proper course for the writer. The writer must create a link between 'sensations' and the 'memories which surround us simultaneously' (Proust 2002f: 197).[6] Patterson translates: 'a unique relationship which the writer has to rediscover in order to bring its two

different terms together permanently in his sentence' (ibid. 198).[7] The
French verb *enchainer*, translated in Moncrieff as 'link together',
appears here as 'bring together', and the dominating verb *retrouver*, for
Moncrieff 'recapture' (Proust 1932b: 1008), is translated as 'rediscover'
by Patterson. These changes are symptomatic of an effort to present
the narrator's deliberations on form in as concise a manner as possible
and to remove Moncrieff's figurative embellishments. However, the
translations frequently favour clarity over charm, empiricism over aes-
theticism. Marcel argues that the 'sensations' and 'memories which
surround us simultaneously' must be enclosed in a special relationship:
'enclose[d] ... in the necessary rings of a beautiful style' ['et les
enfermera dans les anneux nécessaires d'un beau style'] (Proust
1932b: 1008–9). Patterson translates this important directive for the
writer, Proust's translator, as one where the writer 'encloses them
within the necessary *armature* of a beautiful style' [my emphasis]
(Proust 2002f: 198). Might this, once again, be suggestive of an
assimilation of a post-structuralist rhetoric inaugurating a violence of
the sign and of the aesthetic in the work of the translator? The shaping
of Proust's text according to the demands and implications of a critical
discourse still under the aegis of post-structuralism's negative epistemology often reveals a questionable sharpness and mechanicity in the
new translation.

The Proustian metaphor's resistance to codifiable translation works
to foreground Proust's own motivations for writing and for the elaboration of his guiding metaphor of reading for self-awareness. Post-
structuralism's privileging of misreading and difference cannot ultimately guide the task of the translator who must read so closely as to
offer other readers some core elements of an artwork. If translation has
suffered at the hands of post-structuralist theory then ethical theory's
newfound affinity for 'ethical formations' and for an attention to forms
of language that are considered to enhance ethical discussion is
important. It affords literary criticism the opportunity for rediscovering
that capacity where it can 'réveille entre deux images disjointes des
harmonies oubliées' (Proust 1994b: 89) and in doing so foster a new
interdisciplinarity with ethical theory. The new translations reveal how
metaphor's work is never done. As 'the rhetorical equivalents of the
real' (Beckett 1999: 88), Proust's freshly translated metaphors effort-
lessly exhibit the century's critical and literary evolutions; they act as
the rings on language's bough. Each successive translation must present a text that is symbiotic with its time, thereby voicing the 'lost times'
of language's evolution. The narrator informs us at the conclusion of

Du Côté de Chez Swann of 'la contradiction que c'est de chercher dans la réalité les tableaux de la mémoire' ['what a contradiction it is to search in reality for memory's pictures' (Proust 2002a: 430)] (Proust 1999: 342) as '[l]es lieux que nous avons connus n'appartiennent pas qu'au monde de l'espace où nous les situons pour plus de facilité'.[8] Memories assume their distinct quality by being incorporated into our person, by being incarnated. The 'lost time' that I have read the new translations as both revealing and contributing to Proustian time is similar to the memory, or seemingly lost sense, we had of Proust prior to reading these new translations. The memories we had of Proust prior to reading these translations can similarly never be found in the 'reality' of these new works. Once again we must learn to read like the Proustian narrator, reading the new translations not as the ideal of the Proustian 'reality' but rather as 'une mince tranche au milieu d'impressions contiguës' (Proust 1999: 342). We must learn to see that 'le souvenir d'une certaine image' of Proust is 'le regret d'un certain instant', for that moment fleeting, 'hélas, comme les années', when we felt we had recaptured ourselves in being captured by *À la recherche du temps perdu*.

Intersubjectivity, memory and incarnation

How, then, does Proust's use of metaphor and his understanding of the artwork interiorize the theme of incarnation that Julia Kristeva argues is so important for him? As we have seen, Kristeva believes that the figure of the incarnation gives modernist writers 'the motivation without precedent for an artistic expansion'; for Proust it is 'the figure for the indissociable, interconfessional passion of the felt and the feeling, of the Word and the flesh. The intermediary between the two – a state of grace – becomes a possible space. It is this time-space of faith as imaginary experience and, inversely, the experience of the imaginary as an imperative reality' that attracts these writers to these religious figures (Kristeva 1984: 545). Proust, we recall, also conceived of the work of the artist in terms of an incarnation. A letter to Lucien Daudet from November 1913 describes a manner of writing 'where the supreme miracle, the transubstantiation of the irrational qualities of matter and life into human words, is accomplished' (ibid. 374–5). The narrator's sense of suffering and sacrifice, whether for his art, or in regard to what must be relinquished for the prospected marriage to Albertine, is regularly regarded as an 'oblation', or Eucharistic process that commemorates the notion of a Living Presence (Proust 2002d: 520).

In possibly the most revealing section on literature from *Finding Time Again*, Proust describes the precise nature of these 'irrational qualities of matter and life' in terms of the 'inner book of unknown signs' (Proust 2002f: 187). It is the transubstantiation of these into human words, into writing, that the narrator is wholly concerned with as he strives to become a writer in departing from the 'infertile' 'failed life' (ibid. 212) he believes he has inhabited for so long. The Proustian understanding of representation is governed by memory and metaphor. For Proust, 'a representation, such as a seascape by Elstir, will always be a *metamorphosis*: not simply a name, but because of the means whereby one name is substituted for another, an *incarnated* metaphor' (Kristeva 1984: 376). The incarnated metaphor and the transubstantiation that the narrator only contemplates, is, of course, in itself, the accomplishment of this transubstantiation and of the incarnated metaphor for the reader. The presentation of the criticism of art, literature and artistic motivation coalesces with the elaboration of the proper course for writing, in this section added between 1909 and 1912, to ensure the section has a special relevance for Proust criticism. It was originally entitled, *L'Adoration perpétuelle* (an early version of the Princesse de Guermantes's last matinée), and George Painter reminds us of how the 'title draws a parallel between the Catholic rite of perpetual adoration of the Real Presence in the Blessed Sacrament and the Narrator's discovery of the undying truth of Time Regained' (Painter 1983: 559). The paralleling of 'Real Presence' and perpetual adoration with the writer's revealing of the mysteries of Time Regained takes up the themes of ascetic practice and transubstantiation between flesh and word that, as we have seen, Jacques Rancière also regards as central to Proust's understanding of language.

Since the narrator criticizes those who wish to make of the novel a 'cinematographic stream of things' (Proust 2002f: 191), what might very well describe an aspect of Joycean style, and while Proust has privileged, like Joyce, the aspect of transubstantiation implicit in writing, it is worthwhile plotting the course of the narrator's spiritual evolution towards writing in this section. The narrator first advises that sensations felt within, that spark ecstatic moments of involuntary memory leading to an intention to isolate 'time in its pure state' (ibid. 180) (what is elsewhere referred to as 'Lost Time' (185)) must be interpreted while their accompanying feeling is converted into a 'spiritual equivalent' (187). However, there are more important signs and these are found in the 'inner book of unknown signs' (187). There are no rules for interpreting these signs. It is for each individual to interpret them and to trace 'the impression' that 'ideas that may have been left in us by our life' have made on us (188). In a sense, then, we are mediators of a book of signs that Nature, 'or real life', has written inside us and only meticulous self-scrutiny can reveal its state so that readers 'might subsequently draw nourishment from it' (208). In fact, the narrator goes so far as to state that because 'art exactly reconstructs life', (206) '[r]eal life' in its 'uncovered and clarified' state, 'the only life in consequence lived to the full', is 'literature' (204). And yet, the kind of experience that the narrator perpetuates, or describes as ecstatic, and that enables him to discover the truths that will lead him to an artistic creation, and that are now, in his contemplative stop-gap, only providing him with an extended meditation on how art can reveal 'real life', are always found by obliterating what others might perceive as 'real life'. In the desperate attempt to tap further into the moment that will reveal ever greater truths about isolating 'time in its pure state', the narrator, in one moment of involuntary epiphany, at the risk of making himself 'the laughing-stock of the huge crowd of chauffeurs', continues to stagger rather unnaturally, repeating the 'outward form of this movement' (175), thereby cutting himself off from the natural course of 'real life'. The narrator grows more fond of his attempts to distort 'real life' so that the inner experience, the inner recapturing of the involuntary memory and all it reveals, can be clung to for a little longer.

However, any suggestion that the narrator might be striving to elaborate the 'real life' that lies within at the expense of the 'real life' that surrounds him and that presents him with moments that spark these 'resurrections' cannot, of course, be directed at Proust. Proust is merely setting up the 'miracle of analogy' (180). He presents us with a narrator who is striving to privilege the transubstantiation between these two moments and impressions. Proust's elaboration of the space between the times of different selves can be regarded as his means of catering for intersubjectivity in his sprawling, single-voiced narrative. Natalie Depraz describes the work of memory, according to her phenomenological notion of incarnation, as a movement whereby 'the other is present in the experience of remembering, under the figure of a self, different to my present self, devoted to past, living experiences, in other words, as "the alterity of myself to itself"' (Depraz 1995: 204). For Depraz, in Husserl's later comprehension of temporality, 'the accent is here put, not on the self as a pole of unification of flux, but on the temporal flux within which the self is situated' (ibid. 209) This also describes the narrator's struggles, while staggering, to come to terms with the 'enormous difference between the two impressions' (Proust 2002f: 177) when 'we try by an act of will to represent it to ourselves' (ibid. 177), a struggle that also involves the selves and times of remembering of the reader. Our reading is subservient to the miracle of analogy that Proust's narrator contemplates for his own life. Another phase of real life, the reader's 'nourishment' in this book, is therefore all the time drawn into the 'book of unknown signs' that the narrator strives to recognize and advises us to recognize in our own lives.

The narrator is concerned with the 'being' (179) within and with the 'essence of things' (Proust 2002f: 181). Despite the fact that the narrator recognizes that 'between the memory which suddenly comes back to us and our current state' (ibid. 178) the distance is enough 'to render them incomprehensible to each other' (178), the important thing is that the 'being' within, revived by the momentary 'resurrections' (183) and the resulting 'moments of identity between the past and the present' is able 'to find itself in the only milieu in which it could live and enjoy the essence of things, that is to say outside of time' (179). It must also be remembered that it is partially the remoteness of the original impression, the fact that 'it has kept its distance' (178) for so long, that lends such intoxication to the moment of recapitulation when there is an 'impression' that something is shared (179). This intoxication generated by the remote object also applies, for the narrator, to people: once a 'human body' is loved and something comes to 'alter the position of that soul in relation to us [...] we feel that the cherished creature was a not a few feet away, but inside us', as in the case of Albertine (Proust 2002d: 519).

The contemplation of these moments also reveals how the narrator connects this 'being' with 'action'. We are told that this being only manifests itself to the narrator 'outside of action and immediate pleasure, when the miracle of an analogy had made me escape from the present' (Proust 2002f: 180) and later, that we are powerless 'to realize ourselves in material pleasure or real action' (ibid. 186). So, as with the Joycean epiphany, where the moment of contact with a 'previously unrealised disposition' is experienced through the contact with an object only to be later recorded by the 'man of letters', these 'resurrections' that privilege an inner being's self-realization through the movement beyond action and time in the apprehension of 'a little bit of time in its pure state' (180) are to be interpreted as 'the signs of so many laws and ideas' (187). The narrator refers to this 'method' as the 'making of a work of art' (187). The implication is, then, that the future act of creating the 'work of art' through the interpretation of these signs, or 'of those truths written with the aid of figures' (187), will transubstantiate, or be the realization of, these truths for the reader. However, since the reader is only presented with the motivations for what is always represented as an act-to-come and therefore only the formulation for an unrealized artwork, she always has the impression that she is caught up in, and is contributing to, its realization.

Even though the narrator denigrates action, his commitment to procrastination and to the description of what incites him to work – 'I had a considerable appetite for living now that a real moment of the past had just, on three separate occasions, been recreated within me' (180) – sets up a circuitry between the reader and the artwork that is presented as a preparation for writing a 'work of art'; the reader is caught off guard and is confronted with the 'dizzying uncertainty' (183) of locating the boundary between the two impressions of the artwork that are set up within her – one prospected by the narrator and the other detailing the narrator's ambitions. The narrator's emphasis on the renunciation of 'real life' action in the charting of the inner being is transferred to the reader, who is called upon to invest in a careful analysis of her own impressions in order to disentangle the 'real life' actions of Proust, the writer of *À la recherche*, from the kind of 'action' the narrator denigrates. Proust further unsettles any clearly demarcated boundary between narrative time and real time by employing the reader's position as a figure for emotions felt by the narrator: the narrator's unhappiness is described as 'like that which we get from reading a novel' (Proust 2002d: 518) and his desire to get beyond his grief over Albertine, so as to 'attain to that real world', depends on his having no more regard for the feelings she raises than a reader would have for the 'imaginary heroine of a novel after we have finished reading it' (ibid. 518). The 'time-space of faith as imaginary experience' that Kristeva argues is mediated for Proust through the figure of incarnation, encompasses the reader, as the reader is made to invest part of themselves in the work, the reading of which is bound up with the artwork whose preparation *À la recherche* also documents.

This purported incarnation of the 'real life' of the reader in the words of the narrator who denigrates real life for the contemplation of the inner being, where even words themselves 'sometimes get in the way' (Proust 2002f: 194), is reflected in the manner in which the narrator describes reading. The static contemplation of the 'pure instant of time' outside time that the narrator wills upon himself, influences his understanding of reading. We are reminded that the writer must discover the relationship between 'sensations and the memories which surround us' (ibid. 197) in order 'to bring its two different terms together permanently in his sentence' (198). However, this union, or incarnation, that is bound up with metaphor for the narrator, where the writer brings together a quality shared by two sensations, must draw out 'their common essence by uniting them with each other, in order to protect them from the contingencies of time' (198). In other words, the notion that action must be exempt from the contemplation of the inner being is transferred, presumably by the 'miracle of analogy', to the work of the writer and ultimately to the work of reading. The notion that a metaphor might serve to exempt the sign from 'the contingencies of time' would be unacceptable to most modern theories of reading.

Marcel also regards reading as revealing another secret self that also appears to be exempt from the 'contingencies of time'. When the narrator is in the Guermantes library for the last time, he spots an edition of George Sand's *François le Champi* and he recalls the night when his mother read the book to him as a child 'until it was almost morning' (192). The narrator is upset in his train of thought by a 'stranger' who is no other than the child within:

> [I]f in the library I take down *François le Champi*, a child immediately rises up within me and takes my place, the only one who has the right to read the title *François le Champi* and who reads it as he read it then, with the same impression of the weather outside in the garden, the same dreams as he formed then about other countries and about life, the same anxiety about the future. Or again, if I see a thing from another time, it will be a young man who rises up. So that my character today is nothing but an abandoned quarry, thinking everything it contains to be monotonous and identical, but out of each memory, like a sculptor of genius, makes countless statues. (Proust 2002f: 194)

The passage describes how the experience of rereading a book possesses something of the timeless quality that the narrator has already assigned to the proper contemplation of the inner being and to the writer's proper method. However, it is precisely the 'abandoned quarry' that describes the reader's character in the moment of taking up the book again that offers her the conditions for a very different reading from the one originally experienced through the book. How often are we disappointed upon returning to books that were special to us in our youth? However, despite the narrator's admission that he is no longer susceptible to the 'world of mystery' that literature offers, his descriptions of writing and reading are strongly influenced by the state of timelessness that he seeks in order to reveal the real truths of our own inner being. Of course, Proust is under no such illusions. Allowing his narrator to have such thoughts, in the universe that is inhabited by the reader of À *la recherche*, is suggestive of a sensitivity towards the infinite number of temporal landscapes of different readers. Each reader brings his or her store of visual histories and impressions to the task of translating the narrator's meaning for themselves. But Proust's creation of such impressions in the narrator only serves to make the reader more aware of her own very different impressions of reading and writing. The reader is once again caught in the swirl of Proust's 'miracle of analogy'. Like the narrator, we are transfixed by a 'dizzying uncertainty', the result of our heightened awareness of the distance we have travelled for our momentary union with the self of the narrator, a distance travelled beyond 'the enormous difference between the true impression we have had of a thing and the artificial impression we give ourselves of it when we try by an act of will to represent it to ourselves' (Proust 2002f: 177).

The narrator, or Marcel, is, of course, a very different character to Bloom. Bloom does not look forward with certainty to a future time when he will write the great work that will 'nourish' future readers, or transcribe the dead 'into a universal' and 'permanent' language (Proust 2002f: 212). Whereas the narrator believes that the 'only true paradise is a paradise that we have lost' (ibid. 179), Bloom looks forward, before he sleeps, to the modest paradise of a 'thatched bunga-lowshaped 2 storey dwellinghouse of southerly aspect' (*U*: 837–8). The narrator also describes a 'being' that has been resuscitated in him as a result of the 'resurrections' (Proust 2002f: 183) that leave him in a state of 'dizzying uncertainty', yet reveal 'fragments of existence' which 'had escaped from time', the contemplation of which was 'fugitive' and offered the only pleasure that 'was both real and fertile' (ibid. 183). Bloom, on the other hand, is caught up in a stream of consciousness narration that has little time to linger on such fragments of existence that have escaped from time. There is so much of existence incessantly inciting new streams of word-thoughts in his conscience that he is constantly subjected to conscious and unconscious drives and invo-luntary memories. Bloom is, at times, desperate to cling to the here and now as he navigates around the painful reminders of his somewhat alienated existence as a middle-aged cuckold.

The narrator's description of other characters recalls the phenomenological account of self-alterity Natalie Depraz configures in terms of incarnation. On numerous occasions the narrator refers to the 'being' and the 'stranger' that is made manifest *within* through the interaction with the 'essence of things'. The contact with this inner 'being' (Proust 2002f: 180) or 'true self' (ibid. 181), that is reborn within, leads the narrator to 'cling on to this contemplation of the essence of things' (184). However, the only way to 'understand them more completely', 'within myself', is 'to make them transparent enough to see right down into their depths' (185) and draw them out 'of the obscurity within' (188). The narrator recognizes that 'we live our lives heedless of ourselves' (205) and that art can reveal this self-alterity, through the incarnation of secret and undiscovered contemplative truths that can alter the pattern of life. The rejuvenated understanding of inner 'being', or self-alterity, can then be transformed into a kind of 'nourishment' for future readers by the 'man of letters' (208):

> Thus my life was in contact with the forces that would bring about its maturation, and those who might in after years draw sustenance from it would know nothing of what had been done for their nourishment, just as those who eat the edible grains little know that the rich substances they contain first nourished the seed and made possible its development. (Proust 1932b: 1016)

Once again, I have used the Moncrieff translation here as the new translation becomes quite awkward at this point: 'And those who might subsequently draw nourishment from it for themselves would have no idea, any more than people do when they eat food grains, that the rich substances which they contain were made for its nourishment, had first nourished the seed and enabled it to ripen' (Proust 2002f: 208). Even though the narrator looks forward to a form of contact and union with others through the 'life' that will be mediated through the words of his future creation – the narrator explicitly refers here to the reader's incarnation in the artwork as a means for its maturation – the writer will not be consigned to the same fate as those, now dead, who also will populate his book. The narrator argues that 'since we live our lives detached from individual beings, since after a few years our strongest feelings [...] are forgotten, since they mean no more to us than words we cannot understand', these individual beings eventually become like forgotten words. The transubstantiation of these legions of dead into 'forgotten words' offers only one solution to the narrator. In order to 'understand these forgotten words' we must transcribe them 'into a universal, but, permanent, language' making out of 'those who are no longer with us, in their truest essence, an acquisition of lasting value for all human beings' (ibid. 212). The artwork that is still the 'life' of the narrator, or artist-to-be, is also a 'nourishment' for future readers, in that they assist in its 'maturation', and also the incarnation of the forgotten dead as 'forgotten words' that are to be transcribed as a universal, permanent language.

The narrator will ultimately say of others that the 'whole art of living is to use the people who make us suffer simply as steps enabling us to obtain access to their divine form and thus joyfully to people our lives with divinities' (207). But since the narrator is especially made to suffer by those loved people (Albertine and his grandmother) who have died, the implication would appear to be that the creation of the artwork must be preceded by practising an 'art of living' whereby these people are used 'as steps' en route to a form of interaction that regards them as 'divine forms'. A sense of community grounded on such a notion of interaction will surely suffer disillusionment when others are seen to fall short of these divine forms. The narrator's predisposition to per- ceive life and intersubjectivity in terms of how best to free the con- templation of their moments from 'real life', 'the contingencies of time' and the human form of others would then seem to be the reason for why he believes 'we have no freedom at all in the face of the work of art' (189). Since the narrator has a preconceived notion of how best to shape the raw materials of art that are essential for the 'being' that it must bring to life, it leaves us wondering whether a certain freedom of expression might not elude him when he comes to write.

Metaphor as incarnation

Walter Benjamin has described Proust's sentences as the 'entire mus- cular activity of the intelligible body' (Benjamin 1987: 70). He believes that Proust's asthma, his physical malady, became 'part of his art – if indeed his art did not create it' (ibid. 69). However, he also suggests that, as a result, loneliness is mediated in a particular way in Proust. For Benjamin, Proust's attentiveness to 'self-absorption' results in his debunking of friendship and intersubjective encounter, to the extent that an important gesture of these relationships, namely 'physical contact', becomes impossible: 'To no one is this gesture more alien than to Proust. He cannot touch the reader either' (68). In employing 'physical contact' as a metaphor for reading, Benjamin quotes from Ramon Fernandez's study of Proust: '[d]epth, or, rather, intensity, is always on his side, never on that of his partner' (68). Benjamin foregrounds the political in his readings of literature and his reading of Proust is no exception. He regards Proust as turning his whole 'limitless art into a veil for this one most vital mystery of his class: the economic aspect' (66). In allowing, then, for the possibility for 'touch' between Marcel and the reader, by using the metaphor of 'physical contact' for reading, he is putting forward a distinct notion of the 'lifework' under the aegis of this 'economic aspect' (59). In recognizing that *À la recherche*, as the 'image of Proust', is 'the highest physiognomic expression which the irresistibly growing discrepancy between literature and life was able to assume' (59), he is speaking for his time and for its slow dismembering of the possibility of creating anything akin to a 'lifework'. Theodor Adorno has perhaps described this process most clearly: he argues that 'the reification of relations between humans would contaminate all experience and literally become absolute' (Adorno 1997: 67). The somewhat incongruous appearance, therefore, of a 'lifework' still capable of evoking the symbiosis of life and literature at such a time, speaks for why the 'image of Proust' has become representative of a lost time in the history of the artwork.

However, there is an aspect of 'physical contact' that is integral to Benjamin's account of the 'lifework' that Proust suggests the reader can reclaim. The 'nourishment' Proust regards as central to his work is a nourishment that privileges the reader's access to depth and intensity as it is mediated through language. We have seen Natalie Depraz describe phenomenological language by way of a process of incarnation, or a 'passage from the corporeal sensible to the conscious lived sense' (Depraz 1995: 275). The sense of corporeity implicit in a reading of Proust that regards his physical maladies as integral to his art, or creative of his art, also privileges this 'passage from the corporeal sensible to the conscious lived sense' (ibid. 275), but with the reader as mediator. The physical world and the world of the novel coalesce to such an extent that Proust's acceptance of his death, his refusal to accept all medical remedies in his final weeks, can be regarded as the result of his realization that his cure lay in the 'beyond', or in the 'nourishment' he offered his readers. In being the cause of his malady, his narrative also possesses its cure. It is only transformed into art through the reader. The ultimate expression of the 'physical contact' Benjamin believes Proust denies himself would then be the giving up of his life to the care of the reader. Only the reader can sustain a life that has become inextricably bound to its narration. Proust told Jaloux and Curtius in September 1922 that '[w]e must never be afraid to go too far, for truth lies beyond' (Painter 1983: 670) and Proust had already recognized that the cure he now sought lay beyond any represented dichotomy between 'experienced event' and 'remembered event' (Benjamin 1987: 60).

Proust has taken as far as he can the kind of sacrifice Jacques Rancière assigns to the 'truth proven by transforming the pages of the book into living, suffering flesh' (Rancière 2004: 120). However, Rancière believes that Proust's 'stubborn determination to want the individual to be embodied in people, to want the blind certainty of the human species to be transformed into a happy relationship of individual to individual' is ultimately disrupted in Proust (ibid. 121). Rancière argues that this model must give way eventually to the truth from 'outside', to a new version of the 'incarnate truth', what he believes Proust finally gives in to by including references to the 'truth' of the war in his final sections. However, the belief that the narrative gives 'nourishment' is reciprocated by the reading that takes up and rejuvenates again and again the life that is now inextricably bound to this narrative of 'living, suffering flesh'. This acts as another version of the 'incarnate truth' from 'outside' that Rancière believes must finish the work.

Of course, such a reading can be accused of assigning too much of Proust's afflictions to the life of the book, to the 'self' that gives us the book, thereby succumbing to a reading that employs the 'method of Sainte-Beuve', a method that fails to recognize that 'a book is the product of a self other than that which we display in our habits' (Proust 1994a: 12). This self, Proust argues, is unrelated to the vices of the author. However, Benjamin's understanding of a 'lifework', in Proust's case, would appear to be the kind of artwork that is marked by the life the artist led. He argues that Proust's life is not a 'model life in every respect' due to its 'unusual malady, extraordinary wealth' and 'abnormal disposition' (Benjamin 1987: 59). The close alignment of the life of the author with that of the narrator, as a means for understanding the work, is questioned by Proust, who, as we have seen, employs reading as a metaphor for events in the fictional world of the novel. However, René Girard's description of the Proustian metaphor may suggest that Proust is present in his novel in a more duplicitous manner. Girard argues that Proust's 'metaphors deflect our attention from the object and direct it to the mediator' (Girard 1987: 93) and it is metaphor's capacity for 'discovering profound connections between two ideas or sensations' (Proust 1994a: 92) that is mediated by a desire that works through memory. The youthful narrator privileges the desire that 'summons' the 'chord that will resolve' the disparity between past memories and the sounds, or objects, that spark these memories in the present, but as the novel progresses this mode of epiphanic reunification becomes less and less content with 'profound connections' between two moments of narrated time.

In narrating more and more ingeniously what Girard describes as the 'hatred' and 'adult rivalry' of 'snobs and lovers' (Girard 1987: 77), the narrator's formal separation from such vice comes into question, especially since he acknowledges that other people, 'by disappointing or fulfilling their desires' rid themselves 'of their pretension or their bitterness' (Proust 2002f: 244). The reader begins to regard the style of narration, therefore, as a barrier to a complete understanding of the 'self' that is presented as exemplary – a 'self' distinct from the author – that gives us the book. In a sense, the lack of vice in the life of the narrator leads to a questioning of the transparency of the narrator's voice. Unlike Bloom, who masturbates to Gerty, writes his own 'dirty letters' and is accused of being a bit uppity by other Dubliners, Proust's narrator is never the subject of gossip, and his virtue is rarely, if ever, questioned.[9] If there is any hint of vice in the life of the narrator, it may only be found in his treatment of Albertine, and the narrator justifies this treatment to himself through such an exhaustive examination of all-consuming jealousy that the reader can only accept the justification. The narrator is so susceptible to memory's influence on action and intersubjective relations that the giving up of time to the recording of memories, what we must presume the narrator practises for his future artwork, comes to resemble a kind of vice.

Memory intrudes on the ability to act and on the ability to engage in intersubjective relations to the extent that his mother is frequently mistaken for his grandmother, and Albertine's presence is scarcely recalled, or her name uttered, before she is imagined breast to breast with Andrée – 'I recalled all of a sudden what Cottard had said to me in the ballroom of the little casino, and as if an invisible chain had managed to connect an organ to the pictures in my memory, that of Albertine leaning her breasts against those of Andrée gave me a terrible pain in my heart' (2002d: 273–4) – or with her clothes themselves toying with the narrator – 'And confronted by Albertine's rubber waterproof, in which she seemed to have become another person [...] I snatched at this tunic that was jealously moulding a longed-for bosom' (Proust 2002d: 264). This training towards a greater susceptibility to memory is a result of the privileging of memory and of the recording of memories, of the privileging of a lost time that encourages and strengthens the work of memory, thereby leading the narrator to deny others any reciprocation of affection because of jealousy's enhancement through memory.

A contrast is set up, then, between the earlier privileging of the prolonged contemplation of the 'pure essence' of time, revealed through the careful reunification of spots of time, and the meticulous recording and examination of sexual acts and social graces that privilege spontaneity, faddishness and the time of the 'consumer'. The self-abnegating representation of the work of memory leads the reader to suspect that the meticulous detailing of vices represents a form of vicarious living that feeds the narrator until he is sated and ready to find solace in the 'grace' that the contemplation of a Lost Time affords. As we have seen, Proust is careful to unsettle any clear demarcation between narrative time and lived time, and the surveillance of the narrator becomes an accomplice to the 'vices' that initially appear as a humorous interruption to the unravelling of the 'inner book of signs'. Marcel's involvement in the 'vices' he perceives can be examined in the first part of *Sodom and Gomorrah*. Marcel describes the frustrated 'solitary' invert who languishes on station platforms in terms of an orchid and as a 'sterile jellyfish that will perish on the sand', waiting for his 'brilliant luminescence' to be spotted by the unique powers of perception of another of his 'race', an 'adept' (Proust 2002d: 30). They will then have the opportunity for sharing the 'unusual tongue' of their 'race'. However, after describing this 'solitary' and his tell-tale demeanour, what is only apparent to another sexual invert, one belonging to this 'race', the narrator then falls into a first-person voice: 'Jellyfish! Orchid! When I was following only my instinct, the jellyfish repelled me at Balbec; but had I known how to look at it, like Michelet, from the point of view of natural history and of aesthetics, I would have seen a delectable girandole of azure' (ibid. 30). Marcel moves into a lengthy description of the unique shape and appearance of both jellyfish and orchids. He appears frustrated that he did not look beyond what his instinct was protecting him from as a youth. Marcel has presented himself as an 'adept', as one who has assumed, after a struggle with his instinct, the talents of the 'adept' of the previous passage, one who is capable of recognizing solitary inverts, representatives of a 'race' that would appear to reserve these talents for themselves. He will also later describe 'effeminate' inverts as those who 'have inside them an embryo [of the 'feminine sex'] they are unable to make use of' (33). In this context, it is interesting to note that Albertine, Marcel's long-time lover, whom he is ultimately 'unable to make use of', is consistently described as being 'inside' Marcel. In reading between the lines here, it is interesting to speculate on how elements of Proust's own 'inversion' on occasion seep into Marcel's charting of desire.

An early extract from Proust's 'End of Jealousy' casts some light on how desire plays itself out in metaphor for him:

> While dressing for dinner his thoughts were unconsciously hanging on the moment when he would see her again, just as an acrobat already touches the distant trapeze as he flies toward it, or as a musical phrase seems to reach the chord that will resolve it, drawing it across the distance separating them by the very force of the desire that presages and summons it. (Proust 1984a: 193–4)

As the narrator matures, his understanding of the nature of 'real life' alters, and his treatment of the language that must mediate this 'real life' and how its moments are stretched 'across the distance that separates them' by the force of the desire between our imagining of a moment and its realization alters. 'Real life' is no longer that against which the 'inspired moments' as a 'sort of communication of all that our being has left of itself in monuments past' (qtd. in Carter 261) move. In these early notes for *Jean Santeuil*, from 1898–9, Proust is already prefiguring this movement. He believes that 'such moments of vivid, spontaneous memory and their conscious application in the creative process' (Carter 2000: 261) are the 'real life' and that our usual daily life is a sham existence.

Towards the end of *A la recherche* we read a passage where the dividing line between what is evoked as real, and what is evoked as a remembrance, becomes unclear. Marcel has retired to bed following a reception at the house of the Guermantes, and the tinkling of the bell on the door to announce the departure of guests reminds him of a former time with his parents when the tinkling bell would announce the moment when the last guest had left and hence the moment when he would receive his goodnight kiss from his mother:

> Then, thinking over all the events that necessarily ranged themselves between the moment when I heard those sounds and the Guermantes reception, I was startled at the thought that it was, indeed,

this bell which was still tinkling within me and that I could in no wise change its sharp janglings, since, having forgotten just how they died away, to recapture it and hear it distinctly, I was forced to close my ears to the sound of the conversations the masks were carrying on around me. To endeavour to listen to it from nearby, I had to descend again into my own consciousness. (Proust 1932b: 1122–3)

How has this state *as* remembrance become more real than the lived reality of the moment? Does the '[f]ortunate forgetfulness' (Proust 1932b: 1118) that the narrator has recently been alluding to displace the work of involuntary memory? If the remembered state becomes more lived than the reality through which it shines and that it re-appraises, how are we to employ the force and efficacy of this act of remembrance for the re-evaluation of the narrator's, and in turn the reader's, 'reality'? There is a sense that the 'spots of time' have been so tirelessly reworked that they have assumed the flavour of textual moments of inspiration modelled on a fading sense of reality. They have come to find the energy for their recording in the state of pro-longed remembrance, what has always been an intention of the narrator:

And if I was going to live apart from the people who would complain of not seeing me, was it not precisely so that I might devote myself to them – more thoroughly than I could have done in their company – seek to reveal them to themselves, to arrive at their true natures? (Proust 1932b: 1079)

The strategies that reveal the readers to themselves are reliant on the figurative movements involuntary memory comes to act as a metaphor for. The narrator tells us that the creative person within could be regarded as 'coming to life only when there was disclosed some general characteristic common to several things, which constituted his suste-nance and delight' (Proust 1932b: 888). The willingness to describe states of immanence with such precision displays an ability and con-fidence to reveal 'the general characteristic common' to all readers, that will bring readers to his work, a confidence that allows the narrator to feel he can now begin to write.

Chapter 4

Incarnation and impotence: Joyce, Proust and desire

Impotentiality and Impotence[1]

The leading men of *Ulysses* crave meaningful human intercourse. The paralysis that has already left so many of Joyce's men, from the old pederast of 'An Encounter' to Gabriel Conroy, and from Richard Rowan to James Duffy, silently submissive to the workings of a truncated desire, still haunts his last clearly defined characters. One clear victim of this male demise is paternity. Julia Kristeva has suggested that Joyce's *Finnegans Wake* challenges paternal authority 'not only ideologically, but in the workings of language itself, by a return to [pre-Oedipal] semiotic rhythms connotatively maternal' (qtd. in Henke 1990: 7) and it is a challenge to paternity that takes root much earlier in Joyce. However, Joyce challenges and figuratively rephrases received representations of paternity, not solely to mediate 'rhythms connotatively maternal'. He presents us with the true face of paternal impotence and passivity, to the extent that characters imbibe some of the paternal instinct that Joyce transferred to his vision of 'paternal *authority*', an *authority* that manages and oversees the fluid semantics of the word.

Leopold Bloom makes do with a defunct and sublimated 'paternal authority'; the subjects of this authority are either dead (Rudy), in absentia (Milly), or cuckolding the supposed possessor of such authority (Molly). Bloom's duplicitous role as an Everyman who is removed from every opportunity for practising anything akin to 'paternal authority' has, for some critics, meant that he has become representative of a universalist, incarnated paternity, which I have examined in another light through Shem the Penman in Chapter 2. Harold Bloom has written, in a recent critical edition devoted to Poldy, that 'Poldy was not a person, but only language, and that Joyce, unlike myself knew this very well. Joyce knew very well that Bloom was more than a person, but only in the sense that Poldy was a humane and humanized God, a God who had become truly a bereft father, anguishing for his lost Rudy' (Bloom 2004: 4). Poldy embodies both creative and miscreant potentiality. Joyce's depiction of him as an impotent 'bit of an artist' melds the two possibilities, setting Poldy up as a figure for universal creativity; he becomes a type of man-God symbolizing both the material and immaterial aspects of genesis, thereby interrogating any typical sense of 'paternal authority' we might assign to him.

There is a complex nexus of fathering at work in Joyce. Vicki Mahaffey's reading of Joyce argues that he systematically splinters any established loci of authority, one of the most splintered being paternity: 'What I found was that Joyce systematically splintered the power of an established authority, using language and style to produce an interplay of different "author" -ities' (Mahaffey 1995: xiii). She continues: '[t]he ideal of the Father seems to be unitary, but it is embodied in alternative ways: the spiritual father opposes the biological one, and in the reading of the *Odyssey* reflected in *Ulysses*, the false father opposes the helpful one' (ibid. 8). However, these readings of paternity brush over how Bloom configures for himself the workings of a disillusioned paternal instinct that suffers, through him, to maintain some modicum of order in the face of interiorized feelings of impotence.

The reading of paternity and male sexuality given here examines how Joyce describes the end of the movement from procreative paternity to empathetic paternity, from its early manifestation through force and potency to its later realization in resignation, impotence and Bloomian universal love or empathy. In its reflective state, it can be seen to transfer to the 'workings of language' aspects of the empathy and care that we have seen different phenomenologists locate in language. Readings of impotence in Joyce usually stop at equating the 'impotent/castrated' with the 'woman(ish)/inadequate' (Reizbaum 2004: 92). I extend Marilyn Reizbaum's comparison of Stephen, as an 'impotent' 'most finished artist' (ibid. 90), with the 'impotent' Bloom, into an examination of the manner in which Bloom's interiorization of impotence affects his self-image and his understanding of other aspects of creativity. If there are elements of Joyce in Bloom, then Joyce's analysis of figures, his detailing of a character's introspective awakening, and his attention to the word, are also representative of an interrogation and sublimation of desire through the acceptance of im-potentiality. There is a sense of physical impotence and im-potentiality that recurs time and again in *Ulysses* and *Finnegans Wake*. It is integral to the Joycean aesthetic that gives rise to the development of characters and non-characters who exist either wholly in their own deliberations, or within a language of willful obscurity that removes them from a locus of meaningful interaction or communication. The interrogation of physical union that impotence affords the subject leads to an interrogation of all forms of human interaction, ultimately splintering the association that exists between desire and human interaction.

However, the influence of 'deconstructive criticism of Joyce' has led critics to suggest that Joyce either replays cultural hierarchies or presents us with a pessimistic paralysis. Vicki Mahaffey writes:

> Joyce's work, like that of many deconstructionists and feminists, reflects a deep interest in the dynamic processes of polarization and reunion that allow systems such as society and language to change, and a serious concern with the pressure to stabilize – and paralyze – such change by hardening the distinction between opposites in order to privilege one term over its counterpart. (Mahaffey 1995: 4)

David Tracy also sees Joyce's 'language of ordered relationships articulating [both] similarity in difference' (Tracy 1991: 408) and a 'deadening univocity' (ibid. 413). However, this 'deadening univocity' and purported 'hardening' of the 'distinction between opposites' is a moment Joyce surpasses through a careful rendering of the empathy that a resignation towards the potential of the 'corporeity *within*' affords. Joyce's presentation of a truncated movement toward meaningful communication is the *re*presentation of the inspiration and contact that has already taken place between the artist and the word. Joyce invests in a rhetoric of creativity, a practice that evolves throughout his work and that ultimately evokes the vast potential integral to any artistic project conceived in terms of a metaphorics of the flesh made word. The figure of the embodied text offers great potential for the writer to examine, through his characters, self-reflexivity and the desire unique to the mediation of the word.

Luce Irigaray believes the 'sexual relation' is 'impossible' (Irigaray 1985: 105) and that man has invented, in its place, 'elegant' substitutes such as 'courtly love' (ibid. 104). However, because male discourse, exemplified by 'psychoanalytic discourse', determines 'the real status of all other discourses' (104), Irigaray believes that man can play out his desire 'alone' in language (104). This means that there is only such a thing as 'feminine pleasure' because 'men need it in order to maintain themselves in their own existence'. For Irigaray, it 'helps them [men] bear what is intolerable in their world' (98). However, we recall that Bloom is a 'womanly man' and that Joyce's letters describe himself and Nora as possessing 'one flesh' (Maddox 1988: 169). Marcel's descriptions of Albertine also frequently describe her as being 'inside me' (Proust 2002d: 508). I would argue, therefore, that Joyce and Proust do take up this masculine trait of playing with themselves in language, but for a different reason. Bloom and Marcel *are* left to play out their desires 'alone' in language because, for them, the 'sexual relation' is also impossible. However, Joyce and Proust detail an alternative act of union through their play with language that offers the potential for sharing a desire that remains immanent to itself. The nourishment that is offered to the reader, and the prospective reading that nourishes the writer, are grounded on a desire for the word that can be shared.

Irigaray describes the potential for union between man and woman in terms of incarnation. For Irigaray, incarnation describes both a heightened moment of union for the lovers and also a momentary auto-affection for the individual: 'Scent or premonition between my self and the other, this memory of the flesh as the place of approach means ethical fidelity to incarnation' (Irigaray 2004: 179). This 'memory of the flesh' is, as I have argued, also important for Joyce and Proust as they desire an incarnated word. Irigaray's reading is, of course, grounded on a belief that phallogocentric thinking, i.e. philosophy in general, has never admitted a proper thinking of the body. Philosophy is, therefore, left to ponder 'mere survival': 'Who or what can move us out of mere survival except a return to the bodily-fleshly values that have never yet come to full flower? In order to unfold them "voluntarily". Since the great rhythms of incarnation, respiration, circulation of the blood, have never been taken on by man' (ibid. 122). Irigaray incorporates the theological sense of incarnation into her philosophy of the 'here and now' in a manner that offers the most viable route for interconfessional dialogue between theology and philosophy: 'And why do we pay least heed to those texts which speak of the return or the coming of God, of the other, as phenomena of the incarnation which are still unknown to us? [...] Why do we assume that God must always remain an inaccessible transcendence rather than a realization – here and now – in and through the body? [...] [L]ike a ressurrection that would not involve the disappearance of this world. With the spirit impregnating the body in and through a lasting alliance' (124–5).

It is the fleshy sense of incarnation that is most important for Irigaray. Irigaray privileges a language that itself incarnates the body of woman. She charts a 'remaking of immanence and transcendence, notably through this *threshold* which has never been examined as such: the female sex. The threshold that gives access to the *mucous*' [Irigaray's emphasis] (17–8). It is the 'memory of the flesh' in terms of the 'mucous' and 'lips' of the female sex that she evokes. The lips are 'strangers to dichotomy and oppositions', they 'offer a shape of welcome but do not assimilate, reduce or swallow up', and they designate 'the very place of uselessness, at least as it is habitually understood' since they 'serve neither conception nor jouissance' (18). One might well ask, therefore, whether Bloom and Marcel have a strong enough 'memory of the flesh' in these terms to share in this description of incarnation. Bloom has not known Molly intimately for over ten years and Marcel never suggests that he might have an intimate knowledge of the female sex. However, I believe that Bloom, in particular, embodies an understanding of the female imaginary that enables him to envisage for himself and Molly, and for language itself, something akin to Irigaray's notion of incarnation. In the next section I argue that his feelings of emasculation become so strong at times that he sees himself in terms of an impotent woman. He also regards his sex as that which designates a similar 'place of uselessness'. However, these states are incarnated within Bloom to the extent that they affect his understanding of intersubjectivity. Bloom is still a 'lover', but a lover of humanity and universal love. Although he does remain 'alien to the intimacy of the mucous, [in] not crossing the threshold' (Irigaray 2004: 157), he does not, as Irigaray believes the subject of the Levinasian caress does, remain alien to 'the most inward locus of the feeling and the felt, where body and flesh speak to each other' (ibid. 157).

Irigaray believes sexuality has always been examined in relation to a privileging of procreation, with fatherhood being regarded as a '*proof of his potency*' (ibid. 54). She develops her understanding of the female sex, which designates 'the place of uselessness, at least as it is habitually understood' (18), in relation to male impotence. We recall that she regards the 'sexual relation' as 'impossible'. However, for Irigaray, this realization has not led men to be more accepting of 'feminine pleasure': 'The problem is that they [men, epitomized in this instance as psychoanalysts] claim to make a law of this impotence itself, and continue to subject women to it' (Irigaray 1985: 105). Men are regarded as transferring the previously problematized logocentric performativity onto their appraisal of impotence, making a virtue of necessity while failing to examine the true nature of this 'lack'. Julia Kristeva describes another kind of 'impotence' in the typical Joycean encounter. She refers to the Joycean language as an 'antilanguage' in that it is no longer communicative because it seeks to mediate 'displacements and facilitations of energy, discharges, and quantitative cathexes that are logically anterior to lingusitic entities and to their subject mark[ing] the constitution and the movements of the "self"' (Kristeva 1980: 102). This chapter investigates how impotence and impotentiality can reveal, more completely, how Joyce and Proust employ a philosophy of incarnation for mediating desire.

It is very likely that a subject will refrain from communication when it becomes too painful, and when it becomes associated with the emotional and physical feelings of impotence. How is desire represented by writing that must mediate a state of anguish resulting from the interiorization of im-potentiality or impotence? Does the writer transfer his desire to the word? Derrida's reading of Rousseau and masturbation deals with one possible response. For Derrida's Rousseau, pleasure 'is thus lived as the irremediable loss of the vital substance, as exposure to madness and death' (Derrida 1998: 151), produced 'at the expense of their [of writers'] health, strength, and sometimes, their life'. In a letter to Harriet Shaw Weaver dated 24 June 1921, Joyce writes: 'I have not read a work of literature for several years. My head is full of pebbles and rubbish and broken matches and lots of glass picked up most everywhere' (Joyce 1957: 167). Joyce seems to be suggesting that the reading of literature was once a rich experience for him. It might have served as an antidote to the detritus of lived experience now populating his 'head'. In reading further into the extract, it is possible that writing had now become a substitute for the kind of experience such reading always recalled for Joyce. Derrida's commingling of textual and libidinal desire suggests that reading

> must always aim at a certain relationship, unperceived by the writer, between what he commands and what he does not command of the patterns of the language that he uses. This relationship is not a certain quantitative distribution of shadow and light, of weakness or of force, but a signifying structure that critical reading should *produce*. [Derrida's emphasis] (Derrida 1998: 158)

Reading is therefore a productive, or creative, experience for Joyce and Derrida. However, an acknowledgement of impotentiality may have led Joyce to relinquish the lack of 'command' implicit in reading in favour of the potential of writing, a production that affords the writer greater control.

Leopold Bloom may appear somewhat introverted and compelled through impotence to sublimate his sexual instincts for a plethora of new objects, aims and practices. Impotence and im-potentiality are concepts that have received much philosophical attention in recent years. In a section entitled 'Potentiality and Law' from *Homo Sacer: Sovereign Power and Bare Life*, Giorgio Agamben gives new readings of potentiality and im-potentiality:

> Potentiality (in its double appearance as potentiality to and as potentiality not to) is that through which Being founds itself *sovereignly*, which is to say, without anything preceding or determining it (*superiorem non recognoscens*) other than its own ability not to be. (Agamben 1998: 46)

Agamben reads potentiality as that which only founds itself *sovereignly* through its 'ability not to be' or through its 'im-potentiality', so as to return to man the ability to claim his own life. He informs us that an act is sovereign 'when it realizes itself by simply taking away its own potentiality not to be, letting itself be, *giving itself to itself* [my italics] (Agamben 1998: 46). This is reminiscent of Michel Henry's understanding of the *pathētik* and of how radical passivity is described in his later works.[1] It is suggestive of a move to recover for man an ability to admit to the loss of all presupposed relations to Being conceived as realized potential. Heidegger's work on the notion of an 'authentic potentiality-for-Being' is an important antecedent to Agamben's notion of im-potentiality. According to Heidegger, 'potentiality-for-Being' is integral to Dasein. In describing the importance of 'potentiality-for-Being' for Dasein, Heidegger characterizes conscience as a 'call'. He argues that such a call, or such an understanding of 'potentiality-for-Being', becomes disrupted when Dasein fails to 'hear itself' and suffers from a 'lostness' because it is unable to 'find itself'. Hearing itself as a call is therefore integral to Dasein so that it will not get distracted from the multitude of 'possibilities' that prevent it from finding its 'authentic potentiality-for-Being' (Heidegger 1997: 315–6). The language of this phenomenology of care is an integral part of Heidegger's philosophy in *Being and Time*. Potentiality's relationship with self-communication is also important for Joyce's understanding of the conscience. Joyce transforms the interiorization of a state of emasculation and impotence into a new kind of potentiality-for-Being where self-communication offers endless potential for communication and union between the flesh and the word. Through these interpretations of potentiality and im-potentiality the subject is able to understand desire as that which is eternally '*giving itself to itself*'.

Agamben aligns impotentiality with immanence. He reminds us that '[t]o be potential means: to be one's lack, *to be in relation to one's own incapacity*. Beings that exist in the mode of potentiality *are capable of their own impotentiality*; and only in this way do they become potential' (Agamben 1999: 182). To be capable of our own impotentiality is a uniquely human attribute, since without it, 'potentiality would always already have passed into act and be indistinguishable from it' (ibid. 215). Impotentiality enables the subject to understand potentiality as that which is '*giving itself to itself*'. This leads to a new understanding of immanence that Agamben believes is important for the late works of Gilles Deleuze. Deleuze, Agamben argues, wants to devise a new conception of 'life' where nature is regarded as 'desire's variable field of immanence' (qtd. in Agamben 1999: 235). For Agamben, Deleuze does not conceive of desire, in his later writings, in terms of 'alterity' or 'lack', but in terms of how it is 'possible to conceive of a desire that as such remains immanent to itself' (ibid. 236). Joyce and Proust work through this evolution, from impotentiality's acceptance, through immanence, to a new understanding of desire. As Bloom and Marcel resign themselves to the pleasures of self-reflection, their authors transfer their desire to the word, to a word that has become incarnated or consubstantial with such immanence, thereby immanentizing desire and offering it up to the reader as nourishment.

The impotence of Bloom and Marcel

Impotentiality is important for Joyce and as with all philosophical themes in Joyce, it is examined in the context of the body. For Joyce, it manifests itself as a physical impotence that is then internalized by the character. Impotence is generally considered to be an impediment to instinct. Freud informs us that instincts refer to 'the physical representation of an endosomatic, continuously flowing source of stimulation' (Freud 1991: 310). When a course of action presumed necessary by the subject possessive of such a 'physical representation' is frustrated due to impotence, there is a tendency 'to linger over the preparatory activities' (ibid. 299). Stream of consciousness narration and interior monologue are generally creative of somewhat self-conscious characters who display a predilection for 'preparatory activity', whether it be in regard to interpersonal encounter or communicative action.

Bloom appears most content in the 'Calypso' chapter of *Ulysses* where he prepares for the day to come by administering to Molly and the cat while preparing breakfast. The word that guides the chapter is the polyvalent *metempsychosis*, a word that inculcates a semantic flow in the chapter whereby characters segue into one another. Molly's 'sleepy soft grunt', 'Mn' (*U* 67), merges with the cat's 'Mrkrgnao!' (*U* 66), and Bloom's thoughts of Milly merge with memories of Molly. A discussion on reincarnation and metempsychosis leads us to an archetypal description of the feminine that almost presents Milly as a reincarnation of Molly:

> *Those lovely seaside girls*
>
> Milly too. Young Kisses: the first, Far away now past. Mrs Marion. Reading lying back now, counting the strands of her hair, smiling, braiding.
>
> A soft qualm regret, flowed down his backbone, increasing. Will happen, yes. Prevent. Useless: can't move. Girl's sweet light lips. Will happen too. He felt the flowing qualm spread over him. Useless to move now. Lips kissed, kissing kissed. Full gluey woman's lips. (*U* 81)

Bloom, transfixed in an emotional stupor, yearns for a sensuous life now past even as he feels uneasy about the sensuous life yet to be experienced by Milly. Joyce's incorporation of the theme of reincarnation into the description of early morning activity in the Bloom household charges the words of Bloom's interior monologue with a protean and restless semantic agency. Bloom, the father of an absent daughter and a deceased son, lingers over the 'preparatory activities' that should ultimately lead to his wife's sexual fulfilment. However, he merely administers the 'fore-pleasure'. The sexual fulfilment, or 'end-pleasure', is provided instead by Blazes Boylan at about four in the evening later that day. Bloom's dread in regard to his daughter's sensual coming of age provides an outlet for his somewhat repressed dread in regard to his own coming of age as a cuckold.

There are signs of how this sensuous exchange affects Bloom in the language of the chapter. While returning home to fry a kidney, Bloom's deliberations on the plight of his ancestor's nomadic life fills him with a feeling of '[d]esolation' (*U* 73). He is reduced to a sensual existence that has to be content with glimpses of Molly's 'tossed soiled linen' (*U* 75) and her 'mocking eye' (*U* 77) while he tends to her domestic needs. He must resign himself to being 'near her ample bedwarmed flesh. Yes, yes' (*U* 74). Molly also teases him, asking for another book by Paul de Kock because he has a 'nice name'. On a whole other level, one might read Molly's *yes* as standing in for the kind of response that Bloom as 'other' will never respond to, in the deconstructive sense. The kind of *yes* Bloom and Molly have not shared, possibly since five weeks before the birth of Rudy, is the orgasmic *yes*, or the vocal climax of sexual union. Their solitary rehearsals of yes and their accompanying flights of self-performativity are then sublimations for the response they are denied. But even as the 'womanly', impotent man that he is, Bloom will still never embody the 'simple' way of understanding Molly desires. Carnal intercourse has been incomplete between them for over ten years, and 'complete mental intercourse' has not taken place for over nine months (*U* 869). This leads Bloom to feel 'a limitation of activity, mental and corporal' (*U* 869).

Bloom's latent feelings of inadequacy, due to an implied lack of sexual prowess, surface spasmodically in the aporias of his monologue. A woman he follows from Dlugacz'z sausage shop turns off to the right, slipping from view: 'The sting of disregard glowed to weak pleasure within his breast. For another: a constable off duty cuddled her in Eccles Lane. They like them sizeable. Prime sausage. O please, Mr. Policeman, I'm lost in the wood' (*U* 71). Bloom realizes he is not large, not of prime sausage, and that he feels lost in a policed and regulated sexual space where images of virility come to haunt him. Some moments later, Bloom reads about a planter's company seeking to buy land from the Turkish government for cultivation. He falls into a reverie on his ancestor's homeland bordering the Dead Sea, a thought-association leaving a sensation of '[g]rey horror sear[ing] his flesh' (*U* 73). Why does he have such an adverse reaction to the depiction of his people's fatherland? A close reading might offer some clues:

> The oldest people. Wandered far away over all the earth, captivity to captivity, multiplying, dying, being born everywhere. It lay there now. Now it could bear no more. Dead: an old woman's: the grey sunken cunt of the world. (*U* 73)

Bloom describes the generative work of his ancestors in biblical terms that revolve around the theme of genesis. The irony of his charting of a trail of fertility lies in the fact that it began with his speculations on the 'Dead Sea', a lifeless, motionless sea of salt that 'lay there now'. If a reading of this section imbibes the protean tendency of the chapter's guiding noun, its 'metempsychosis', and if it is also mindful of the semantic multi-layering of the Joycean sentence, then the passage also works on another level. 'It lay there now' can also refer to Bloom's resigned manhood, the sense of inadequacy driving his word associations and the motif of 'dead meat' running through the chapter. Bloom, who can 'bear no more', is a metaphor for the barren land of a nomadic people. His member is '[d]ead: an old woman's'. Not only is he emasculated, but he is one with the guiding theme of the chapter, its metempsychosis. His 'dead' sex is a 'grey sunken cunt of the world', the reincarnation of a trail of fertility that is coloured by his feelings of inadequacy.

The theme of metempsychosis that weaves its way through the chapter enables the reader to invoke all kinds of parallels at this point. The barren motif recalls Joyce's own physical ailments that had caused him to stop reading and writing so frequently, cutting him off from the life that was becoming his only object of desire and his only sustenance. This barren motif will resurface at the end of the next chapter where Bloom, in his bath, refers to his penis as a 'limp father of thousands, a languid floating flower' (*U* 107). These passages evoke a sense of sexual inadequacy, but they also acknowledge that the male sex can also be regarded as the 'very place of uselessness, at least as it is habitually understood' (Irigaray 2004: 18), that Irigaray assigns to the woman's sex. Bloom's acceptance of such 'uselessness' reminds us that humans are unique in being '*capable of their own impotentiality*' [Agamben's emphasis] (Agamben 1999: 182).

Bloom's envy towards the end of Ithaca as he disrobes for bed also clearly expresses his desire *for* desire: 'the anticipation of warmth (human) tempered with coolness (linen), obviating desire and rendering desirable: the statue of Narcissus, sound without echo, desired desire' (*U* 859). In a beautifully staged reply to one of the chapter's questions, Joyce references one of literature's great symbols to adultery. Bloom is granted Molly's 'secondbest bed', recalling Shakespeare's parting gift to Anne Hathaway:

With circumspection, as invariably when entering an abode (his own or not his own): with solicitude, the *snakespiral* springs of the mattress being old, the brass quoits and pendent viper radii loose and tremulous under stress and strain: prudently, as entering a lair or ambush of lust or adder: [...] reverently, the bed of conception and of birth, of consummation of marriage and of breach of marriage, of sleep and of death. [my emphasis] (*U* 862)

This homage to the bed allegorizes the relationship between Bloom and Molly: quoits are brass rings that are thrown so as to encircle pins in a form of entrapment, and the 'pendent' of the 'viper radii' is something that hangs dependent upon something else. Viper is also a word favoured by Shakespeare to describe villainy and treachery in *Coriolanus, Henry V* and *Pericles, Prince of Tyre*.[2] Its use usually augurs a fall from grace or the transformation of a character's godlike status into that of a lowly commoner. Bloom, like Christ and Coriolanus, is made to answer for the deeds of men who have passed before. Bloom's very personal fall from grace is at least granted the comfort of a homecoming of sorts, whereas for Coriolanus and Christ, the transformation is more complete. In *Coriolanus*, the change of fortunes brings sterility and other misfortunes that will 'depopulate the city'. Vipers traditionally connote treachery. In being used to describe the 'radii' of Bloom's bed, it strengthens the tones of entrapment, dependence and deception their marriage bed symbolizes. Bloom's and Molly's relationship has literally become 'tremulous under stress and strain'.

Bloom lists the men that have slept with Molly. He then experiences the 'antagonistic sentiments' (*U* 864) of envy, jealousy, abnegation and equanimity, an emotional odyssey that culminates in the most explicit account of Bloom's impotence. Bloom is envious of possessors

> of a bodily and mental male organism specially adapted for the superincumbent posture of energetic human copulation and energetic piston and cylinder movement necessary for the complete satisfaction of a constant but not acute concupiscence resident in a bodily and mental female organism, passive but not obtuse. (*U* 864)

It is only Bloom's equanimity that enables him to accept this state of affairs. Bloom can only console himself with the fact that it is 'not more abnormal than all other altered processes of adaption to altered conditions of existence, resulting in a reciprocal equilibrium between the bodily organism and its attendant circumstances' (*U* 865).

There are also intimations of sexual inadequacy in *Finnegans Wake*. In Part II Chapter IV, after HCE has just passed out, the tale of the voyage of Tristan and Iseult is interrupted by what appear to be HCE's unconscious fears. Tristan appears unable to perform as a hero should. We learn that the 'vivid girl', who is 'deaf' with love, took control of his 'flattering hend' and with a 'queeleetlecree of joysis crisis she renulited their disunited, with ripy lepes'. Then, with an 'aragan throust' (organ, or arrogant, thrust) she 'druve', 'quick is greaseed pigskin', the 'massive of virilvigtoury flshpst the/both lines of forwards' and into the 'goal of her gullet' (*FW* 395–6: 27–2).

The initiative is very much with the 'vivid girl' in this exchange. The other character, a character whose 'joysis crisis' may connote a physical crisis in Joyce's own life, wills himself on to finish the 'virilvigtoury' deed, only to later ask '[a]nd pullit into yourself, as on manowoman do another!' (*FW* 396: 4–5). It seems that he cannot direct the virile member home and must have the 'vivid girl' assist. Whether HCE is asking that we read the sexual act as one by a 'mano[n]woman', or as 'on[e] mano[f]woman do another' is uncertain. However, the male needs assistance to 'druve' the 'virilvigtoury flshpst the both lines of forwards'. The concern in the section is for the young woman, or the 'Irish prisscess' (*FW* 396: 8), who must put up with 'so tiresome old milkless a ram' with his 'tiresome duty peck' (*FW* 396: 15–16). Once again, the 'ram', or the male, must be content with his 'duty peck' while the 'vivid girl' seeks her 'goal' elsewhere.

Shaun's earlier appearance as Jaun, as a kind of John the Baptist to Shem's Jesus, has him preaching on love and intercourse. Jaun advises that 'canalised love [...] does a felon good, suspiciously if he has a slugger's liver [...] (and after the lessions of experience I speak from inspiration)' (*FW* 436: 18–21). '[C]analised love', or love through any canal, is recommended for the 'slugger' (hard-hitter) or big drinker who can't very well manage sex while soaking his 'liver'. The bracketed section leads us to wonder whether it is an aside from the author, or from Shaun as Jaun, the prophet of the universal writer. This voice speaks after 'the lessions of experience'; the lessons of love and sex have become lesions or wounds. Is Joyce intimating that his impotence, his 'joysis crisis', makes the recollection of sex painful and uncomfortable? Is it so painful for the writer that he must now merely 'speak from inspiration' and describe as obscurely as possible a sexual act that is all in the past, in the 'memory of the flesh', and that it can only now be vicariously experienced through the creation of text?

In Part III Chapter IV the voices of the four evangelists describe the various sexual positions of HCE and ALP. Once again, HCE seems to lament the loss of some previous strength:

I fear lest we have lost ours [...] respecting these wildy parts. How is hit finister! How shagsome all and beastful! [...] I show because I

> must see before my misfortune so a stark pointing pole [...] I am
> hather of the missed. (*FW* 566: 33–6)

It is a somewhat poignant extract that compares coitus and writing; the
authorial voice asks whether it is worth continuing with the labour of
writing or with life, when the 'wildy parts' appear long gone ('[h]ow is
it finister!'): 'I show because I must see before my misfortune so a stark
pointing pole'. Joyce is willing himself on here when all strength, all
'wildy parts' have been 'lost'. Even though all still appears 'shagsome'
and 'beastful', the writer, HCE, or Joyce, must ask themselves, '[w]hat
do you show on?' It seems that the body has lost all ability to be altered
by the life and sensuality that it is privy to. No longer having the power
to imitate the 'beastful', the only alternative is, for Joyce (the writer, or
eternal consciousness), to 'show', or create for the reader, an image for
what he recalls as 'shagsome'. Joyce sees before his 'misfortune so a
stark pointing pole'. Pole refers to both the ends of the earth, and the
phallus as a symbol of fertility and strength. In order to continue the
task of writing his life's work, he must overcome the sense of 'misfortune so', and accept that impotentiality is integral to the 'wildy
parts'. The voice then refers to itself as the 'hather of the missed', what
can be taken to mean 'father of the missed', or 'hather' (he who has
had) of what is yearned for.

Some of HCE's final words before the soliloquy of Anna Livia are on
marriage and intercourse:

> Humperfeldt and Anunska, wedded now evermore in annastomoses
> [...] . [...] who so shall separate fetters to new desire, repeals an act
> of union to unite in bonds of shismacy. O yes! O yes! Withdraw your
> member. Closure. This chamber stands abjourned. (*FW* 585: 22–7)

This passage, of course, works on a number of levels. 'Humperfeldt
and Anunska' are the latest incarnations of HCE and ALP who embody
so much of Joyce and Nora. They are wedded, the '[t]otumvir and
esquimeena', in 'annastomoses', and we recall that anastomosis is the
'strucural concept' that Clive Hart believes is essential to the 'duality of
being' Joyce privileges (Hart 1962: 153). However, 'annastomoses' also
describes a kind of saintly union of an '[A]nna' to a '[M]oses'. If the
separation in question here is one that 'repeals an act of union' unique
to the 'wedded', then it is most likely disrupting the sexual act sanctioned by marriage. A marriage without sex might be regarded as
reducing the marriage bonds to little more than 'bonds of shismacy'.

'Shismacy' describes a troubled intimacy: its first syllable combines 'she' and 'his' while also connoting 'schism' or 'sham', and it ends like 'intimacy'. 'Who so shall separate' the 'wedded' lovers in repealing the 'act of union' is only then fettered or shackled 'to new desire'. The killing of the 'act of union' does not kill off desire itself. It leads to a celebration of such 'shismacy', or to a parodying of the sexual climax: 'O yes! O yes!' The desire to live in wedlock without sex is itself shackled by the legal and religious laws that will always remind the 'wedded' of what they lack. The Act of Union between Great Britain and Ireland is also referenced here. It is also made to sound like a schism or politically motivated act of intimacy that only further entrenched national differences. Joyce parodies these legal and political themes by then assuming a legal register that advises: 'Withdraw your member. Closure. This chamber stands abjourned'. The 'act of union' can be repealed, when 'Humperfeldt', HCE, or the writer, withdraw their members. However, it only brings a temporary end to proceedings. The legal '[c]losure', or adjournment, very often only postpones the right to appeal. '[A]bjourned' can also refer to the verb abjure. Joyce knew, only too well, that to abjure means to swear perpetual absence from one's country. Joyce's longings for his lost homeland became inextricably bound up with his longing for the word, a word that had sustained, for decades, all memories of this homeland. All desires for the homeland and for the word are mediated, then, through this description of the loss integral to a marriage that has repealed its 'act of union'.

In Part III Chapter II, Shaun as Jaun is admonished by the omniscient voice of the unconscious: 'The pleasures of love lasts but a fleeting but the pledges of life outlusts a lifetime' (*FW* 444: 23–4). Joyce's letters to Nora are often revealing about his private life. Brenda Maddox argues that the letters reveal how, '[a]lways she [Nora] was to be the dominant partner, he the passive recipient' (Maddox 1988: 144). Maddox argues that the Joyces' heated sexual activity may have cooled around the time of the writing of *A Portrait*: '[T]he Joyces' sexual relationship continued strong at least until 1912' (ibid. 169) and she argues, in relation to *Ulysses*, that '[t]he speculation is irresistible that Joyce excluded it from his book because he had excluded it from his life' (223).

However, Joyce's union with Nora was complete. In a letter from 1912 he writes: 'I wish you were here. You have become a part of myself – one flesh' (Maddox 1988: 169). This emphasizes the themes of reconciliation and incarnation examined earlier. Joyce does not privilege difference and radical alterity even in the face of despair, but rather a commitment towards union and notions of 'the one'. Joyce's tendency to regard himself and Nora as 'one flesh' further complicates any sense of impotence that we might impart to either party in such a relationship. Nora's 'gynaecological difficulties' (ibid. 153) could only then be regarded as characteristics of his own self, just as any impotence on his part would be shared with Nora. Maddox concludes that '*Ulysses* is not so much a book about impotence and cuckoldry as it is about love: married love' and that '[w]hat Bloom and Molly are left with is comfort, trust, companionship and solicitude' (272).

However, while *Ulysses* is undoubtedly a book about love, it is only by examining Joyce's treatment of desire that we can appreciate the nature of this love. *Ulysses* describes a kind of 'comfort' grounded on the still vital emotions of jealousy, regret and resignation and on a persistent questioning of desire. *Ulysses* foregrounds themes of sexual inadequacy and introspection; Bloom reinforces what little contentment and 'comfort' there is to be had from his married life with the fruits of his artistic and scientific speculation, his memories of lost times, and his irrepressible embodiment of universal love, evidenced at the end through his care for Stephen. It is through his inordinate capacity for contextualizing his own plight – '[a]s not more abnormal to altered conditions of existence, resulting in a reciprocal equilibrium between the bodily organism and its attendant circumstances, foods, beverages, acquired habits, indulged inclinations, significant disease. As more than inevitable, irreparable' (*U* 865) – that Bloom remains generally content.

In *À la recherche* Marcel also privileges what Deleuze has argued is implicit in impotentiality, namely a desire that strives to remain 'immanent to itself' (quoted in Agamben 1999: 236). Marcel regularly reduces other people, and his experiences with them, to facets of his own being: 'wordly conversation' 'reduces us' to 'the level of simple "medium"' (Proust 2002d: 209); his grandmother becomes, during his mourning, nothing more 'than the reflection of my own thoughts' (ibid. 184) and he regularly suggests that it is possible, even beneficial, to be in a state where one has no 'contact with the outside world' (Proust 2002e: 18). Marcel does not admit to the 'sexual inversion' that he examines in Charlus and Jupien. Since the narrator does intimate, on occasion, that his name and the author's can be used interchangeably – 'Now she began to speak; her first words were "darling" or "my darling", followed by my Christian name, which, if we give the narrator the same name as the author of this book, would produce "darling Marcel" or "my darling Marcel" ' (ibid. 64) – then, pre-sumably, his reflections on desire are somewhat duplicitous. A desire 'immanent to itself' is essentially a desire that requires no object. Marcel moves all of the customary objects of desire inside where they become 'the reflection' of his 'own thoughts'. I argue here that the process is a reaction to the acknowledgement of impotentiality.

When the narrator realizes that Albertine is beginning to fill him with 'something like a desire for happiness' (Proust 2002d: 185), he admits that he is '[i]ncapable [...] as yet of again experiencing phy-sical desire' (ibid. 184). Later, he recalls his experiences with the girls who stopped before him on the beach, and how his desire for them bore within it a destructive 'first step': 'between my desire and the action that would be my asking to kiss her, there lay the whole inde-finite "blank" of hesitation and timidity' (238). He is unable to act on his impulses. Directing his desire towards the objects that lie outdoors only draws his attention to his desire's destructive 'first step'. Albertine is also caught up in this nexus of desire. Even in her confined state – Marcel admits that he only occasionally releases her 'from the cage where I had kept her for days on end' (Proust 2002e: 440) – she still causes him great pain because his desire for her cannot be completely internalized. As the narrator's art evolves, he comes to regard other people and societal events solely in relation to the artistic truths or 'inner book of unknown signs' that he must chart. Even Albertine, or to be more precise, the memory of Albertine, one of his final attach-ments to the 'outdoors', is more often than not 'used' for how she can further the artistic process:

> [F]or so many years I had looked for people's real lives and thoughts only in the direct expressions of them that they deliberately pro-vided, but now, thanks to them, I had come to do the opposite, to attach importance only to those statements that are not a rational, analytical expression of the truth; I relied on words only when I could read them like the rush of blood to the face of a person who is unsettled, or like a sudden silence. [...] Albertine sometimes left such loose ends trailing in her speech, precious compounds which I hastened to 'process' so as to turn them into clear ideas. (Proust 2002e: 77)

He realizes that 'it was inside me that all Albertine's actions took place' (Proust 2002e: 231). The object of the narrator's desire gradually becomes completely internalized. The hesitation and timidity that prevents him from fulfilling his desire with that which lies outside himself, epitomized by the lovely seaside girls, turns him inward. Now he will devote himself to examining how sketches of other people, as a 'reflection of my own thoughts', can further his desire for the word. He wants to immerse himself in the consubstantiality of word and body, in his own being, until he is able to rely only on 'words' read 'like the rush of blood to the face'. The 'loose ends' left trailing in other people's expressions are now to be garnered as 'precious compounds' to be processed and transformed into 'clear ideas'. To acknowledge that these people have 'real lives' away from such artistic processing would now be a destructive 'first step' for a desire that has turned inwards. The narrator acknowledges that this artistic process is further removing him from that which lies outside, but he is unwilling to interrupt 'the unrolling of the living frieze':

> To understand what I was losing by always being shut indoors, and to measure the riches the day was offering, I would have had to stop the unrolling of the living frieze and catch one girl carrying her laundry or her milk, frame her, like a silhouette in a moving decoration, between the uprights of my door and focus on her, making sure to obtain enough information about her to be able to find her again another day, like the tags that ornithologists and ichthyologists attach to birds' legs or fishes' fins before freeing them to study their migrations. (Proust 2002e: 123–4)

The 'living frieze' is the narrator's life. The young girls that once alerted him to his desire's impotentiality are now extraneous objects of the 'outdoors', distractions from the charting of a desire that looks inwards, remaining immanent and 'giving itself to itself' in the form of an incarnation between inner sense and word. As representations of what lies outdoors, the laundry girl and the milk girl are now only specimens that may never be incorporated into the writer's experiments.

While still believing that Albertine will return to him, shortly before he is informed of her death, the narrator admits that it is only the 'elimination of desire' that can grant happiness. Desire leads people to forget that '[t]he links between another person and ourselves exist only in our minds' (Proust 2002e: 418). Proust details a new conception of desire in relation to the plotting of the 'inner book of unknown signs'. The narrator, however, has not yet started writing and he believes that memory weakens these links with other people as it fades.

The nature of the narrator's painful struggle with memory and involuntary memory is therefore revealed as a means for greater self-awareness, since he admits that '[m]an is a being who cannot move beyond his own boundaries, who knows others only within himself' (ibid. 418). Of course, the 'nourishment' the reader finds in Proust's novel breaches these boundaries that the narrator, in not having begun to write, cannot yet explicitly claim as his own. The narrator's transformation of desire into something that seeks an internal object as opposed to something external appears to be almost complete when he admits that 'people and things started to exist for me only when they took on an individual existence in my imagination' (ibid. 479).

Marcel admits that '[l]ove, no, pleasure well rooted in the flesh helps literary work because it cancels out other pleasures, the pleasures of social life, for example, which are the same for everyone' (Proust 2002e: 165). However, the presumption that life, what becomes inseparable from writing for Proust, ultimately gives up a 'social life' that is the 'same for everyone' is grounded on a distinct understanding of intersubjectivity. Desire is useful to the 'man of letters' because it keeps him 'at a distance from other men' and because it restores 'some movement to a spiritual machine which otherwise, beyond a certain age, tends to seize up' (ibid. 166). However, even though the narrator uses desire to keep others 'at a distance', he does assign their actions to an inner world. The profound immanence he strives to describe through the 'real journey' to 'see the hundred universes that each of them can see' (ibid. 237) presumes that he can first separate, inside him, their universes from his universe. He invests in a state of self-alterity where the 'double' he possesses inside for 'every being' (231) he knows is separated from his sense of himself. Located in 'memory', these doubles are 'external to ourselves' (231–2), or external to our sense of ourselves, yet their actions have 'no more painful impact on us than an object placed some distance away' (232).

In another section the narrator sets up a frustrating sense of dualism for himself as he laments that 'Nature' had not provided for the 'interpenetration of souls' (Proust 2002e: 357). He realizes that even though Albertine's 'body was in the power of my body, her thought constantly escaped from my thought's grasp' (ibid. 357). The experience of others that could lead to a more engaging 'interpenetration of souls', as we recall, has become too painful for him, partially as a result of the social dynamic he has consigned himself to, whereby others have to be kept 'at a distance'. How can there be an 'interpenetration of souls' when desire is used to preserve distance? We have seen in the last chapter that Proust has invested in an alternative experience of the 'interpenetration of souls' through the nourishment that the reader and himself can offer each other. However, unlike Proust, the narrator has not yet attained such enlightenment. The narrator reveals how the state of immanence he is beginning to privilege protects him from the true nature of an embodied understanding of intersubjectivity. In recalling an incident where Charlus described his house as 'ugly' because he was not a collector, he admits that 'statues' and 'pictures' contemplated with detachment could have given him 'access to that way out of oneself' that leads to 'the life of others' (Proust 2002e: 358). However, it is an understanding of intersubjectivity and of the path to the 'life of others' that is only known through 'how we have first suffered by it' (ibid. 358). Living in communion with the 'life of others' ultimately brings pain. The sense of impotentiality that Agamben has aligned with the possibility of conceiving 'of a desire that as such remains immanent to itself' (Agamben 1999: 236) is examined in Proust by a writer-to-be who contemplates imparting so much of himself to the word that the resulting incarnation will discover an 'interpenetration of souls' between himself and the reader.

Incarnating criticism: creative force and critical act

In 'Force and Signification' Jacques Derrida argues that impotence is integral to literary criticism. In deconstructing Jean Rousset's structuralism, and indeed structuralism itself, Derrida argues that literary criticism is structuralist in every age, but that it is 'only now' becoming aware of this fact: 'Criticism has not always known this, but understands it now, and thus is in the process of thinking itself in its own concept, system and method' (Derrida 2002a: 3). For Derrida, 'form', what connotes structuralism for him, 'fascinates when one no longer has the force to understand force from within itself. That is, to create' (ibid. 3). For Derrida, force is bound up with the creative act of writing literature – the kind of writing criticism depends on. Derrida suggests that criticism, sublimating the repressed energy it feels by being removed from such force, inaugurates a 'separation' between 'the critical act and [the] creative force' (ibid. 380 footnote) and then sets about 'gravely and profoundly proving, that separation is the condition of the work, and not only of the discourse on the work' (ibid. 3). Separation is, then, what criticism inaugurates as a structural necessity implicit in the critical act and the creative force, or in the reading and writing of criticism and literature. Criticism has brought this notion of separation to literature and, for Derrida, it implies that '[i]mpotence, here, is a property not of the critic but of the criticism' (ibid. 380 footnote). The failures of structuralism are implicit in all criticism, since criticism is 'structuralist in every age'. However, Derrida believes that criticism can throw off what is responsible for such separation, namely its 'Platonism', metaphysical intentionality and its failure to 'permit the conceptualization of intensity or force' (ibid. 32), what are all components of the writing, or account of language that he wants to resist 'as far as is possible' (33). Due to its phenomenological roots structuralism has been ineffective 'in thinking [...] the mysterious failures called crises' (32). However, in questioning the potential of a 'force of weakness' in the roots of 'modern structuralism', Derrida argues that 'it can only be articulated in the language of form, through images of shadow and light' (32–3). He does not examine how this 'force of weakness', what recalls Agamben's suggestion that 'Beings that exist in the mode of potentiality *are capable of their own impotenti-ality*' (Agamben 1999: 182), is implicit in any creative force mediated by the body.

Derrida locates the 'force of weakness', once again, in Husserl's problematic account of genesis that was examined in Chapter 1. He questions the appearance of this 'weakness' in Husserl, because he sees it as integral to an 'oppositional couple' (Derrida 2002a: 33) of force and weakness that will never explain force itself. Derrida argues that structuralism's 'dependence' on phenomenology has meant that criticism has inherited an inability to permit the conceptualization of power as the '*tension* of intentionality' (ibid. 32). This difficulty results in a metaphysical short-sightedness that Derrida again phrases in terms of an incarnation; criticism inherits phenomenology's 'difficulties [...] of accounting for the successful or unsuccessful incarnation of *telos*' (32). Such an incarnation of telos is bound up with Derrida's belief that a 'structuralist reading' must appeal to the 'theological simulta-neity of the book' (28), that, for him, amounts to the 'myth of a total reading' that is 'promoted to the status of a regulatory ideal' (29). In other words, there is little acceptance of notions such as deferral, erasure or difference in this account of reading. Derrida's description of this simultaneity as 'truth within reading' replays the kind of immanence that he has critiqued in speech where the 'phenomen-ological voice' is taken to be a 'spiritual flesh that continues to speak and be present to itself – *to hear itself* – in the absence of the world' (Derrida 1973: 16). However, in examining Derrida's notes on criticism in relation to the opposition he works through here – he admits that 'our discourse irreducibly belongs to the system of meta-physical oppositions' (Derrida 2002a: 22) – I want to contrast the description of his means for overcoming this opposition, and for overcoming the impotence integral to criticism, what he describes as a violent means, with the method of Proust and Joyce.

Derrida describes his intentions in the essay as follows:

> Our discourse irreducibly belongs to the system of metaphysical oppositions. The break with this structure of belonging can be announced only through a *certain* organization, a certain *strategic* arrangement which, within the field of metaphysical oppositions, uses the strengths of the field to turn its own stratagems against it, producing a force of dislocation that spreads itself throughout the entire system, fissuring it in every direction and thoroughly *delimiting* it. (Derrida 2002: 22)

This is a decidedly violent process that Derrida describes, one that can only then set up another kind of opposition between this underlying process and the recognition of 'impotence' and 'weakness' that also assist Derrida in moving towards a force of 'resistance' that challenges structuralism and, hence, all forms of criticism. Derrida wants criticism to see itself as more than the 'philosophy of literature' (ibid. 33) and he looks forward to a day when it will no longer, in its 'exchange with literary writing', have to wait for such 'resistance' to be 'first organized into a "philosophy" which would govern some methodology of aes-thetics whose principles criticism would receive' (33). However, the violence of the approach suggested here, and the manner in which Husserl's recognition of a 'force of weakness' is questioned, creates another opposition between such impotentiality and the creative or 'dislocating' force that it must accompany. This reluctance to embrace weakness in proposing a systemic deconstruction that would appear to work by brute force alone, may lead to its own 'delimiting' examination of criticism's potential for appraising 'embodied meaning'.

Joyce and Proust give us criticism within the artwork, thereby unsettling the separation that Rousset and Derrida describe. Theodor Adorno describes Proust's novel as 'an artwork and a metaphysics of art' (Adorno 1997: 63). Joyce and Proust inaugurate in their work a very different sense of critical impotence that does not align the acknowledgement of impotentiality, or impotence, in writing with a violent process of 'dislocation' and systemic 'fissuring'. All 'criticism' and aesthetic theory in their work is mediated through characters who chart exhaustively the loss and failure of physical desire, and the recognition of impotentiality. Joyce's 'epic of the human body' and Proust's 'inner book of unknown signs' have 'critical acts' incorporated into them that are directly influenced by their respective characters' internalizations of these physical states. Viscerally examining the conditions of impotence and impotentiality, they bridge the gap between 'critical act' and 'creative force' through a writing that details these states. Joyce and Proust give rigorous analyses of the creative act, of 'force', and of form, from within the literary work. They give some of the potential for creative force back to criticism by incarnating it within the artwork, by making the creative force consubstantial with the critical act.

À la recherche is saturated with aesthetic theory that displays a rigorous understanding of its literary predecessors. It is an understanding that was worked towards, as it was for Joyce, in early pieces of criticism. The voice of much of the early criticism is indistinguishable from the later Proustian 'literary writing'. Do we read the narrator's literary criticism in *À la recherche*, which influences how we read his novel, differently from his description of a ball gown, a church, or a moment of enlightenment? Proust's understanding of aesthetic practice questions the role of the critic. William C. Carter argues that:

> [I]n his critical remarks about Saint-Beuve, Proust is writing as himself in a fictional situation, imagining a conversation with his mother before she died. This invented setting for a real person (Proust) commenting on another real person and his work (Sainte-Beuve) served as the incubator for the emergence of the Narrator's full voice. (Carter 2000: 467)

Stephen Dedalus's aesthetic theories require 'a new terminology and a new personal experience' (*P* 176), and the criticism that provides this 'new terminology' takes up a good part of Joyce's early novel. In the final volume of *À la recherche*, Marcel's reflections on his lack of 'literary talent' unleash what can only be described as an extensive critical evaluation of literature. The reader is asked to assess critical remarks on literature – 'that literature which is satisfied to "describe objects", to give merely a miserable listing of lines and surfaces, is the very one which, while styling itself "realist", is the farthest removed from reality' – while catching glimpses of her own 'inner book of unknown signs' that only the book, as literature, can reveal to her. However, the motivations for unsettling any divide between 'critical act' and 'creative force' are never described as a violent force, for to do so would then set up a contradiction in the work between this violence and the impotentiality that is always foregrounded. Later in his essay 'Force and Signification', Derrida describes force as 'a certain pure and infinite equivocality which gives signified meaning no respite' (Derrida 2002a: 29) and this lies closer to what Joyce and Proust achieve.

Their acknowledgement and foregrounding of impotentiality does not lead them to suggest that 'there is no phrase' 'which does not pass through the violence of the concept' (Derrida 2002a: 185). In doing so, they would jeopardize the consubstantiality they have privileged between word and life. The life they incarnate in their writing is not a life that will reveal the true nature of force through an opposing 'force of dislocation that spreads itself throughout the entire system fissuring it in every direction and thoroughly *delimiting* it' (ibid. 22). Their careful balancing of creative force and critical act instead works to privilege empathy and purity, what grounds reading and writing for them. One of Michel Foucault's last seminars, given at the College de France in 1982, examines how desire is played out in literature in terms of purity. For Foucault, life as a beautiful work obeys the idea of a certain style, or form of life, what I have argued Joyce and Proust incarnate in their work. Foucault argues that proof is more important than abstinence for the individual concerned to develop life as art, or as *tekhnê*. He claims that any proof requires a questioning of the self that is not found in the 'simple application of abstinence', what is 'only a voluntary privation' (Foucault 2001: 412). Life lived according to proof must privilege an 'interrogation of the self' (ibid. 413) and an appreciation of *tekhnê*, or an 'art of the self' (429).

The adherence to such a form of life becomes, for Foucault, the living of life *as* proof. Foucault believes that the Greek 'novel', epitomized in the Odyssean quest, marks the 'appearance of this theme that life must be a proof, a formative proof' (431). Such formative proof must lead, he argues, not to 'a reconciliation with the gods' but to a 'self-purity' that must be treated with 'vigilance' and 'self-possession' (431). The heroic quest, then, becomes a template, or proof, for such life, because, according to Foucault, the essential question that the novel raises is 'the question of virginity' (431), or personal purity, and this is the ideal state the author must strive to preserve. All the proofs that authors invest in and live out through their heroes and heroines are enacted, therefore, for the service, and for the staging of virginity and personal purity. The result is that the preservation of such a state of personal purity becomes a metaphoric figure in literature for the relationship with one's self. In other words, the novel as genre is proof for a certain concept of consciousness, one that it mediates through the metaphor of a narrative-that hinges on the question of virginity, a virginity that is 'a metaphor for the relationship with the self' (431). The lifeworks of Joyce and Proust embody this notion of 'life as proof'. In recognizing the potential to be gained from an acknowledgement of impotentiality, their unsettling of all myths attached to force enables them to forge a new 'concept of consciousness', one grounded on the belief that 'personal purity', 'profound reciprocity' (Depraz 1995: 226) and intersubjective empathy will ultimately enable them to offer the reader a share in their incarnation of 'life as proof'.

The staging of such personal purity and virginity, what mediates a new 'concept of consciousness' that is grounded, I believe, on an awareness of 'profound reciprocity', takes the subject beyond force and unsettles the regular course of desire. The subject becomes impervious to states, such as jealousy, that are linked to desire as force. The purity Marcel intends to capture is 'time in its pure state' (Proust 2002f: 180), even as he admits that he is 'taking up my work on the eve of my death' (Proust 1932b: 1119), what epitomizes impotentiality's role in potentiality. The 'conception of time as incarnate, of past years as still close held within us' (ibid. 1123) sustains him when he is about to put his creative force to work as his critical self-examination nears its end. Readers sustain Proust's rendering of 'time in its pure state' when they attach his metaphysics of time to their conceptions of consciousness, thereby supporting Proust's 'incarnate' time as 'they touch simultaneously epochs of their lives' through him (ibid. 1124).

The impotence Joyce's characters tackle in the face of desire also influences their alignment of the 'critical act' and the 'creative force'. Bloom and Richard Rowan have come to terms with the jealousy their wives' affairs bring and their version of 'purity' is a Bloomian 'universal love'. Rowan's thoughts on possession are most clearly expressed to his son Archie: 'But when you give it, you have given it. No robber can take it from you. *[He bends his head and presses his son's hand against his cheek.]* It is yours then for ever when you have given it. It will be yours always. That is to give' (Joyce 1979: 55). These characters share a belief in 'universal love', what Luce Irigaray has described in terms of 'indwelling': 'The act of love is neither an explosion nor an implosion but an indwelling. Dwelling with the self, and with the other – while letting the other go' (Irigaray 2004: 175). It is only the writer's letting go of the work that allows him any such 'indwelling', when he can eternally give and finally 'begin to forget it', so that the work 'will remember itself' through its readers 'from every sides, with all gestures, in each our word' (*FW* 614: 20–1).

Notes

Introduction

[1] James K. Smith argues that the 'question of incarnation' is really a question about Platonism and that Derrida's critique of Husserl is essentially a critique of Husserl's Platonism. For Smith, Derrida argues for 'an incarnational account of language as constituted by both presence and absence – a 'manifestation' (Kundgabe) which both "announces" and "conceals"' (Smith 2002: 218).

[2] Aryeh Botwinick argues that 'the key terms in his ethical vocabulary in this work [*Otherwise than Being*] are: passivity, incarnation, and substitution' (Botwinick 2002: 106). I examine Levinas's use of these terms in relation to his understanding of incarnation in Chapter 1.

[3] Ricoeur seeks a means of communication between the religions of the 'biblical Great Code' and 'other religious consciousnesses' (Ricoeur 2000: 145). He asks how 'this religious consciousness, informed by the biblical Great Code, could be open to other religious consciousnesses, informed by other scriptural codes, and how it could communicate with the latter [...] under the title interconfessional hospitality of one religion to another' (ibid. 145–6). My examination of the figure of the incarnation in literary and philosophical texts responds to Ricoeur's fundamental concern for interconfessional hospitality.

[4] Dominique Janicaud contests what he regards as a problematic development in the phenomenological tradition: 'It is a question here of analysing the methodological presuppositions permitting a phenomenologist (or by which a phenomenologist might believe him- or herself permitted) to open phenomenological investigations onto absolute Transcendence while putting aside the Husserlian concern for rigor and scientificity.

Emmanuel Levinas's *Totality and Infinity* is the first major work of French philosophy in which this theological turn is not only discernible, but explicitly taken up within a phenomenological inspiration' (Janicaud *et al.* 2000: 35–6).

[5] Gargani claims that 'religion has not enjoyed the same emancipation of the discursive field as other cultural disciplines' (Gargani 1998: 112). He wants to abandon what he calls the 'metaphysical commitments regarding the ontological status of the referents of theological discourse' so that 'objects of the religious tradition' might become figures for an interpretative perspective

on life' (ibid. 114). I argue that Joyce and Proust employ religious figures in a similar manner for the aesthetic. This is not so as to return religion to itself but rather so as to 'think through' the 'signs of the religious tradition' (Gargani 1998: 114). It is suggestive of a similar 'linguistic turn' to that described by Gianni Vattimo in terms of a distinct 'liberation of metaphor' unleashed through the demise of metanarratives: '[T]he renewed possibility of religious experience' has taken the 'guise of the liberation of metaphor' (Vattimo 2002: 16).

[6] Bergson questions philosophies that 'regard perception as a kind of contemplation': 'But this is what our opponents are determined not to see because they regard perception as a kind of contemplation, attribute to it always a purely speculative end, and maintain that it seeks some strange dis-interested knowledge, as though, by isolating it from action, and thus severing its links with the real, they were not rendering it both inexplicable and useless' (Bergson 1991: 68). Even though it can be argued that the contemplative aspect of perception is important for Proust and Joyce, they have a very different understanding of action. Each recalling of a moment of perception in Joyce and Proust is accompanied by a string of narrative shifts or tangential interior monologues that scrupulously record in a literary work the action integral to the contemplation of perceptions. Since these recordings appear in the narrative of a literary work, then the real/imaginary dichotomy that Bergson evokes above is unsettled further by the potential these narratives possess to allow the reader to re-embody or re-enact alternate worldviews that a reader might feel he or she can 'step into', so to speak.

[7] Merleau-Ponty refers to the body's capacity to express 'existence at every moment, this is in the sense in which a word expresses thought', as the body's 'incarnate significance'. He argues that this 'incarnate significance is the central phenomenon of which body and mind, sign and significance are abstract moments' (Merleau-Ponty 2003: 192).

[8] Joyce's interest in the notion of epiphany is well documented. The epiphany refers, for many, to the recording of a moment where a character is infused with a previously unrealized disposition through the encounter with some aspect of humdrum existence. While it must be acknowledged that the epiphany was, for Joyce, a specific literary form, this book argues that the aesthetic theory that underpins the epiphanies evolves within Joyce's later work while never wholly relinquishing this interest in the capacity of religious figures to contribute to the literary imagination.

[9] Robert Eaglestone takes Levinas 'at his word' in making a 'clear distinction' between Levinas's 'philosophical and confessional texts' (Eaglestone 1997: 5). However, Alphonso Lingis notes in his introduction to *Otherwise than Being or Beyond Essence* that, 'in transferring religious language to the ethical sphere, Levinas no doubt divinizes the relationship with alterity' (Levinas 1981: xxxix).

[10] See Peter Trifonas's *The Ethics of Writing: Derrida, Deconstruction, and Pedagogy* (Lanham, Md.: Rowman and Littlefield, 2000).

[11] Thomas Docherty argues: '[T]he ethics of alterity disposes a reading subject-in-process towards a historical futurity in which she or he constantly defers the production of identity or of an empirically determined self-present selfhood' (Docherty 1996: 41).

[12] Depraz argues that 'the first texts of *Husserliana XV* [dating from 1929] stick to a strictly egological problematic in which the mode of access remains Cartesian: in this way text 3 puts forward the idea of "the apodicticity of the ego" and "the notion that the apodicticity of the alter ego is only hypothetical" '. Depraz continues: '[I]n the first months of 1930 appears, on the other hand, texts that make way for the idea of an intersubjective reduction distinct from the egological reduction'. (Depraz 1995: 219)

Chapter 1: Phenomenology and incarnation

[1] Extracts from this section are taken from: O'Sullivan, M. (2006), *Michel Henry: Incarnation, Barbarism and Belief.* Oxford: Peter Lang.

[2] My examination of incarnation in this chapter responds to Hent de Vries's belief that by 'renegotiating the limits and aporias of the ethical and the political in light of the religious and theological, we can rearticulate the terms and oppositions in which the most pressing and practical present-day cultural debates are phrased' (de Vries 1999: xii).

[3] Badiou writes in 'Mathematics and Philosophy': 'And it is by donning the contemporary matheme like a coat of armour that I have undertaken, alone at first, to undo the disastrous consequences of philosophy's "linguistic turn"; to demarcate philosophy from phenomenological religiosity; to re-found the metaphysical triad of being, event and subject; to take a stand against poetic prophesying' (Badiou 2006: 17).

[4] In 'Experience and Language in Religious Discourse' Ricoeur seeks a means of communication between the religions of the 'biblical Great Code' and 'other religious consciousnesses' (Ricoeur 2000: 145). He asks how 'this religious consciousness, informed by the biblical Great Code, could be open to other religious consciousnesses, informed by other scriptural codes, and how it could communicate with the latter within the horizon of the regulative idea evoked at the beginning of this study under the title interconfessional hospitality of one religion to another' (ibid. 145–6). He argues that the religious consciousness mediated through the 'Jewish then Christian Scriptures' hinges on the 'concrete figure' that is the 'reciprocity between the triad of the call and that of the response' (145). My examination of the figure of the incarnation in literary and philosophical texts responds to Ricoeur's fundamental concern for the figure as a means for offering interconfessional hospitality.

[5] Kant suggests that the theologian 'leaps over the wall of ecclesiastical faith'

when he ventures into the realm of allegory, thereby fleeing into the 'free and open field of private judgement and philosophy' (Kant 1992: 286).

⁶ One of the central arguments in *The Essence of Manifestation* revolves around what Henry refers to as 'ontological monism'. Henry argues that the 'uniqueness' of this approach to philosophy, the presuppositions of which 'ruled the development of occidental philosophical thought', can only be questioned by 'surpassing monism' (Henry 1973: 74). Even though Greek thought is dualist for Henry in its thinking about the body (it posits a trans-cendental soul and a 'perishable' body), it is ontologically monist. In other words, it takes for granted its 'Being-given rather than considering it in and for itself'; it 'considers a being as it offers itself to us' without questioning its givenness (ibid. 74). Henry believes that the Cartesian philosophy of con-sciousness corrected this ontological oversight through its '*opening of another dimension of existence and essence*' (74). However, Henry argues that it also inaugurated another species of dualistic thought. What has become 'classical' since Descartes's time is the opposition 'between consciousness and the thing'. Henry asks whether this opposition can be 'made equivalent, as has been done currently [he is thinking here, for example, of Heideggerian philosophy], to the opposition between consciousness and Being'. *The Essence of Manifestation* attempts to override this opposition by returning to an examination of the basic presuppositions of ontological monism. Henry seeks to dispense with this opposition between consciousness and the 'thing' and to describe it instead in terms of a unique sense of 'unity': 'Understood in its unity with the essence which constitutes its foundation, is the thing still an anti-thetic term for con-sciousness, or rather, *is not consciousness precisely the very thing-ness of the thing and as such the essence of it?* (75).

⁷ Desire is capitalized, for Levinas, once he has described it as the kind of desire that 'desires beyond everything that can complete it' (Levinas 1969: 34).

⁸ The term 'auto-affection' translates Henry's '*auto-affection*'. Whereas Susan Emmanuel, in her translation of *I am the Truth*, translates it as 'self-affection', in *Michel Henry: Incarnation, Barbarism and Belief*, I retain 'auto-affection' because it relates more clearly to the notion of 'auto-affection' that Derrida critiques in the work of Husserl. The juxtaposition of these two versions of auto-affection becomes important for the examination of representation. Girard Etzkorn also translates the French '*auto-affection*' as 'auto-affection' in his translation of *L'Essence de la manifestation*. In *The Essence of Manifestation* we read: '[s]elf-affection' 'co-constitutes auto-affection' (Henry 1973: 188). It is therefore a slightly broader concept than self-affection. Auto-affection refers to both an individual's '[a]*ffection by self*' (ibid. 189) and to the essential movement of temporality. For Henry, time is not 'affected by a being' (187), but instead by 'time itself *under the form of the pure horizon of Being*' (187).

Chapter 2: Joyce and the incarnation of language

[1] See Valery Larbaud's preface to the 10/18 edition of Dujardin's *Les Lauriers sont coupés*, p. 8. This conversation took place in 1920. Dujardin's novel dates from 1887. For Gérard Genette's descripion of this style see *Narrative Discourse: An Essay in Method* (1988), p. 173.

[2] Clive Hart informs us of Joyce's interest in Vico's cyclical understanding of history: 'Joyce was always an arranger rather than a creator, for, like a medieval artist, he seems superstitiously to have feared the presumption of human attempts at creation. The medieval notion that the artist may organise but cannot under any circumstances create something really new is, of course, capable of universal application but it is more than usually relevant to Joyce' (Hart 1962: 44). Hart continues: 'Vico's theories are based on a tripartite formula, with a short interconnecting link between the cycles; nearly every Indian system uses a primarily four-part cycle, with or without a short additional fifth Age'. Joyce 'extends Vico's fourth age, on the analogy of the Indian cycles, and gives it a great deal more detailed attention than it receives in the *Scienza Nuova*. He still adheres to the general Viconian progress – Birth, Marriage, Death and Reconstitution'. Hart also regards Shem's chapter, Chapter 3.1 of *Finnegans Wake*, as 'the easiest to demonstrate the Viconian 4 cycles' as it is represented in Shaun's 'four watches of the night' (ibid. 50).

[3] Bergson writes: 'The *actuality* of our perception thus lies in its *activity*, in the movements which prolong it, and not in its greater intensity: the past is only idea, the present is ideo-motor. But this is what our opponents are determined not to see because they regard perception as a kind of contemplation, attribute to it always a purely speculative end, and maintain that it seeks some strange disinterested knowledge, as though, by isolating it from action, and thus severing its links with the real, they were not rendering it both inexplicable and useless' (Bergson 1991: 68).

[4] John Bishop draws our attention to the fact that 'Joyce said "there [were] no characters"' in *Finnegans Wake*, where all traits featuring the 'chiaroscuro coalesce', their contraries eliminated, in one 'stable somebody' (*FW* 107: 29–30)' (Bishop 1993: 306).

[5] Joyce's early review of J. Lewis McIntyre's *Giordano Bruno* (London: Macmillan, 1903) cites Coleridge in arguing for Bruno's fundamental concern with nature's 'tendency to reunion'. The extract from Coleridge reads: 'Every power in nature or in spirit must evolve an opposite as the sole condition and means of its manifestation; and every opposition is, therefore, a tendency to reunion' (*The Friend* [1818] Essay xiii). The argument appears in Joyce's review, 'The Bruno Philosophy' (Barry 2000: 93–4).

[6] W. Y. Tindall argues: '*Ulysses* and *Finnegans Wake* are great epiphanies, disclosing their whatness and the whatness of reality' (Tindall 1950: 73).

[7] In a letter to Constatine Curran from July 1904 Joyce refers to his motivations for *Dubliners* in relation to the notion of *epiclesis*: 'I am writing a series

of epicleti – ten – for a paper. I have written one. I call the series *Dubliners*, to
betray the soul of that hemiplegia or paralysis which many consider a city'
(Ellmann 1972: 169). Ellmann describes *epiclesis* as follows: 'The word epicleti,
an error for *epicleses* (Latin) or *epicleseis* (Greek), referred to an invocation still
found in the mass of the Eastern Church, but dropped from the Roman ritual,
in which the Holy Ghost is besought to transform the host into the body and
blood of Christ. What Joyce meant by this term, adapted like *epiphany* and
eucharistic moment from ritual, he suggested to his brother Stanislaus: [Ellmann
also refers the reader here to Stanislaus Joyce's *My Brother's Keeper* (1958), pp.
103–4] "Don't you think there is a certain resemblance between the mystery of
the Mass and what I am trying to do? I mean that I am trying ... to give people
some kind of intellectual pleasure or spiritual enjoyment by converting the
bread of everyday life into something that has a permanent artistic life of its
own ... for their mental, moral, and spiritual uplift" ' (Ellmann 1972: 169).

   [8] Weldon Thornton argues that 'one of the most striking things about
Finnegans Wake is the absence in it of anything like individual characters'
(Thornton 1994: 61).

   [9] Scholes famously restricts the use of the term epiphany to 40 sketches of
Dublin life, recorded by Joyce in a notebook between 1900 and 1903, 22 of
which reside at the State University of New York at Buffalo.

   [10] It is very likely that Joyce borrowed this notion of emotions being 'mirrored perfectly' in a 'lucid supple periodic prose' from Aquinas. Hans Georg
Gadamer reminds us in *Truth and Method* of Thomas's 'brilliant metaphor' for
how the 'perfect word' is created: 'The perfect word, therefore, is formed only
in thinking, like a tool, but once it exists as the full perfection of the thought,
nothing more is created with it. Rather, the thing is then present in it. Thus it
is not a real tool. Thomas found a brilliant metaphor for this: the word is like a
mirror in which the thing is seen. The curious thing about this mirror, however, is that it nowhere extends beyond the image of the thing. In it nothing is
mirrored except this one thing, so that the whole mirror reflects only the
image (similitudo). What is remarkable about this metaphor is that the word is
understood here entirely as the perfect reflection of the thing – i.e., as the
expression of the thing – and has left behind it the path of the thought to
which alone, however, it owes its existence. This does not happen with the
divine mind' (Gadamer 1995: 425). In the above passage, Stephen prefers the
perfect mirroring of 'individual emotions', one imagines, in an 'inner world'
of 'lucid supple periodic prose' to the 'glowing sensible world' as it is reflected
through a language 'many-coloured and richly storied'. What is important
here is that Stephen does not want his emotions to be reflected through a
process that disperses the emotion into various ornate streams, but rather to
mirror the emotions perfectly inwardly through 'contemplation' before
proceeding.

   [11] Even before this point, the narrator most regularly refers to her as 'Mrs

Conroy' or 'Gabriel's wife'. While Gabriel does call her by her name in their final words to each other, the narrator continues to employ 'she'.

[12] Stephen Spender extends his reading of Joyce to a discussion of the formal expression of intersubjectivity in *Ulysses*: 'Joyce does not objectify his world by seeing it from the outside, but by seeing several characters through each others' eyes, from the inside. *Ulysses* is a series of introspective studies of people who are outside each other, so they are externalised not in their own, but in each others' minds' (quoted in Deming 1970: 749).

[13] In one of the unpublished Zurich notebooks, Joyce reveals his thoughts on metaphor: 'Good diction: tria – metaphor, antithesis, energy. Metaphor prefer to comparison. Comparison makes folks wait and tells you only what something is like' [Noon's punctuation] (quoted in Noon 1957: 63).

[14] Richard Ellmann's biography records that for the first half of 1925 Joyce was dogged by both dental and opthalmological difficulties that made any work on *Work in Progress* incredibly difficult: 'Early in April the fragment of tooth was removed, and in the interval between dentist and opthalmologist Joyce had just enough sight to be able, with the aid of three magnifying glasses and his son, to revise Chapter V (104–25) for the *Criterion*, where it was published in July. He submitted to the seventh operation on his left eye in the middle of April and remained in the clinic for ten days. There were not many visitors' (Ellmann 1972: 581).

[15] Joyce complained to Harriet Shaw Weaver in a letter of November 1930 that the 'first draft of about two thirds of the first section of Part II [of *Finnegans Wake*] came out like drops of blood'. He also explains that for the next two years he did almost nothing (Joyce 1957: 295).

[16] Joyce writes this in a letter to Harriet Shaw Weaver on 1 May 1935 (Joyce 1957: 366).

[17] Joyce describes his daughter's condition in a letter to Constantine Curran on 10 August 1935 (Joyce 1957: 378–9).

Chapter 3: Proust and the incarnation of language

[1] This essay originally appeared as: O'Sullivan, M. (2005), 'Metaphor's Lost Time: Notes on the New Translations of Proust', *Nottingham French Studies*, 44, (2), (Summer), 31–41.

[2] All extracts from *À la recherce du temps perdu* are taken from Jean-Yves Tadié's revised edition (Paris: Gallimard, 1999).

[3] 'This is because lost time is not only passing time, which alters beings and annihilates what once was, it is also the time one wastes (why must one waste one's time, be worldly, be in love, rather than working and creating a work of art?). And time regained is first of all a time recovered at the heart of time lost, which gives us an image of eternity; but it is also an absolute, original time, an actual eternity that is affirmed in art' (Deleuze 2000: 17).

⁴ The original French reads: 'Mais, quand d'un passé ancien rien ne sub-
siste, après la mort des êtres, après la destruction des choses, seules, plus frêles
mais plus vivaces, plus immatérielles, plus persistantes, plus fidèles, l'odeur et
la saveur restent encore longtemps, comme des âmes, à se rappeler, à
attendre, à espérer, sur la ruine de tout le reste, à porter sans fléchir, sur leur
gouttelette presque impalpable, l'édifice immense du souvenir' (Proust 1999:
46).

⁵ Terence Kilmartin's revision reads: 'But when from a long-distant past,
nothing subsists, after the people are dead, after the things are broken and
scattered, taste and smell alone, more fragile but more enduring, more
unsubstantial, more persistent, more faithful, remain poised a long time, like
souls remembering, waiting, hoping, amid the ruins of all the rest; and bear
unflinchingly, in the tiny and almost impalpable drop of their essence, the vast
structure of recollection' (Proust 1989: 50).

⁶ The original reads: 'un certain rapport entre ces sensations et ces souve-
nirs qui nous entourent simultanément' (Proust 1999: 2280).

⁷ The original reads: 'rapport unique que l'écrivain doit retrouver pour en
enchainer à jamais dans sa phrase les deux termes différents' (Proust 1999:
2280).

⁸ The translation of this line and the passage it is taken from also offers
room for consideration. Lydia Davis's translation of the larger passage reads:
'The reality I had known no longer existed. That Mme Swann did not arrive
exactly the same at the same moment was enough to make the avenue different. The places we have known do not belong solely to the world of space in
which we situate them for our greater convenience. They were only a thin slice
among contiguous impressions that formed our life at that time; the memory
of a certain image is only regret for a certain moment; and houses, roads,
avenues are as fleeting, alas, as the years' (Proust 2002a: 430).

The original reads: 'La réalité que j'avais connue n'existait plus. Il suffisait
que Mme Swann n'arrivât pas toute pareille au même moment, pour que
l'Avenue fût autre. Les lieux que nous avons connus n'appartiennent pas
qu'au monde de l'espace où nous les situons pour plus de facilité. Ils n'étaient
qu'une mince tranche au milieu d'impressions contiguës qui formaient notre
vie d'alors; le souvenir d'une certaine image n'est que le regret d'un certain
instant; et les maisons, les routes, les avenoues, sont fugitives, hélas, comme les
années' (Proust 1999: 342).

Here we find the narrator almost lamenting the fact that reality does not
present us with the means for recapturing memories, for finding 'dans la
réalité les tableaux de la mémoire'. Moncrieff's translation translates the
second sentence above as '[t]he places that we have known belong now only to
the little world of space on which we map them for our own convenience'
(Proust 1932a: 325). The emphasis in Davis's translation favours that space
that is beyond our immediate control and beyond our 'convenience'. The
passage, however, appears to be emphasizing the contrived nature of memory,

its capacity to unsettle any sense of 'reality' our misconceptions of memory connote. The collective sense of the passage appears to lean towards Moncrieff's translation where reality is to be relinquished for belief in a 'world of space' that is arranged for our convenience. The narrator relieves reality, therefore, of any aura or authenticity it might be seen to possess above memory. Memory is concerned here, it seems, with 'regret' and with the 'image', and not with a reality or other space beyond convenience.

[9] This is all the more surprising since the narrator recognizes the 'psychological value' of gossip: 'It prevents the mind from falling asleep over the fictitious view that it takes of what it believes things to be like, which is only their outward appearance. It turns the inside out with the magical dexterity of an idealist philosopher and quickly offers us an unsuspected corner of the reverse side of the fabric' (Proust 2002d: 441–2).

Chapter 4: Incarnation and impotence: Joyce, Proust and the incarnation of desire

[1] 'Impotentiality' and 'Im-potentiality' are taken from Giorgio Agamben for whom both terms appear to refer to the same idea. 'Impotentiality' appears first in the section entitled 'On Potentiality' from his 1999 collection Potentialities ('On Potentiality' was held as a lecture in 1986): 'Beings that exist in the mode of potentiality are capable of their own own impotentiality' (182). In *Homo Sacer*, which appeared in English in 1998, Agamben argues that when 'what is potential' 'sets aside its own potential not to be' it is setting aside its 'im-potentiality' (46). In this book both terms refer to a state invested with this 'potential not to be'. In general, 'impotentiality' is used throughout the book, the hyphenated version only being used for direct quotations.

[2] Susan Emmanuel writes: 'Throughout the text, Michel Henry uses French pathos and pathétique in what amounts to the sense of these words' Greek roots. For pathos, that semantic domain extends from "anything that befalls one" through "what one has suffered, one's experience" (including its negative inflection in something like English "suffering"), to "any passive state or condition". The adjectival form – which we spell "pathētik" – has nearly reversed the meaning of its root, so that it applies to the object that arouses feeling rather than to the one who undergoes emotion – means "subject to feeling, capable of feeling something"' (Henry 2003: ix).

[3] In *Coriolanus* the epithet references both a sense of incarnation and impotence. Sicinius asks, in relation to the despotic Coriolanus who is viewed by the rabble as stepping well beyond the mark of righteous rule, '[w]here is this viper / That would depopulate the city and / Be every man himself?' (Shakespeare 1926: 840).

Bibliography

Adorno, T. (1997), *Aesthetic Theory*, eds G. Adorno and R. Tiedemann. Theory and History of Literature, Vol. 88. Minneapolis: University of Minnesota Press.

Agamben, G. (1998), *Homo Sacer: Sovereign Power and Bare Life*, trans. D. Heller-Roazen. Stanford: Stanford University Press.

—— (1999), *Potentialities: Collected Essays in Philosophy*, ed. and trans. Daniel Heller-Roazen. Stanford: Stanford University Press.

—— (2005), *The Time That Remains: A Commentary on the Letter to the Romans*, trans. Patricia Dailey. Stanford: Stanford University Press.

Attridge, D. and Ferrer, D. (1984) (eds), *Post-structuralist Joyce: Essays from the French*. Cambridge: Cambridge University Press.

—— (2000), *Joyce Effects: On Language, Theory, and History*. Cambridge: Cambridge University Press.

Auerbach, E. (1984), *Scenes from the Drama of European Literature: Six Essays*. New York: Meridian.

Badiou, A. (2001), *Ethics: An Essay on the Understanding of Evil*, trans. P. Hallward. London: Verso.

—— (2003), *Saint Paul; The Foundations of Universalism*. Stanford: Stanford University Press.

—— (2006), *Theoretical Writings*. London: Continuum.

Baldwin, T. (2003), *The Cambridge History of Philosophy 1870–1945*. Cambridge: Cambridge University Press.

Barry, K. (2000) (ed.), *James Joyce: Occasional, Critical, and Political Writing*. Conor Deane (trans.). Oxford: Oxford University Press.

Beckett, S. (1999), *Proust and Three Dialogues with George Duthuit*. London: John Calder.

Beja, M. (1971), *Epiphany in the Modern Novel*. London: Peter Owen.

Benjamin, W. (1987), 'The Image of Proust', in H. Bloom (ed.), *Marcel Proust: Modern Critical Views*. New York: Chelsea House Publishers, pp. 59–71.

Bergson, H. (1991), *Matter and Memory*, trans. N. M. Paul and W. S. Palmer. New York: Zone Books.

Bishop, J. (1993), *Joyce's Book of the Dark*. Wisconsin: University of Wisconsin Press.

Bloom, H. (1986), *James Joyce.* Modern Critical Views. New York: Chelsea House Publishers.

—— (1987), *Marcel Proust.* Modern Critical Views. New York: Chelsea House Publishers.

—— (1988) (ed. and introd.), *Dubliners: Modern Critical Interpretations.* New York: Chelsea House Publishers.

—— (2004) (ed. and introd.), *Leopold Bloom.* Philadelphia: Chelsea House.

Bosinelli, R., Bollettieri, M. and Mosher, H. F. (1998) (eds), *Rejoycing: New Readings of Dubliners.* Lexington: Kentucky University Press.

Botwinick, A. (2002), 'Emmanuel Levinas's Otherwise than Being, the Phenomenology Project, and Skepticism'. *Telos*, 20, 95–117.

Bowen, Z. (1981) 'Joyce and the Epiphany Concept: A New Approach'. *Journal of Modern Literature*, 9 (1), 103–14.

Bramly, S. (1994), *Leonardo: The Artist and the Man*, trans. S. Reynolds. London: Penguin.

Brown, R. (1988), *James Joyce and Sexuality.* Cambridge: Cambridge University Press.

Budgen, F. (1960), *James Joyce and the Making of Ulysses.* Bloomington: Indiana University Press.

Burke, K. (1970), *The Rhetoric of Religion: Studies in Logology.* Berkeley: University of California Press.

Carter, W. C. (2000), *Marcel Proust: A Life.* New Haven: Yale University Press.

Cixous, Hélène (1976), *The Exile of James Joyce*, trans. S. Purcell. London: John Calder.

Clark, K. (1993), *The World of Leonardo.* London: Penguin.

Critchley, S. (1992), *The Ethics of Deconstruction: Derrida and Levinas.* Oxford: Blackwell.

Cross, R. (2002), *The Metaphysics of the Incarnation: Thomas Aquinas to Duns Scotus.* Oxford: Oxford University Press.

Davis, S. T., Kendall, D. and O'Collins, G. (2004), *The Incarnation.* Oxford: Oxford University Press.

Deleuze, G. (1976), *Proust et les signes.* Paris: Presses Universitaires de France.

—— (2000), *Proust and Signs*, trans. R. Howard. European Thinkers. London: The Athlone Press.

Deleuze, G. and Guattari, F. (2004), *Anti-Oepidus: Capitalism and Schizophrenia.* London: Continuum.

De Man, P. (1979), *Allegories of Reading: Figural Language in Rousseau, Nietzsche, Rilke and Proust.* New Haven: Yale University Press.

—— (1984), 'Autobiography as De-Facement', in *The Rhetoric of Romanticism.* New York: Colombia University Press, pp. 67–82.

Deming, R. H. (1970) (ed.), *James Joyce: The Critical Heritage.* Vol. 2. 1928–1941. London: Routledge & Kegan Paul.

Depraz, N. (1995), *Transcendence et Incarnation: Le Statut de l'intersubjectivité comme alterité à soi chez Husserl.* Paris: J. Vrin.

Derrida, J. (1973), *Speech and Phenomena: And Other Essays on Husserl's Theory of Signs*, trans. and introd. D. B. Allison, preface by Newton Garver. Evanston: Northwestern University Press.

—— (1974) 'White Mythology: Metaphor in the Text of Philosophy'. *New Literary History*, 6, 11–74.

—— (1982), *Margins of Philosophy*. A. Bass (trans.). Chicago: University of Chicago Press.

—— (1984), 'Two words for Joyce', trans. Geoff Bennington, in D. Attridge and D. Ferrer (eds), *Post-structuralist Joyce: Essays from the French*. Cambridge: Cambridge University Press.

—— (1987), *The Post Card: From Socrates to Freud and Beyond*. Chicago: University of Chicago Press.

—— (1989), *Edmund Husserl's Origin of Geometry: An Introduction*, trans., preface & afterword J. P. Leavey, Jr. Lincoln: University of Nebraska Press.

—— (1992a), *Acts of Literature*, ed. D. Attridge. London: Routledge.

—— (1992b), 'Ulysses Gramophone: Hear Say Yes in Joyce', in D. Attridge (ed.), *Acts of Literature*. London: Routledge, pp. 253–309.

—— (1992c), *Given Time: 1. Counterfeit Money*, trans. Peggy Kamuf. Chicago: Chicago University Press.

—— (1998), *Of Grammatology*, trans. G. C. Spivak. Baltimore: Johns Hopkins University Press.

—— (2002a), *Writing and Difference*, trans. and introd. A. Bass. London: Routledge.

—— (2002b), *Acts of Religion*, ed. G. Anidjar. London: Routledge.

—— (2003), *The Problem of Genesis in Husserl's Philosophy*, trans. M. Hobson. Chicago: University of Chicago Press.

Derrida, J. and Vattimo, G. (eds) (1998), *Religion*. Stanford: Stanford University Press.

De Vries, H. (1999), *Philosophy and the Turn to Religion*. Baltimore and London: The Johns Hopkins University Press.

—— (2002), *Religion and Violence: Philosophical Perspectives from Kant to Derrida*. Baltimore: The Johns Hopkins University Press.

Docherty, T. (1996), *Alterities: Criticism, History, Representation*. Oxford: Clarendon Press.

Droit, R.-P. (1987), 'Un essai de Michel Henry La Barbarie des temps modernes', *Le Monde*, 1 January.

—— (2002), 'Michel Henry: Un philosophe du sujet vivant', *Le Monde*, 7 July.

Eaglestone, R. (1997), *Ethical Criticism: Reading After Levinas*. Edinburgh: Edinburgh University Press.

Eco, U. (1984), *Semiotics and the Philosophy of Language*. London: Macmillan.

Eide, M. (2002), *Ethical Joyce*. Cambridge: Cambridge University Press.

Ellmann, R. (1972), *James Joyce*. New York: Oxford University Press.

Ellmann, R. (ed.) (1975), *The Selected Letters of James Joyce*. London: Faber and Faber.

Florindi, L (2003), 'Two Faces of Scepticism', in T. Baldwin (ed.), *The Cambridge History of 1870–1945*, pp. 533–43.

Foucault, M. (1994), *The Order of Things: An Archaeology of the Human Sciences*. New York: Vintage.

—— (2001), 'L'hermeneutique du Sujet, Cours du 17 Mars 1982', *Cours au College de France 1981–82*. Cours du 17 mars. Paris: Seuil, pp. 395–434.

French, M. (1993), *The Book as World: James Joyce's Ulysses*. New York: Paragon House.

Freud, S. (1991), *The Essentials of Psycho-Analysis: The Definitive Collection of Sigmund Freud's Essays*, ed. and introd. A. Freud, trans. J. Strachey. London: Penguin.

Frye, N. (1973), *Anatomy of Criticism: Four Essays*. Princeton: Princeton University Press.

Frymer-Kensky, T. S., Novak, D., Ochs, P., Sandmet, D., Signer, M. and Cherry, E. T. (2000), *Christianity in Jewish Terms. Radical Traditions*. Boulder: Westview Press.

Gadamer, H. G. (1995), *Truth and Method*, trans. J. Weinsheimer and D. G. Marshall (2nd revised edn). New York: Continuum.

Gana, N. (2005), 'The Poetic of Mourning: The Tropologic of Prosopopoeia in Joyce's "The Dead"'. *American Imago*, 60, (2), 159–78.

Gargani, A. (1998), 'Religious Experience as Event and Interpretation', in J. Derrida and G. Vattimo (eds), *Religion*. Stanford: Stanford University Press, pp. 111–35.

Genette, G. (1988), *Narrative Discourse Revisited*. New York: Cornell University Press.

Gilbert, Stuart (1969), *James Joyce's Ulysses*. London: Faber and Faber.

Girard, R. (1987), 'The Worlds of Proust' in H. Bloom (ed.), *Marcel Proust. Modern Critical Views*. New York: Chelsea House Publishers, pp. 71–95.

Groden, M. (1977), *Ulysses in Progress*. Princeton: Princeton University Press.

Halbertal, M. (1997), *People of the Book: Canon, Meaning and Authority*. Cambridge, MA: Harvard University Press.

Hart, C. (1962), *Structure and Motif in Finnegans Wake*. London: Faber and Faber.

Hayman, D. (1990), *The 'Wake' in Transit*. New York: Cornell University Press.

—— (1998), 'The Purpose and Permanence of the Joycean Epiphany'. *James Joyce Quarterly*, 35.4/36.1 (Summer/Fall), 633–55.

Heidegger, M. (1997), *Being and Time*, trans. J. Macquarre and E. Robinson. London: Blackwell.

Henke, S. A. (1990), *James Joyce and the Politics of Desire*. London: Routledge.

Henry, M. (1965), *Philosophie et phénoménologie du corps: essai sur l'ontologie biranienne*. Paris: Presses Universitaires de France.

—— (1973), *The Essence of Manifestation*, trans. G. Etzkorn. The Hague: Martinus Nijhoff.

—— (2000), *Incarnation: Une philosophie de la chair*. Paris: Seuil.

—— (2002), *Paroles du Christ*. Paris, Seuil.

—— (2003), *I am the Truth*, trans. S. Emmanuel. Stanford: Stanford University Press.

—— (2004a), *Phénoménologie de la vie. Tome I. De la subjectivité*. Paris: Presses Universitaires de France. Épiméthée.

—— (2004b), *Phénoménologie de la vie. Tome II. De la phénoménologie*. Paris: Presses Universitaires de France. Épiméthée.

—— (2004c), *Phénoménologie de la vie. Tome III. De L'art et du politique*. Paris: Presses Univesitaires de France. Épiméthée.

—— (2004d), *Phénoménologie de la vie. Tome IV. Sur l'éthique et la religion*. Paris: Presses Universitaires de France. Épiméthée.

—— (2004e), *Phénoménologie matérielle*. Paris: Presses Universitaires de France.

—— (2004f), *Auto-donation: Entretiens et conférences*, ed. M Uhl. Paris: Beauchesne.

—— (2005), *Entretiens*. Arles: Sulliver.

Husserl, E. (1965), *Phenomenology and the Crisis of Philosophy*, trans. and ed. Q. Lauer. New York: Harper and Row.

—— (1970a), *Logical Investigations*. Vol. 1, trans. J. N. Findlay. London: Routledge and Kegan Paul.

—— (1970b), *Logical Investigations*. Vol. 2, trans. J. N. Findlay. London: Routledge and Kegan Paul.

—— (1970c), *The Crisis of European Sciences and Transcendental Phenomenology: An Introduction to Phenomenological Philosophy*, trans. and introd. D. Carr. Evanston: Northwestern University Press.

—— (1970d) *Cartesian Meditations: An Introduction to Phenomenology*, trans. D. Cairns. The Hague: Martinus Nijhoff.

—— (1977), *Phenomenological Psychology: Edmund Husserl Lectures (Summer Session) 1925*, trans. J. Scanlon. The Hague: Martinus Nijhoff.

Irigaray, L. (1985), *This Sex Which Is Not One*, trans. C. Porter with C. Bourke. New York: Cornell University Press.

—— (2004), *An Ethics of Sexual Difference*. London: Continuum.

Iser, W. (1978), *The Act of Reading: A Theory of Aesthetic Response*. London: Routledge and Kegan Paul.

Jaarsma, A. S. (2003), 'Irigaray's *To Be Two*: The Problem of Evil and the Plasticity of Incarnation'. *Hypatia*, 18, (1), 44–62.

Janicaud, D., Courtine, J.-F., Chrétien, J.-L., Marion, J.-L., Henry M. and Ricoeur, P. (2000), *Phenomenology and the 'Theological Turn': The French Debate*, trans. B. G. Prusak and J. L. Kosky. New York: Fordham University Press.

Jaurretche, C. (1998), *The Sensual Philosophy: Joyce and the Aesthetics of Mysticism*. Wisconsin: University of Wisconsin Press.

Johnson G. A. and Smith, M. B. (eds) (1990), *Ontology and Alterity in Merleau-Ponty*. Evanston: Northwestern University Press.

Joyce, J. (1957), *Selected Letters*, ed. S. Gilbert. London: Faber and Faber.

—— (1963), *Stephen Hero*. New York: New Directions. [*SH*]

—— (1975), *The Selected Letters of James Joyce*, ed. R. Ellmann. London: Faber and Faber.

—— (1979), *Exiles*. London: Panther.

—— (1991) *Poems and Shorter Writings including Epiphanies, Giacomo Joyce and 'A Portrait of the Artist'*, eds R. Ellmann, W. Litz and J. Whittler-Ferguson. London: Faber and Faber.

—— (1992a), *Dubliners*. London: Penguin. [*D*]

—— (1992b), *Ulysses*. London: Penguin. [*U*]

—— (1999), *Finnegans Wake*, introd. J. Bishop. New York: Penguin. [*FW*]

—— (2000), *A Portrait of the Artist as a Young Man*. Oxford: Oxford University Press. [*P*]

Joyce, S. (1958), *My Brother's Keeper: James Joyce's Early Years*, ed. and introd. R. Ellmann, preface by T. S. Eliot. New York: Viking Press.

Kant, I. (1992), *The Conflict of the Faculties*, trans. M. J. Gregor. Lincoln: University of Nebraska Press.

Kenner, H. (1973), *The Pound Era*. Berkeley: University of California Press.

—— (1978), *Joyce's Voices*. Berkeley: University of California Press.

Kierkegaard, S. (1992), *Either/Or: A Fragment of Life*. London: Penguin.

Kristeva, J. (1980), *Desire in Language: A Semiotic Approach to Language and Art*. London: Basil Blackwell.

—— (1984), *Le temps sensible: Proust et l'expérience littéraire*. Paris: Gallimard.

Lacan, J. (1977), *Écrits*, trans. A. Sheridan. New York: Norton.

Laoureux, S. (2005), *L'immanence à la limite: Recherches sur la phénoménologie de Michel Henry*. Paris: Cerf.

Lawlor, L. (2002), *Derrida and Husserl: The Basic Problem of Phenomenology* Bloomington: Indiana University Press.

Le Lannou, Jean-Michel (2002), 'Le "renversement de la phénoménologie" selon Michel Henry'. *Critique*, 58, (667), 968–85.

Levin, H. (1960), *James Joyce*. London: Faber and Faber.

Levinas, E. (1969), *Totality and Infinity: An Essay on Exteriority*, trans. A. Lingis. Pittsburgh: Duquesne University Press.

—— (1990a), *Difficult Freedom: Essays on Judaism*, trans. Sean Hand. London: Athlone Press.

—— (1990b), 'Intersubjectivity: Notes on Merleau-Ponty', in G. A. Johnson and M. B. Smith (eds), *Ontology and Alterity in Merleau-Ponty*. Evanston: Northwestern University Press, pp. 55–60.

—— (1990c), 'Sensibility', in G. A. Johnson and M. B. Smith (eds), *Ontology and Alterity in Merleau-Ponty*. Evanston: Northwestern University Press, pp. 60–6.

—— (1993), *Time and the Other [and additional essays]*, trans. R. A. Cohen. Pittsburgh, PA: Duquesne University Press.

—— (2006), *Otherwise than Being, or Beyond Essence*, trans. A. Lingis. Pittsburgh, PA: Duquesne University Press.

Lingis, A. (1970), 'Intentional and Corporeality', in A.-T. Tymieniecka (ed.),

Annalecta Husserliana, Vol. 1. Dordrecht: D. Reidel Publishing Company, pp. 75–90.

Lovibond, S. (2002), *Ethical Formation*. Cambridge, MA: Harvard University Press.

MacCabe, C. (1979), *James Joyce and the Revolution of the Word*. London: Macmillan Press.

Maddox, B. (1988), *Nora*. London: Hamish Hamilton.

Mahaffey, V. (1995), *Reauthorizing Joyce*. Florida: University Press of Florida.

Marion, J.-L. (1998), *Reduction and Givenness: Investigations of Husserl, Heidegger, and Phenomenology*, trans. T. A. Carlson. Studies in Phenomenology and Existential Philosophy. Evanston: Northwestern University Press.

Mensch, J. R. (2003), *Postfoundational Phenomenology: Husserlian Reflections on Presence and Embodiment*. Pennsylvania: The Pennsylvania State University Press.

Merleau-Ponty, M. (1964), *Signs*, trans. and introd. R. C. McCleary. Evanston: Northwestern University Press.

—— (2003), *Phenomenology of Perception*, trans. C. Smith. London: Routledge.

Milesi, L. (2003), *James Joyce and the Difference of Language*. Cambridge: Cambridge University Press.

Mohanty, J. N. (1996), *Phenomenology: Between Essentialism and Transcendental Philosophy*. Northwestern University Studies in Phenomenology and Existential Philosophy. Evanston: Northwestern University Press.

Mulder, A.-C. (2002), 'Incarnation: The Flesh Becomes Word'. *Paragraph*, 25, (3), 173–83.

Nadel, I. (1996), *Joyce and the Jews: Culture and Texts*. Florida James Joyce Series. Florida: Florida University Press.

Natanson, M. (1998), *The Erotic Bird: Phenomenology in Literature*. Foreword by Judith Butler. Princeton: Princeton University Press.

Noon, W. T. (1957), *Joyce and Aquinas*. New Haven: Yale University Press.

O'Sullivan, M. (2005), 'Metaphor's Lost Time: Notes on the new translations of Proust'. *Nottingham French Studies*, 44, (2), 31–41.

—— (2006), *Michel Henry: Incarnation, Barbarism and Belief*. Oxford: Peter Lang.

Painter, G. D. (1983), *Marcel Proust*. London: Penguin.

Proust, M. (1932a), *Remembrance of Things Past*, trans. C. K. Scott Moncrieff. Vol. 1. New York: Random House.

—— (1932b), *Remembrance of Things Past*, trans. C. K. Scott Moncrieff and F. A. Blossom. Vol. 2. New York: Random House.

—— (1984a), *Pleasures and Regrets*. New York: The Ecco Press.

—— (1984b), *Correspondance: Tome XII –1913*, ed. P. Kolb. Paris: PLON.

—— (1989), *Remembrance of Things Past*, trans. C. K. Scott Moncrieff and T. Kilmartin. Vol. 1. London: Penguin.

—— (1994a), *Against Sainte-Beuve and Other Essays*, trans. J. Sturrock. London: Penguin.

—— (1994b), *Essais et articles*, introd. T. Laget, eds P. Clarac and Y. Sandre. Paris: Gallimard.

—— (1999), *À la recherce du temps perdu*. Revised single edition. Paris: Gallimard.

—— (2002), *In Search of Lost Time*. New Edition. Gen. ed. C. Prendergast. 6 vols. London: Allen Lane, The Penguin Press.

—— (2002a) *The Way by Swann's*, in C. Prendergast (ed.), *In Search of Lost Time*. Vol. 1, trans. L. Davis. London: Allen Lane, The Penguin Press.

—— (2002b) *In the Shadow of Young Girls in Flower*, in C. Prendergast (ed.), *In Search of Lost Time*. Vol. 2, trans. J. Grieve. London: Allen Lane, The Penguin Press.

—— (2002c) *The Guermantes Way*, in C. Prendergast (ed.), *In Search of Lost Time*. Vol. 3, trans. M. Treharne. London: Allen Lane, The Penguin Press.

—— (2002d) *Sodom and Gomorrah*, in C. Prendergast (ed.), *In Search of Lost Time*. Vol. 4. trans. J. Sturrock. London: Allen Lane, The Penguin Press.

—— (2002e) *The Prisoner and The Fugitive*, in C. Prendergast (ed.), *In Search of Lost Time*. Vol. 5, trans. C. Clarke and P. Collier. London: Allen Lane, The Penguin Press.

—— (2002f) *Finding Time Again*, in C. Prendergast (ed.), *In Search of Lost Time*. Vol. 6, trans. I. Patterson. London: Allen Lane, The Penguin Press.

Purcell, M. (2006), *Levinas and Theology*. Cambridge: Cambridge University Press.

Rabaté, J.-M. (1991), *James Joyce, Authorized Reader*. London: The Johns Hopkins University Press.

—— (2001), *James Joyce and the Politics of Egoism*. Cambridge: Cambridge University Press.

—— (2002), *The Future of Theory*. London: Blackwell.

Rancière, J. (2004), *The Flesh of Words: The Politics of Writing*. Stanford: Stanford University Press.

Rapaport, H. (1989), *Heidegger and Derrida: Reflections on Time and Language*. Lincoln: University of Nebraska Press.

Reizbaum, M. (1999), *James Joyce's Judaic Other*. Stanford: Stanford University Press.

—— (2004), 'Weininger and the Bloom of Jewish Self-Hatred in Joyce's *Ulysses*', in H. Bloom, *Leopold Bloom*. Philadelphia, PA: Chelsea House, pp. 87–95.

Reynolds, J. (2004), *Merleau-Ponty and Derrida: Intertwining Embodiment and Alterity*. Athens, OH: Ohio University Press.

Ricoeur, P. (1976), *Interpretation Theory: Discourse and the Surplus of Meaning*. Fort Worth: Texas Christian University Press.

—— (1983), *The Rule of Metaphor: Multi-Disciplinary Studies of the Creation of Meaning in Language*, trans. R. Czerny with K. McLaughlin and J. Costello. London: Routledge and Kegan Paul.

—— (1984), *Time and Narrative*. Vol 1, trans. K. McLaughlin and D. Pellauer. Chicago: University of Chicago Press.

—— (2000), 'Experience and Language in Religious Discourse' in D. Janicaud, J.-F. Courtine, J.-L. Chrétien, J.-L. Marion, M. Henry and P. Ricoeur, *Phenomenology and the 'Theological Turn'*. New York: Fordham University Press, pp. 127–46.

Robbins, J. (1999), *Altered Reading: Levinas and Literature*. Chicago: The University of Chicago Press.

Rossi, M. (1977), *The Hidden Leonardo*. Chicago: Rand McNally.

Roughley, A. (1999), *Reading Derrida Reading Joyce*. Gainesville, FL: University Press of Florida.

Scholem, G. (1997), *On the Possibility of Jewish Mysticism in Our Time and Other Essays*, ed. and introd. A. Shapira, trans. J. Chipman. Philadelphia: Jewish Publication Society.

Scholes, R. E. (1964), 'Joyce and the Epiphany: The Key to the Labyrinth?', *Sewanee Review*, 72 (Winter), 65–77.

—— (1965), *The Workshop of Dedalus: James Joyce and the raw materials for A Portrait of the Artist as a Young Man*, eds R. Scholes and R. M. Kain. Evanston: Northwestern University Press.

Shakespeare, W. (1926), *The Complete Dramatic and Poetic Works of William Shakespeare*. Philadelphia: The John C. Winston Company.

Smith, J. K. (2002), 'A principle of incarnation in Derrida's (Theologische?) Jugendschriften: Towards a confessional theology', *Modern Theology*, 18, (2), (April), 217–30.

Thornton, W. (1994), *The Antimodernism of Joyce's Portrait of the Artist as a Young Man*. Syracuse: Syracuse University Press.

Tindall, W. Y. (1950), *James Joyce: His Way of Interpreting the Modern World*. New York: Scribner's.

Todorov, T. (1982), *Theories of the Symbol*, trans. C. Porter. Oxford: Basil Blackwell.

Tracy, D. (1991), *The Analogical Imagination: Christian Theology and the Culture of Pluralism*. New York: Crossroad, 1991.

Trifonas, P. (2000), *The Ethics of Writing: Derrida, Deconstruction and Pedagogy* Lanham, Md.: Rowman and Littlefield.

Turner, A. R. (1995), *Inventing Leonardo: The Anatomy of a Legend*. London: Papermac Macmillan.

Valéry, P. (1919), *Introduction à la méthode de Léonard de Vinci*. Paris: Éditions de la Nouvelle revue française.

Vattimo, G. (2002), *After Christianity*. New York: Columbia University Press.

Wallace, R. (1966), *The World of Leonardo 1452–1519*. New York: Time-Life Books.

Walsh, R. (2003), 'Fictionality and Mimesis: Between Narrativity and Fictional Worlds'. *Narrative*, 11, (1), January, 110–21.

Whelan, K. (2002), 'The Memories of "The Dead" ', *The Yale Journal of Criticism*, 15, (1), 59–97.

Index

Lightning Source UK Ltd.
Milton Keynes UK
UKOW05f0612240414

230501UK00001B/81/P